D1061254

Organizational Change

Foundations of Communication Theory

Series Editor
Marshall Scott Poole (University of Illinois, Champaign-Urbana)

The *Foundations of Communication Theory* series publishes innovative textbooks that summarize and integrate theory and research for advanced undergraduate and beginning graduate courses. In addition to offering state-of-the-art overviews in a broad array of subfields, authors are encouraged to make original contributions to advance the conversation within the discipline. Written by senior scholars and theorists, these books will provide unique insight and new perspectives on the core sub-disciplinary fields in communication scholarship and teaching today.

Published
Organizational Change: Creating Change Through Strategic Communication, Laurie K. Lewis

Forthcoming
An Invitation to Communication Theory, Robert Craig
Foundations of Intercultural Theory, Deborah Cai and Ed Fink
Foundations of Media and Communication Theory, Leah Lievrouw
Managing Privacy, Sandra Petronio
Foundations of Organizational Communication, Linda Putnam and Scott Poole
Theorizing Crisis Communication, Timothy Sellnow and Matthew Seeger

Laurie K. Lewis

Organizational Change
Creating Change Through Strategic Communication

WILEY-BLACKWELL

A John Wiley & Sons, Ltd., Publication

Blackwell Publishing was acquired by John Wiley & Sons in February 2007. Blackwell's publishing program has been merged with Wiley's global Scientific, Technical, and Medical business to form Wiley-Blackwell.

Registered Office
John Wiley & Sons Ltd, The Atrium, Southern Gate, Chichester, West Sussex, PO19 8SQ, United Kingdom

Editorial Offices
350 Main Street, Malden, MA 02148-5020, USA
9600 Garsington Road, Oxford, OX4 2DQ, UK
The Atrium, Southern Gate, Chichester, West Sussex, PO19 8SQ, UK

For details of our global editorial offices, for customer services, and for information about how to apply for permission to reuse the copyright material in this book please see our website at www.wiley.com/wiley-blackwell.

Library of Congress Cataloging-in-Publication data

Lewis, Laurie K.
  Organizational change : creating change through strategic communication / Laurie K. Lewis.
    p. cm. – (Foundations in communication theory ; 2)
  Includes bibliographical references and index.
  ISBN 978-1-4051-9190-6 (hardback) – ISBN 978-1-4051-9189-0 (paperback)
1. Organizational change. 2. Communication in organizations. I. Title.
  HD58.8.L4934 2011
  658.4′5–dc22
                                                                    2011001786

A catalogue record for this book is available from the British Library.

This book is published in the following electronic formats: ePDFs (9781444340341); Wiley Online Library (9781444340372); ePub (9781444340358)

Set in 10 on 12.5 pt Century by Toppan Best-set Premedia Limited

1 2011

This book is dedicated to Mikyla, Parker, and Craig,
whose patience, encouragement, and love made this book possible,
and to Pat, Bob, and Mark who taught me to love ideas

Contents

Contents in Detail

Introduction

Only the wisest and the stupidest of men never change
Confucius

If you don't change direction, you'll end up where you're headed
Chinese proverb

Change is a prominent feature of organizational, civic, and personal life. Change is something we sometimes seek, sometimes resist, and often have thrust upon us. It would not be an overstatement to suggest that society is rife with change and questions about how, when, and in what ways change ought to occur. Goal achievement, progress, and even the avoidance of crisis very often involve implementing planned changes. Change can serve as means to address many important challenges such as those related to policy, governance, rule of law, philosophy, and distribution of information, rights, and resources; challenges of efficiency, effectiveness, quality, and competitiveness; and challenges hinged on shared values, understanding, and cooperation. These challenges span across many sectors of society including private sector organizations upon which we depend for goods, services, and the basis of our economy; public sector organizations that run our community,

Organizational Change: Creating Change Through Strategic Communication,
First Edition. Laurie K. Lewis.
© 2011 Laurie K. Lewis. Published 2011 by Blackwell Publishing Ltd.

state, national, and international governance; and non-governmental or nonprofit organizations that promote community and leisure activity as well as provide for numerous humanitarian, scientific, professional, cultural, and social services.

Change is sometimes necessary to correct past failures and accomplish learning and improvement. And, although decision-makers can often agree on problems to be solved, the principles involved in solving them, and even the specific changes to be made in a given situation, making the change happen – through implementing ideas and improvements – can be incredibly challenging. For example, in the aftermath of Hurricanes Katrina and Rita or after the 9/11 tragedy, hindsight produced many ideas and suggestions for improvement in preventive measures, security measures, and procedures of first responders among others. In order to realize those changes in time to be prepared for the next hurricane or attack, leaders needed to not only vet the ideas, but figure out how to install changes, deal with conflicting opinions about the changes, provide for necessary adjustments to the ideas as they were introduced, and cope with the unexpected consequences of changes made. These are all tasks of implementation. Failure to implement change as a result of organizational learning can result in repeated failure. One could argue that failure to implement change as a result of what was learned from the Exxon Valdez oil spill in Alaska may have led to the BP oil spill disaster in the Gulf of Mexico years later.

Change is sometimes important because it provides opportunities for growth, development, increasing resources, and seizing a moment that if missed may have negative consequences. Leaders who are frozen in the process of implementing change, who are not able to act efficiently and effectively in bringing an innovative idea into practice soon enough, may be unable to realize the benefits of even the best of ideas. In some cases, being second or third with a great idea is worthless; in some cases resources are so scarce and timing so critical that delays in getting innovation up and running can mean a missed opportunity. If companies, governments, and other collectives who are trying to innovate are not able to swiftly and smoothly bring new ideas into the marketplace or operations the window for innovation may close. Successful implementation is key to realizing the potential of most great ideas.

Alternatively, change processes are sometimes wrong-headed, faddish, unnecessary, and potentially disastrous in their consequences. Huge investments in time, money, physical resources, and social and political capital can be wasted if spent on flawed, misguided changes that have little value or high negative consequences. The period of implementation is the last stopgap period where poor decisions to adopt changes can be recognized and corrected before lasting damage results.

Many factors give rise to change processes in organizations. Organizations seek to be innovative; give in to pressures to follow the "pack" or an industry or sector leader; or are coerced by forces of public opinion, regulatory force, or marketplace mechanisms to attempt change. The success of change in organizations can be measured by a variety of perspectives – those who seek the change; those who are asked to alter their practice; those whose stakes are most impacted by old and new ways of doing; and bystanders of the process among others. However we come to those assessments, the process of implementing change – of putting ideas into practice – is a major determinant of outcomes. This book is about that process.

State of the Art

Many theorists, researchers, and consultants have written about the implementation process. Expertise from many disciplines and sub-disciplines has been offered to explain implementation, including management, psychology, sociology, social work, technology transfer, and communication, to name a few. Important insights into implementation and important components of change are often isolated within disciplines or sub-disciplines. Sometimes similar ideas crop up across disciplines and occasionally researchers have built upon work across disciplinary lines. However, too often, each approach to change has ignored important contributions of those writing in other fields or sub-fields representing different approaches. Even in our isolation, much has been accomplished in furthering our understanding of the implementation process. Since an earlier review I conducted over twelve years ago (Lewis and Seibold, 1998), the study of change implementation has grown considerably in scope, sophistication, and depth. Despite the relative isolation of some of our research on implementation processes, one is struck in a thorough review of the literature that several central themes continue to emerge in the ways that we think, write and research about this process. Some of these themes emphasize some important limitations to our most common approaches to change implementation.

Weaknesses in Current Approaches to Change Implementation

First, we have been overly focused on implementers' strategies and recipients' responses. **Implementers** are those people in organizations who take on a formal role in bringing about the change effort and translating the idea of change into practice. An overemphasis on implementers suggests by our very questions and research approaches that initiators of change play a strategic and central role in communication but other stakeholders are passive and peripheral. *Stakeholders* are those who have a stake in an organization's process and or outputs. The popular press books that provide advice for practitioners nearly exclusively provide instruction for those who will implement change while completely ignoring the role of stakeholders on how to become meaningfully engaged in change or even on how to forestall or alter a change initiative (which at times may be an incredibly valuable role). Even in the books for implementers there is little acknowledgment that other stakeholders will often *strategically* attempt to derail or re-direct a change effort. We ascribe "resistance" behaviors or attitudes as a mere reaction rather than as an affirmative, principled perspective of stakeholders who care about their organizations and a wide array of stakes held by various stakeholders, and whom in their resistance can bring much to enhance and inform change processes. By thinking of non-implementer stakeholders as mere audiences for implementers' messages about change but not as actors who have stakes, insight, and valuable perspective, which they are asserting in organizations, we miss a critically important source of explanation of how change processes unfold in organizations.

Second, and related to the first point, too often we have ascribed the reactions stakeholders (primarily employees) have to change efforts as being due to: (1) emotional response (e.g., stress, anxiety, fear), (2) misunderstanding communication of implementers, (3) direct experience engaging the change in some material way, and/or (4) individual cognitive framing of the change and what it "means" to individuals in their own heads. In doing so we have often overlooked any consideration of the very social aspects of sensemaking and sensegiving relative to change initiatives. We have assumed that individuals react to change for a host of individual reasons – many of them rooted in irrational anxieties, personal interests, and personality flaws. Again, this approach portrays stakeholders as reactionary and not as strategic; as individualistic and not collective; as focused on self-interest and not on shared interests. It implies that we need to deal with recipients of change programs one-by-one in a paternal or therapeutic manner.

Thus, in viewing stakeholders as autonomous individuals who come to understand change only in relation to what they are being told by implementers or through direct experience with change, we've missed altogether or underplayed the influence multiple stakeholders have on one another. In this misplaced focus we miss the strategic attempts *among* stakeholders to influence each others' sensemaking and the products of that joint sensemaking – including the formation of powerful coalitions, rivalries, and schisms. We also miss the processes by which sense is made – that is the "ing" in sensemaking. Too often we've only examined the various understandings stakeholders have of a change at a single point in time – the "sense made." In doing so we gain no understanding of how those "senses" of the change evolve and the important social dynamics that create them.

Third, we've assumed too often that "success" in implementation of change means getting what implementers initially desire. Very little in the popular press literature or even much of the academic literature allows for the possibility that the original idea for change is flawed. The assumption is often made that "success" will be achieved when the change, as originally envisioned by decision-makers, is up and running and institutionalized into practice. Much of the research tradition in implementation of change is focused on figuring out how to make that happen. This approach leaves out important consideration of the processes by which organizations self-correct; avoid groupthink (i.e., insulating themselves from critical voices, disconfirming evidence, or reconsideration of goals); and maximize use of available resources in maintaining vigilance in decision-making. For researchers, as well as consultants, starting with the assumption that any specific change is a good idea is dangerous for making conclusions about best practice as well as for developing strong theory to explain processes of change.

In an effort to address the weaknesses in the state of the art literature in implementation of change as well as build on its strengths, this book provides an integration of theory and research across disciplines. In ranging across a number of theoretical literatures that address institutionalization, persuasion, message design, socialization, identification, roles, participatory practice, knowledge, networks, power, resistance, sensemaking, framing, among others, this book connects pockets of strong theoretical and research traditions to inform important social dynamics of implementation of change. The book embraces a version of Stakeholder Theory and adopts a centrally communicative approach in accomplishing that integration.

Stakeholder Theory has been used to help account for how organizations manage the competing stakes stemming from divergent interests of stakeholders (Freeman, 1984; Jones and Wicks, 1999; Phillips, Freeman, and Wicks, 2003). This collection of theoretical perspectives helps direct attention of scholars and practitioners to the means of identifying important stakeholders; tools to monitor changing stakeholders or stakeholder demands; and issues surrounding balancing bottom-line considerations and ethical considerations in addressing stakeholder demands. More modern approaches to stakeholder theory also have begun to address the tactics of influence that stakeholders use to influence organizations and one another.

A communication perspective on organizing provides a lens by which we can examine and explain organizing activity. Organizations are socially constructed largely through the communicative interactions of internal and external stakeholders. Stakeholders enact the organization as the embodiment of their own purposes, their sense of how activities are related; how people are known; how outcomes arise and how processes unfold. So, we enact the "leader" by engaging with her/him as someone who is deserving of more floor time, whose opinions are turned into policy, and whose requests become mandates. We enact a "club" in a different way than we enact a "business." By emphasizing fun over profit and personal relationships and enjoyable activities over customer satisfaction and market share we create the organizing activity known as a "club." It is more than an exercise of labeling. It involves highly complex ways of interacting and the sense that is given to those interactions.

Thus, by combining a stakeholder perspective that calls attention to the many perspectives and stakes of actors in and around organizations with a communication perspective that highlights enacted reality through interaction, this book hopes to bring a heightened awareness of a host of complex dynamics during change implementation that have thus far received too little attention. This book (a) highlights the strategic behavior of all potential stakeholders, (b) addresses the interaction *among* stakeholders who are not implementers, (c) focuses on the sensemaking and sensegiving activities of all participants in change as they evolve and change over the course of an implementation effort, and (d) threads together many components of the process of implementation of planned organizational change into a holistic model that helps us to explain how various sub-processes and activities influence the outcomes of change.

The next sections of this introduction will lay out more specifics about Stakeholder Theory perspective as well as the general outlines of what a communication perspective brings to the understanding of implementation processes. Finally, I will introduce three case studies that will be used throughout the book to help illustrate various dynamics discussed in each chapter.

A Stakeholder Theory Perspective

Allen went to work on Monday. He stored his lunch in his locker and reported to his line to begin work. His shift supervisor was calling everyone over for an announcement. Allen felt a knot in his stomach. He was told the "news" that everyone had been talking about for months, but the CEO of the company had denied. The company was being merged with another company in the mid-west. The supervisor made the announcement and handed out a sheet with a set of questions and answers on it and then told everyone to get back to work. Allen didn't know what this would mean for his job, his pay, or who he was really working for. He felt anxious the rest of the day.

On a busy day at state university, Allison was preparing for classes and glanced at the clock to realize that she was late for a faculty meeting. After rushing to get there, she sat down as a discussion about "The Commission" was taking place. One of the University business officers was briefing the faculty on the important potential implications of some report issued out of the Department of Higher Education. Allison was irritated that she had to listen to all this when she had piles of work waiting for her in her office. Geesh, couldn't someone in central administration deal with all of this? What did it have to do with her anyway? The business officer said that if changes didn't come from higher education, they'd likely be imposed – and they wouldn't be ones we want. Allison wondered what that might entail. Surely if this was a big deal more of her colleagues would have been talking about it. It must be the usual bureaucratic nonsense that will blow over.

Letisha and Raul were working on the inter-agency document for application for federal funding for the homeless services in their city. They were very hopeful that the city would get more funding since in the recent years they had been getting small increases. However, they both knew that even though they were rank-ordering ten projects – all critically needed in the city–only two would receive federal support. The reality of scarce funding for homeless services was huge. Competition for grant and private foundation money was fierce, but the people who worked in the service organizations in their city were all committed and trying hard to serve homeless individuals and families. Leaders of the smaller agencies were feeling increasingly jaded and hesitant to participate given their low chances of receiving funding. This year might be different though.

Two university professors had offered to help the local service providers to communicate better. They had provided many organizations with computers, high-speed Internet connections, and some other tools and had given them technical support and training. Letisha hadn't really got a chance to look at any of the tools – she was just too swamped with work. Raul was very comfortable with technology though and was really into using the new listserv set up for the group. He'd been one of the first to subscribe and was a frequent poster. He even used the instant messaging feature – although few in the network were ever on.

Allen, Allison, Letisha, and Raul are all stakeholders in organizational change. Anyone reading this introduction is a stakeholder in organizations, and likely, in organizational change as well. As noted earlier, **stakeholders** are those who have a stake in an organization's process and or outputs. Stakes can come in many forms (e.g., financial, environmental, physical, symbolic). Stakeholders like employees, community members, customers/clients, and suppliers have a variety of different stakes in organizations. Some rely on an organization for products and services. Others provide raw materials and depend on the business as revenue to run their own organization. Others are affected by the organization indirectly in terms of experiencing effects of organizational outputs including pollution, tax revenue, congestion, donations to local causes, advertising, and/or impacts on the economy and culture of the city or country where the organization operates.

We often think of the internal change processes of organizations as something that only impacts those who work there. However, if we start to really think about how organizations affect us, we can better appreciate how the ripple effects of change processes also impact us. Organizations can have many ripple effects in communities in which they operate. **Ripple effects** are the impacts that organizational actions and presence brings to stakeholders within and surrounding the organization. Hershey, PA is an excellent, if extreme, example of the potential of ripple effects of an organization (see Highlight Box 1). In the early 1900s Milton Hershey created a whole town around his chocolate company. Even today, in addition to the world famous chocolate factory, the town boasts multiple Hershey entertainment venues (Hershey Park, Chocolate World, Zoo America, Hershey Golf courses), the Hershey Medical Center, Hershey botanical gardens, Milton Hershey School, and The Milton Hershey Foundation among many other legacies of Milton Hershey's vision. Local stakeholders of this organization experience many ripple effects of the actions of the Hershey company. Hershey created infrastructure, community resources, a tourism trade, and schools among other tangibles. He also created an identity for the town known by his name and forever tied to his chocolate confections and the culture of his company and family. Any significant changes that the company makes have the potential to further impact the local community as well as worldwide customers, suppliers, competitors, and even governments (who rely on Hershey tax revenue, employment of citizens, contributions to local economy, etc.).

All organizations create ripple effects by their actions on both large and small scales. The failure of major industry can crush the economy of a region. As I write this book the automakers in the mid-west United States are struggling to survive an economic crisis. The dire projected ripple effects of their demise hang in the balance. Employees without work cannot pay mortgages, buy goods and services, support local merchants, or pay taxes that support schools. Unemployed families put a strain on health care systems, food pantries, low-income housing options, and a whole string of social support nonprofits. On a smaller scale just the widening of a roadway to make room for a new Walmart can create ripple effects of increased traffic, costs of roadway repair, and the diversion of traffic patterns away from other businesses. Ripple effects can be planned or unplanned, anticipated or unanticipated, positive or negative, but they are a major part of the reason that organizations have such diverse sets of stakeholders – some of whom can be hard to identify until an organization takes a new action, changes the way it operates, or experiences an unexpected event or crisis. For example, in the BP Gulf oil spill in the United States, some individuals who never considered themselves stakeholders of BP were suddenly impacted in tremendously important ways. Business owners in the affected states, Parish governments, fishermen in the Gulf, tourists planning trips to the region, among many others likely never felt they had a stake in BP's actions until the spill occurred. Others may have had their stakes in BP's actions raised due to the crisis. Environmentalists doubtlessly have a heightened sense that BP's current and future actions are even more critical to meeting their goals.

Highlight Box 1: Hershey Builds a Community

Milton Hershey picked rural Derry Township to establish his company. Mr. Hershey envisioned a complete, new community after workmen started digging the foundation for the Hershey chocolate factory in early 1903. Mr. Hershey used other manufacturing communities as a model for his town.

Like other "model towns" Hershey provided its residents with modern educational facilities, and affordable housing. A unique feature of Hershey's town was that he wanted to promote it as a destination for tourists.

By 1905 electric, water, and telephone service were provided. The McKinley School was built and it provided a modern, centralized educational system for grades one through twelve. A bank, general store, post office, and boarding rooms for men, were all located in the Cocoa House. Hershey connected other towns to his town through rail and trolley lines.

Through his encouragement, the town's residents also helped add to the services provided. They established a volunteer fire company, YMCA, and YWCA. A variety of literary and social clubs, the Hershey Band, and local sports teams were also formed. Mr. Hershey supported the local organizations by providing meeting halls, uniforms, and equipment.

The centerpiece of Milton Hershey's provisions for recreation and culture was the Community Building. Originally designed in 1914, the building was finally started in 1929 and completed in 1933. It housed the men's club, a gymnasium and pool, a library, bowling alley, and public meeting rooms. The local hospital (1932–45) and the Hershey Junior College (1938–65) were also housed here. For years the building served as the focal point of community activity.

Source: Adapted from Pamela Cassidy and Eliza Harrison, One Man's Vision: Hershey, A Model Town, Hershey Museum, 1988 (http://www.mhs-pa.org/about/history/hershey-pennsylvania-chocolatetown-is-born/).

Stakeholders often make demands on organizations. Employees ask for better benefits, pay, and working conditions. Clients/customers demand more efficiency, better or different products and services. Suppliers demand smooth working relationships. Watchdog groups, professional associations, and advocacy organizations demand that organizations operate within acceptable standards of ethics, cultural norms, and values of those stakeholders. Demands on organizations to monitor and respond to all those stakeholder demands are critical and tremendous. Also, demands are continually changing as circumstances with stakeholders change. For example, the economic downturn in the United States and around the globe has caused customers to begin to alter their demands for certain products and services. High-end fashion is beginning to be replaced by desire for bargains and affordable necessities. Businesses like Home Depot's home design stores EXPO, Starbucks, and even Macy's are laying off workers and closing stores. As high-end products and services are becoming less desirable and affordable for customers, organizations have to change both the way they represent and market their image as well as, in some cases, what they offer.

As we begin to think about different types of organizations other stakeholders and other sorts of demands can be illustrated. Governmental organizations are expected to provide services (e.g., fire protection, police protection, environmental protection and regulation, road quality, defense); social service organizations are relied upon to address many of society's major problems (e.g., poverty, hunger, homelessness, disaster recovery); other nonprofits provide guidance and leadership around the globe on numerous fronts such as health, peace, international cooperation, and science. Still others are centers for art, history, and culture (e.g., museums, cultural centers, art festivals). When thinking of the processes involved in these organizations and the expected and actual things they produce, many diverse stakeholders come into play.

Many times stakeholders make divergent and conflicting demands on organizations. Employees want more pay and customers want cheaper products. Clients of nonprofits want faster and more comprehensive services, and government funders want more accountability and record-keeping. Many such conflicts occur for organizations. As we noted in the introduction to this chapter, Stakeholder Theory can help us to understand how organizations manage these divergent demands and how stakeholders attempt to influence organizations to meet their demands.

Stakeholder Theory also can be used to help us understand how organizations introduce change. Stakeholders, like Allen, Allison, Letisha, and Raul in the stories opening this introduction, have reactions to changes in their organizational lives. Those changes impact how they feel, how they relate to the organization, what they think they can get from and give to the organization among many other reactions. Further, as discussed next, stakeholders communicate with one another as they confront change in organizations. Those interactions help them to make sense of the change, orient to the possibilities the change may bring, and sometimes show how they will jointly or individually mobilize to accept, support, resist or alter the path of the change efforts.

A Communication Perspective

This book embraces a communication perspective on change implementation and examines how organizational change is accomplished or not accomplished through implementers' interactions with stakeholders, and stakeholders' interactions with each other. As we work through the various chapters of this book I will argue how change processes, as most other organizing activities, are rooted in and enacted through communication.

As discussed in Chapter 1, the very triggers of change stem from communication of key stakeholders who "notice" features of the internal or external environment that then lead them to make a case for a change. As decision-makers work through the adoption of a change (those steps that precede the introduction of it into practice), communication is the means by which they compare their understandings and senses of "what is going on" with competitors, regulators, customers, industry partners, and internal stakeholders such as employees, volunteers, and affiliated national organizations. That input will accommodate various interpretations that serves as the basis of decisions to implement and the manner, timing, and form of implementation. In fact, the ways in which implementers and other stakeholders talk about the change will form the basis of what the change becomes for that organization. For example, just as a group can make a "club" different from a "business," in another organization a change to a new technology can be framed as a new philosophy of who we are (e.g., we are now "modern"). Enacting the reality of becoming "modern" is accomplished through the interaction of stakeholders around the change initiative. In another organization the same new technology could be constructed as just "doing business as usual with a modest update."

In Chapter 2 I will begin to examine the ways in which communication processes and roles within and around organizations are central to how stakeholders influence the course of change implementation. Three general processes of information dissemination, soliciting input, and socialization will be introduced and discussed to show the complexity of how social interaction gives rise to both process and outcomes during change implementation. Social actors strategically participate through formal and informal channels in ways that have a powerful influence on outcomes. These communication processes come to shape the ways in which stakeholders understand and interpret what the change is; how it effects their stakes in organizations; as well as inform their own strategic participation in change.

Implementers play a key stakeholder role in any organizational change effort. *Implementers* are those people in organizations who take on a formal role in bringing about the change effort and translating the idea of change into practice. Implementers design many aspects of the change effort including decision-making; authorization of timing, participation, purchases, procedures, and policy; making official proclamations; and communicating about the change to and with stakeholders. Although implementers are themselves "stakeholders" in change, for clarity we will refer to them as implementers and all others with a stake in the change and the organization as stakeholders.

In Chapter 3 an overview of the stakeholder perspective and a model of the change process in the context of stakeholder interaction is presented. This chapter will further explore Stakeholder Theory and show how it helps us to elaborate a more complex and dynamic picture of implementing change than much of our current literature has done. The model and the use of Stakeholder Theory expands our understanding of the multiple relationships that stakeholders have with one another and ascribes more meaningful, focused, and strategic action to stakeholders than have other approaches that treat stakeholders as mere audiences for change.

Chapters 4 through 8 develop portions of the model and add to explanation of how change implementation unfolds through communication with and among stakeholders. In Chapter 4, I discuss the ways in which we can conceptualize the outcomes of change processes and put that discussion in the context of how organizational outcomes and concepts of "success" and "failure" are developed. Chapters 5 through 8 highlight the strategic messages developed and framed by various participants in change; examine the ways in which resistance and power are constructed in interaction during change and the results those constructions bring to change processes and outcomes; explore the antecedents to stakeholders' and implementers' selections of communication strategies and approaches to change; and assess the critical processes of storying, sensemaking, and framing that serve as the key means by which organizational changes come to exist and be transformed within social contexts. Finally, Chapter 9 will complete the discussion of implementation of planned change by focusing specifically on practice. This final chapter provides both implementers and stakeholders with ideas about how to monitor and strategically communicate across the topics, dynamics, and processes that are discussed throughout the book.

Cases of Organizational Change

As we further explore dimensions of implementation of organizational change throughout this book, we will make use of three extended case studies of organizational change. Each will now be introduced to give some critical background to the organizational and environmental context in which these changes were introduced. These are real-life examples of changes that have been introduced and studied by communication scholars.

Our first case concerns a merger (Laster, 2008). Ingredients Inc. is a food ingredients corporation. It was the result of a merger between two significant players in the industry. The second case (Ruben, Lewis, and Sandmeyer, 2008; Lewis, Ruben, Sandmeyer, Russ, and Smulowitz, unpublished) follows the Spellings Commission on Higher Education and its attempts to create change in institutions of higher education across the United States. The third case (Lewis, Scott, and D'Urso, unpublished; Scott, Lewis, and D'Urso, 2010; Scott, Lewis, Davis, and D'Urso, 2009) describes the implementation of communication technologies in a network of homeless service providers in a major city in the southwest United States. Next, basic background about each case is provided.

Ingredients Incorporated

Midwest Company (MC) and Eastern Company (EC) were high profile mid-sized companies (each employing approximately 300 employees) that merged into Ingredients Inc. As leaders in baking ingredients, food ingredients, and specialty chemicals and equipment MC and EC together generated annual sales upwards of $330 million. In an effort to maximize control of the market, these two organizations merged in January 2007, forming a new organization. MC was located in two large midwestern metropolitan areas while EC was located in several smaller cities near New York City. Both legacy companies included a team of sales representatives dispersed across the United States. MC's corporate office was downtown near the center of the city. EC was located in four physical locations near NYC. Since the merger, Ingredients Inc. has procured a new location in a suburb of Midwest City, where the corporate offices are now located; this location also includes the Research and Development lab for the organization. The entire executive team for the newly formed organization, including the former EC chief executive officer (CEO) and vice presidents are now corporately located in Midwest City. The former MC downtown corporate office is now vacant, and the EC corporate office has been reduced to a small team of administrative personnel; all other (eight in total) production and distribution locations remained unchanged.

The merger took place in the context described by inside stakeholders as friendly and cooperative. It took approximately six months to complete. As a result of negotiations between the two CEOs of the original companies, it was decided that the CEO of MC would become the CEO of the combined firm, and the CEO of EC would become its president and chief operating officer (COO). However, about six months after these decisions were made and about two weeks after the official merger, the CEO of the new organization (the former MC CEO), announced that he would be stepping down to accept a position with another (noncompeting, but industry compliant) company. Other staffing decisions included offering those back-office position-holders (Human Resources, Customer Service, Accounting) in the EC corporate office an opportunity to relocate to Midwest City in a comparable position. EC employees who held duplicated positions and were unwilling to relocate were provided with exit packages.

Spellings Commission on Higher Education

In September 2005 the Department of Education's Spellings Commission began a process that after twelve months resulted in the publication of a 55-page report entitled, "A Test of Leadership: Charting the Future of US Higher Education" outlining an "action plan" for the future of higher education in the United States. In part the Report raised concerns about the state of higher education and the need for change:

> As we enter the 21st century, it is no slight to the success of American colleges and universities thus far in our history to note the unfulfilled promise that remains. Our yearlong examination of the challenges facing higher education has brought us to the uneasy conclusion that the sector's past attainments have led our nation to unwarranted complacency about its future. It is time to be frank. Among the vast and varied institutions that make up US higher education, we have found much to applaud, but also much that requires urgent reform. (US Department of Education, 2006)

The Department's website served as a hub for dissemination of the Report which was widely read. As of January 2008 the Department of Education had distributed nearly 20,000 copies of the Report to stakeholders including states, institutions, governing boards, associations, US college presidents, participants at national and regional higher education summits and town hall meetings, as well as to students and parents (Ruben et al., 2008). According to the Department of Education records, there were nearly 75,000 visits to the Spellings Commission website in 2006 and more than 95,000 in 2007 (Ruben et al., 2008). There was widespread and sustained interest in the Commission's Report.

Reactions to the Report varied and created an impetus to many follow-on interactions and discussions among key stakeholder groups. Faculty, boards, administrators, alumni, students, parents, Congress, state governments, business community, national higher education association, accrediting associations, and media all weighed in on the discussion of how the Report ought be interpreted, the level of its accuracy, its importance and relevance, and the appropriate responses to its recommendations. The Report and the subsequent reactions to it may account for much of the current wave of reform in higher education. As Ruben et al. (2008) argue the commission attracted attention and fostered a large national conversation about the challenges and needs of higher education. For example, national and regional accrediting associations intensified their focus on issues of assessment and transparency, hundreds of US colleges are adopting standards templates for reporting institution outcomes, and many of these are enacting recommendations of the report in the form of increasing use of standardized student-achievement tests, allowing comparisons between institutions and making performance-related data more readily available for public scrutiny (Ruben et al., 2008; NASULGC, 2008).

Homeless Net

Homeless Net is a set of approximately 28 organizations that operate in the same geographic area (surrounding a major southwestern city) providing services to homeless persons. Recent research done by the National Law Center on Homelessness and Poverty estimated 3.5 million homeless people in this country in the mid 2000s. In the specific mid-sized metropolitan city where Homeless Net exists the average daily estimate of homeless persons has been right at 4,000.

Homeless Net organizations provide many varied services. The individual work of these organizations in the community includes helping homeless kids stay in school; helping homeless families navigate the system to secure affordable housing and achieve job training; counseling homeless victims of domestic violence and protecting them from threatening behavior of abusers; assisting abandoned and abused teens to redirect their lives and complete the GED; helping mentally ill homeless persons to gain access to appropriate health care; providing safe and appropriate shelter and transitional housing for those who are seeking to recover from crisis and obtain permanent affordable housing; and providing the most basic of life's needs: showers, laundry, lockers, phone access, food, clothes, diapers, and dental care.

For several reasons collaboration among these organizations is necessary but challenging. First, no single service provider alone can address all these needs, and thus a patchwork of service provision is needed to ensure everything is available. However, agencies and personnel in agencies are sometimes only minimally aware of other agencies and their services. Second, the environment of dwindling financial resources has created a scarcity-induced competitiveness among many providers evidenced by some mutual protectiveness about sources of funding and the tension surrounding these processes. Third, several disagreements exist in terms of philosophy of service-delivery, desire to participate in advocacy efforts, and beliefs about how to target the overall mission of the community of providers. As a result of these challenges, formal and even informal collaboration among the organizations has historically been fairly limited.

In 1999 a pair of researchers from the nearby state university approached The Taskforce on Homelessness to explore the implementation of communication technologies within the network to expand the capacity of the organizations to collaborate. The researchers called their project The Collaborative Technologies for Organizations Serving the Homeless (CTOSH; pronounced "see-tosh"). The purpose of the CTOSH project was to enable these organizations to enhance their ability to work cooperatively in order to maximize a rapidly dwindling supply of financial and other resources. Through grant funding, CTOSH provided a group of organizations with tools for communication. Each of 28 CTOSH organizations was equipped with the appropriate infrastructure (e.g., high speed Internet connections, powerful desktop computers, collaborative software) and provided with training and ongoing technical support. Additionally, a listserv was made available to anyone associated with the homeless provider network in the area. The listserv had the effect of drawing somewhat of a boundary line around an otherwise dispersed and ill-defined community of professionals and organizations. Other tools were also provided including instant messaging, file sharing, a group decision support system, and a customized web. The CTOSH Project followed the implementation efforts of these technologies for four years.

Conclusion

Change is a prominent feature of our lives and the character of many organizations. Changes come in all sizes and configurations from small procedural changes within given units or departments, initiated with no or little formality, to large-scale multi-organizational, multi-part change efforts with uncertain ends. Successful mastery over change is a subject that has received a great deal of attention in scholarly and popular press articles and books. Scholars, consultants, and practitioners alike have sought explanation of how stakeholders can create the most positive implementation processes to bring planned changes to successful conclusion. The importance of mastering organizational change is due to the magnitude of what can be accomplished if change processes are successful and the consequences of failure, delay, poor process, or unwise change. This book examines the implementation of change in the context of stakeholder communication, providing a clear depiction of the complex social dynamics of implementation of planned organizational change as well as presenting important strategic tools that if mastered can further any stakeholder's or implementer's goals in change.

References

Freeman, R. E. (1984) *Strategic Management: A Stakeholder Approach*. Boston, MA: Pitman.

Jones, T. M. and Wicks, A. C. (1999) Convergent stakeholder theory. *Academy of Management Review*, 24, 206–221.

Laster, N. M. (2008) Communicating multiple change: Understanding the impact of change messages on stakeholder perceptions. Dissertation Abstracts International (UMI No. AAT 3342339).

Lewis, L. K. and Seibold, D. R. (1998) Reconceptualizing organizational change implementation as a communication problem: A review of literature and research agenda. In M. E. Roloff (ed.), *Communication Yearbook 21* (pp. 93–151). Thousand Oaks, CA: Sage.

Lewis, L. K., Ruben, B., Sandmeyer, L., Russ, T., and Smulowitz, S. (unpublished) Sensemaking interaction during change: A longitudinal analysis of stakeholders' communication about Spellings Commission's efforts to change US higher education.

Lewis, L. K., Scott, C. R., and D'Urso, S. (unpublished) Development of collaborative communication: A case study of an interorganizational network.

Phillips, R., Freeman, R. E., and Wicks, A. C. (2003) What stakeholder theory is not. *Business Ethics Quarterly*, 1 (4), 479–502.

Ruben, B. D., Lewis, L., and Sandmeyer, L. (2008) *Assessing the Impact of the Spellings Commission: The Message, the Messenger, and the Dynamics of Change in Higher Education*. Washington, DC: National Association of College and University Business Officers.

Scott, C. R., Lewis, L. K., and D'Urso, S. C. (2010) Getting on the "E" list: Email list use in a community of service provider organizations for people experiencing homelessness. In L. Shedletsky and J. E. Aitken (eds.), *Cases on Online Discussion and Interaction: Experiences and Outcomes* (pp. 334–350). Hershey, PA: IGI-Global.

Scott, C. R., Lewis, L. K., Davis, J. D., and D'Urso, S. C. (2009) Finding a home for communication technologies. In J. Keyton and P. Shockley-Zalabak (eds.), *Case Studies for Organizational Communication: Understanding Communication Processes* (2nd edn.). Los Angeles, CA: Roxbury.

Further Reading

Frooman, J. (1999) Stakeholder influence strategies. *Academy of Management Review*, 24, 191–205.

1

Defining Organizational Change

To improve is to change; to be perfect is to change often
Winston Churchill

Life is change. Growth is optional. Choose wisely
Unknown

Wisdom lies neither in fixity nor in change, but in the dialectic between the two
Octavio Paz, Mexican poet and essayist

As these opening quotations hint, change is often considered a sign of progress and improvement. Partly owing to a cultural value, organizations are under extreme pressure to constantly change. Zorn, Christensen, and Cheney (1999) make the case that "change for change's sake" (p. 4) has been glorified to an extent that it has become managerial fashion for stakeholders to constantly change their organizations. If it isn't new,

Organizational Change: Creating Change Through Strategic Communication,
First Edition. Laurie K. Lewis.
© 2011 Laurie K. Lewis. Published 2011 by Blackwell Publishing Ltd.

it cannot be good. If we aren't changing, we must be stagnant. If we don't have the latest, we must be falling behind. If we aren't improving, we must be inadequate. These scholars go on to argue that the cultural and market pressures that demand constant change in competitive organizations can lead to disastrous outcomes including adoption of changes that are not suited to the goals of the organization; ill-considered timing of change; dysfunctional human resource management practices; exhaustion from repetitive cycles of change; and loss of benefits of stability and consistency. It appears that this faddish behavior, like becoming slaves to any fashion, can lead to poor decision-making and poor use of resources.

Communication plays a critical role in fostering the fad of change in organizations. We hear stakeholders in and around organizations making arguments that change is inherently good and that stability is necessarily bad. The continual use of language of change in terms considered positive – improvement, continuous improvement, progressive, innovative, "pushing the envelope," being "edgy" – is juxtaposed against language of stability in negative terms – stagnant, stale, old fashioned, "yesterday's news," "behind the times." The rhetorical force of labeling in this way pushes an agenda that contributes to the faddishness that Zorn *et al.* point out.

Pressure to change also derives from complex organizational environments that put many demands on organizations to adapt and innovate. For example the economic downturn beginning in 2008 has triggered a steady stream of changes in organizations worldwide. Layoffs, restructuring, mergers, store closings, sell-offs, product redevelopment and introduction of new strategies for marketing are increasingly viewed by decision-makers as necessary business survival strategies. Nonprofits also have been hit hard by the economic conditions and struggle for new ways to fund activities and services while dealing, in many cases, with increased needs from those individuals who are spiraling into poverty, homelessness, and financial crises. Governments at all levels struggle to balance budgets, continue to provide necessary services, and maintain staff on payrolls, resulting in some cases to state employee furloughs (where staff are compelled to take unpaid days off from work) and withholding of state income tax returns. Few, if any sectors of industry and society are left untouched by the recent major environmental jolts. And, oftentimes, the rationale that changing circumstances demand changing tactics, responses, and strategies makes it difficult for organizations to resist trying to do something new or at least appear they are doing something new.

Change can be triggered by many factors even in the most calm of financial times. Triggers for change include the need for organizations to stay in line with legal requirements (e.g., employment law, health and safety regulations, product regulation, environmental protection policies), changing customer and/ or client needs (e.g., changing demographics, fashions that spur desire for specific products and services, heightened problems or needs of clients served), newly created and/or outdated technologies, changes in availability of financial resources (e.g., changes in investment capital, funding agencies for nonprofits, administrative priorities for government agencies), and alterations of available labor pool (e.g., aging workforce, technological capabilities of workforce, immigration) among others.

In addition, some organizations self-initiate change and innovation. Change initiated within organizations can stem from many sources including the personal innovation of employees (individuals developing new ideas for products, practices, relationships), serendipity (stumbling across something that works and then catches on in an organization), and through arguments espousing specific directions that stakeholders in and around organizations think should be adopted or resisted. As stakeholders assert their own preferences for what organizations do and how they operate, their interactions produce both evaluations of current practice and visions for future practice that incite change initiatives.

Communication is key in triggering all change. In fact, we can easily argue that none of the other factors that trigger change are truly the direct cause for change until stakeholders recognize them, frame them in terms that suggest change is necessary, and convince resource-holding decision-makers to act on them by implementing change. That is, the necessity for change or the advantage of responding to changing circumstances is one that is created in the interaction among stakeholders. The process is much more subtle than we might assume at first glance. It isn't as simple as noticing that the environment is demanding change or is presenting opportunity for productive change. We actually need to piece together a construction of the environment that suggests this reality.

Karl Weick (1979) suggests "managers [and others] construct, rearrange, single out, and demolish many objective features of their surroundings" (p. 164). He calls this process **enactment**. In this process stakeholders "enact" or "construct" their environment through a process of social interaction and sensemaking. As we encounter our world we attempt to form coherent accounts of "what is going on." We do that by selecting evidence that supports one theory over the other

– like a detective might in solving a murder mystery. However, the process is far from perfectly rational or a lone act of individuals. We have biases about what we want to be the truth of the matter and we are influenced heavily by the enacted realities of those around us (Weick, 1995). Through communication we share our theories of "what is going on" and we purposefully or incidentally influence the process of enactment of others. As Weick (1979, 1995) argues, we simply forget some facts, reconstruct some to better fit the theory of reality we prefer, and look for supportive evidence to bolster our preferred case. He suggests that sensemaking is as much about "authoring" as interpretation.

In this way communication plays a central role in surfacing or suppressing triggers for change. For example, a theory that the economy is in a downturn can be supported and refuted through different ways of looking at evidence, different ways of framing evidence, and constructing evidence through managing meanings that others attach to their observations. An alternate theory can reconstitute observations, history and the narrative around these "facts" in ways that suggest not a downturn but a natural lull or a period of great opportunity. Perceptions that an organization is in a crisis; needs to be responsive to a particular stakeholder; is headed for greatness; exists in a time rich with opportunity; or any number of other characterizations are created through this process.

As discussed more in Chapter 8, communication among stakeholders is at the heart of change processes in organizations because of this highly social process of making sense of what is going on and "spinning" it into narratives and theories of the world around us.

Many attempts at organizational change have met with failure by the standards of stakeholders who served as implementers. Statistics on failures of implementation efforts are significant. Knodel (2004) suggests that 80% of implementation efforts fail to deliver their promised value, 28% are canceled before completion, and 43% are overextended or delivered late. Researchers estimate from data that approximately 75% of mergers and acquisitions fall short of their financial and strategic objectives (see Marks and Mirvis, 2001), as many as 95% of mergers fail (e.g., Boeh and Beamish, 2006), 60–75% of new information technology systems fail (Rizzuto and Reeves, 2007), and estimates of sales force automation failure are between 55 and 80% (Bush, Moore, and Rocco, 2005). A recent global survey of executives by McKinsey consultants revealed that only one-third of organizational change efforts were considered successful by their leaders (Meaney and Pung, 2008). These alarming statistics make one wonder if it is possible to do change well.

The consequences of failure are costly on many levels. Failure of organizational changes may have minor or major consequences for stakeholders associated with an organization and on the ultimate survival of an organization. The energy and resources necessary to undergo moderate to major change are often high. Costs include financial expenditures; lost productivity; lost time in training and retraining workers; confusion, fatigue, and resentment for workers, clients, customers, suppliers, and other key stakeholders; damage to brand; disruption in workflow; and loss of high value stakeholders including workers, supporters, clients/customers, among others. Those costs are not paid off if the change does not yield benefits and/or if it causes additional disruption as the organization retreats to previous practices or moves on to yet another change to replace a dysfunctional one. Change, while common in many organizations, is frequently troublesome and often fails to yield desired benefits.

Most of the failure statistics are generated through official accounts of how organizational leaders and managers judge outcomes. The judgments of failure and success made by non-implementer stakeholders is much more difficult to estimate. Anecdotal evidence in case studies suggest that stakeholders – primarily employees – often have a difficult time during change and that change takes a high toll on stress levels and feelings of commitment to the organization (I will return to this in Chapters 2 and 4). Negative outcomes of change processes in organizations are much more frequently documented than positive ones but rarely are non-implementers asked for their assessments of the results of change programs. Certainly, the ways stakeholders talk about changes that are occurring and have occurred – as failures or successes – impacts their sensemaking about the worthiness of any given initiative. The degree to which implementers and stakeholders agree in framing success and failure can have tremendous impacts on future change initiatives. I will discuss these issues more in Chapter 4.

What Is Organizational Change?

We should examine more closely exactly what this common and troublesome aspect of organizational life entails and what is meant by the concept of organizational change. Zorn *et al.* define change as referring "to any alteration or modification of organizational structures or processes" (1999, p. 10). This and other definitions of change often imply that there are periods of stability in organizations that are absent of change or that a normal state for organizations is marked by routine, consistency, and stability. Although stakeholders may experience organizations as more familiar and stable at some points and as more disrupted and in flux at other points, we can certainly observe that organizing activity is made up of processes and as such is always in motion and always changing. This book is concerned with planned change and periods in organizations where purposeful introductions of change are made in some bracketed moment in the flow of organizing activities. That is, managers and implementers attempt to disrupt what is normal and routine with something else.

The process of implementing change in organizations sometimes begins with processes of innovation and diffusion and nearly always involves a formal adoption process and implementation. **Innovation** is a creative process of generating ideas for practice. Organizational changes are sometimes generated through accidental or intentional innovation processes used by organizations to create new ways of doing or new things to do. However, organizations don't always choose to change based on a self-generated idea. Sometimes, as noted earlier, pressures from environment drive changes or changes are spread through a network (e.g., professional associates) or within a particular context (e.g., industry). **Diffusion** is the process involved in sharing new ideas with others to the point that they "catch on."

Organizational changes may be spread through a diffusion process where important organizational stakeholders or networked organizations select an idea and then others in the network become aware of the choice – typically through communication in social networks. **Adoption** is the term we use to describe the formal selection of the idea for incorporation into an organization. An illustration of the process of diffusion is provided in the stories of the "drive-thru window." As we are all accustomed to now, drive-thru windows are a modern convenience of fast-food restaurants, coffee shops, pharmacies, banks, some liquor stores, and even marriage chapels in Las Vegas! The drive-thru allows customers to do business without leaving their cars. Drive-thru restaurants (different from drive-ins where customers parked and receive service at their car) were invented by In-N-Out Burger in 1948 (In-N-Out Burger Home Page). By 1975 the fast-food giant McDonald's opened its first drive-thru in Sierra Vista, Arizona, followed ten years later by a drive-thru in Dublin, Ireland (Sickels, 2004). The success of drive-thrus in the high profile fast-food company doubtlessly encouraged the diffusion of the practice in other fast-food businesses. As smaller chains sought to mimic the successful practices of McDonalds they were more likely to adopt this practice to remain competitive.

Another pattern is shown in the use of drive-thru banks which, following the 1928 adoption by UMB Financial, increased steadily over several decades and spread internationally.[1] However, in recent years there has been a decline in drive-thru banking due to increased traffic and availability of automated teller machines, telephone, and Internet banking. As these new technologies became available, the drive-thru feature at banks has become less desirable or needed and so is disappearing. **Discontinuance** (Rogers, 1983), the gradual ending of a practice such as the drive-thru innovation, is brought about through the rise in other innovations that are being diffused throughout the banking industry. The convenience of automated teller machines in every mall, many stores, and scattered throughout any person's daily path, makes the convenience of the drive-thru comparatively less desirable. The observations of these changes in the environment as other innovations diffused more and more widely, has led many banks to decrease use of their own drive-thru.

In the story of adoption of drive-thrus by pharmacies we find that some current research indicates that dispensing of medications through drive-thru windows may increase the chance the pharmacist will become distracted, be less efficient, and make more errors.[2] Further, some pharmacists worry that replacing face-to-face interaction with a drive-thru experience will harm both the professional standing of pharmacists and the quality of exchanges between pharmacists and customers. In fact, the American Pharmacists Association put out a statement in 2008 discouraging the use of drive-thru pharmacies unless pharmaceutical care can be adequately delivered.[3] In this case, although the practice of drive-thru convenience is still common, a set of stakeholders from the professional field may eventually bring enough pressure to bear that the use of drive-thrus in this context will be discontinued. This example illustrates the power of communication in both spawning and stalling the spread of change in an environment. Owners of pharmacies will have to balance their observations of what successful competitors are doing, and the desires of customers, with pressures from professionals in their employ and agencies that regulate dispensing of medication. Balancing the demands of different stakeholders while keeping an eye on the diffusion and/or discontinuance of drive-thru pharmacy technology will play a key role in any given pharmacy's decision to maintain this innovation. The means by which organizations keep tabs on such trends is through their communication with stakeholders.

As these examples help illustrate, a key to diffusion is often the social pressure of what other successful organizations in the environment or context are doing and how success is defined. Social pressure is exerted through communicative relationships. For example, Andrew Flanagin (2000) found evidence that nonprofit organizations' self-perceptions of their status and leadership position in their field is positively correlated with adoption of websites. They ascribed this in part to felt pressures to stay on the leading edge. As more and more organizations in a local area or within an industry adopt a specific innovation, the pressure mounts for those who don't have that innovation to try it. However, as powerful stakeholders eschew an idea or find they desire other alternatives, pressure to drop a new idea may mount.

Some ideas provoke more attention as they become more popular (more diffused) in the context or environment in which an organization exists. For example, Total Quality programs became highly popular and started to catch on in the 1980s as a marker of excellence in companies around the world. Having a quality program in your organization became an important indicator that your products, services, and operations were well run, reliable, and continuously being improved (all markers of Total Quality).

Awards are given for organizations that are able to demonstrate evidence of quality programs. The Malcolm Baldridge award (see Highlight Box 1.1), named in honor of the Secretary of Commerce from 1981 until his death in 1987, is the most prominent example of this. The award is recognized internationally as a prominent marker of high quality. Another international standard used in quality management systems is called ISO 9000 and is maintained by the International Organization for Standardization located in Switzerland (see Highlight Box 1.2).

Thousands of companies in over 100 countries have already been certified as ISO organizations. ISO's standards are used to facilitate international trade by providing a single set of standards that people everywhere in the world can recognize and respect. The existence and popularity of these practices and standards create pressure to engage in change because important stakeholders such as major trading partners and customers value them. Accreditation and standards show up in nonprofit and governmental sectors too. For example, universities are accredited through regional accreditation organizations that review practices every few years. Non-accredited universities and colleges risk loss of federal approval and financial support such as aid to students for tuition. These losses would make it very difficult, if not impossible, to operate or to attract grant dollars or students. Independent watchdog

Highlight Box 1.1: The Malcolm Baldrige Award

What is the Malcolm Baldrige National Quality Award?

The Baldrige Award is given by the President of the United States to manufacturing and service businesses and to education, health care, and nonprofit organizations that apply and are judged to be outstanding in seven areas: leadership; strategic planning; customer and market focus; measurement, analysis, and knowledge management; workforce focus; process management; and results. Congress established the award program in 1987 to recognize US organizations for their achievements in quality and performance and to raise awareness about the importance of quality and performance excellence as a competitive edge.

Why was the award established?

In the early and mid-1980s, many industry and government leaders saw that a renewed emphasis on quality was no longer an option for American companies but a necessity for doing business in an ever expanding, and more demanding, competitive world market. But many American businesses either did not believe quality mattered for them or did not know where to begin. The Baldrige Award was envisioned as a standard of excellence that would help US organizations achieve world-class quality.

How is the Baldrige Award achieving its goals?

The criteria for the Baldrige Award have played a major role in achieving the goals established by Congress. They now are accepted widely, not only in the United States but also around the world, as the standard for performance excellence. The criteria are used by thousands of organizations of all kinds for self-assessment and training and as a tool to develop performance and business processes. Several million copies have been distributed since the first edition in 1988, and heavy reproduction and electronic access multiply that number many times.

For many organizations, using the criteria results in better employee relations, higher productivity, greater customer satisfaction, increased market share, and improved profitability. According to a report by the Conference Board, a business membership organization, "A majority of large US firms have used the criteria of the Malcolm Baldrige National Quality Award for self-improvement, and the evidence suggests a long-term link between use of the Baldrige criteria and improved business performance."

Which organizations have received the award in recent years?

2008 Cargill Corn Milling North America, Poudre Valley Health System, and Iredell-Statesville Schools.

2007 PRO-TEC Coating Co., Mercy Health Systems, Sharp HealthCare, City of Coral Springs, and US Army Research, Development and Engineering (ARDEC).

Source: Adapted from http://www.nist.gov/public_affairs/factsheet/baldfaqs. htm.

groups, nonprofit foundation associations, and professional associations that monitor standards of practice and ethical codes (e.g., standards for governance and operating practices) pass judgments on nonprofit organizations. The Independent Sector, a nonpartisan coalition focused on charitable organizations, provides an index to the various standards applied to nonprofits in different sectors (e.g., arts, education, environment, health, human services) and different places nationally and internationally.

In planned organizational change, once organizational leaders adopt an idea, their next task is to implement it. Tornatzky and Johnson (1982) define **implementation** as "the translation of any tool or technique, process, or method of doing, from knowledge to practice" (p. 193). Here again communication plays a tremendous role in that translation. In implementing a change implementers will see a need to convince stakeholders to alter practices, processes, procedures, work arrangements, and often beliefs and values as well. In the examples we just reviewed, implementation would follow the decision to adopt a drive-thru or a quality program. Knowledgeable experts would need to help install the necessary technology; train personnel; explain changes to clients and customers; and redesign work processes around these changes. In

Highlight Box 1.2: ISO Standards

ISO (International Organization for Standardization) is the world's **largest developer** and publisher of **International Standards**.

ISO is a **network** of the national standards institutes of **158 countries**, one member per country, with a Central Secretariat in Geneva, Switzerland, that coordinates the system.

ISO is a **non-governmental organization** that forms a bridge between the public and private sectors. On the one hand, many of its member institutes are part of the governmental structure of their countries, or are mandated by their government. On the other hand, other members have their roots uniquely in the private sector, having been set up by national partnerships of industry associations.

Therefore, ISO enables a **consensus** to be reached on solutions that meet both the requirements of business and **the broader needs of society**.

ISO standards:

- make the development, manufacturing and supply of products and services **more efficient, safer, and cleaner**
- **facilitate trade** between countries and make it **fairer**
- provide governments with a technical base for **health, safety and environmental legislation**, and conformity assessment
- **share** technological advances and good management practice
- disseminate **innovation**
- **safeguard consumers**, and users in general, of products and services
- make life simpler by providing **solutions** to common problems

Source: Adapted from http://www.iso.org/iso/home.htm.

change implementation, communication is a means by which stakeholders describe, persuade, define, instruct, support, resist, and evaluate the new and old practices.

Drive-thrus are a well-known idea that any employee would be familiar with now, but when they were first introduced the very concept must have seemed novel! Explaining to employees and managers how to manage communication tasks with customers at the drive-thru window, working with intercom systems, and coping with problems in the technology, must have presented some initial challenges and perhaps resistance. And, once the employees were trained then the customers had to be taught how to use drive-thru windows so they did not shout into the intercom or become confused about the script of order-taking that might otherwise involve overlapping talk. They needed to learn how to navigate the drive-thru lane, know which window to pay at and which one to pick up at. They had to be ready to give an order when it was asked for and they needed to have money ready at the pay window. Implementers of this change needed to plan for how to train both employees and customers. No doubt implementers in different organizations turned to one another for ideas about how best to accomplish implementation.

The relationship among the concepts raised here – innovation, diffusion, adoption, and implementation – have not always been clearly articulated nor used consistently in much of the scholarly literature on organizational change. For example, adoption sometimes has been used to describe the adoption decision, such as we are using it here, and at other times as an outcome of implementation – the completion of implementation such that the change/idea is part of ongoing normal practice in the organization. Further, the term innovation has been used both to describe the object/idea that is implemented in an organization as well as the process by which it is created.

These concepts have often been viewed and visually represented as a set of phases of the change process within a single organization. Rogers (1995) arrays them in the order of agenda-setting – matching – redefining/restructuring (reinvention) – clarifying – routinizing. The first two phases he considers as "initiation" stages where change ideas are compared against the perceived problems in the organization and the last three he considers part of "implementation" where the changes are brought into use and fit into the existing practices of the stakeholders. The decision to adopt is the dividing line between the first and second phase of the process.

Lewin's classic work (1951) suggests phases of unfreezing – changing – refreezing. These and other similar models and variations on these models share the assumptions that these phases of change are singular, proceed linearly, map the process *within* a given organization, and result in either routinization of use, some variant of use, or nonuse/discontinuance of use. This model grossly oversimplifies the complexity of change. First, it assumes "the change" is agreed upon by stakeholders and has a fixed set of qualities that are immutable. Second, it assumes that the change itself is static and unchanging during implementation and merely needs to be plunked down into ongoing activity in an organization – like placing a rock in a stream.

In fact, the change itself will constantly shift as it is negotiated by the stakeholders who engage about it and with it. For example, one could view the pharmacy drive-thru window as a means to de-emphasize the role of the pharmacist or to deprofessionalize that role. It could also be framed as a means to improve efficiency or as a method to increase speed of customer service without regard to the quality of that service. Different stakeholders will doubtlessly have different takes on what "it" is. They also will interact with one another and influence those perspectives over time, thus shaping and reshaping the conceptualizations of the change over time. This communicative process involved in framing a given change calls into question Lewin's language of freezing.

As we noted at the start of this section, one could make similar observations about the "frozen" state of organizations prior to periods of change. This language implies that organizations are at one moment stable and at another in flux. In fact, organizations are constantly in flux. Further, stakeholders have multiple versions of the organization in mind as they construct what the organization is and reconstitute those notions as they interact with other stakeholders who may view it differently. In the case of a pharmacy, for example, the pharmacists may see it as a medical dispensing organization staffed with professionals to guide patients in order to improve health practices, while the owners may view it as a store that sells things to customers with the aim of gaining a profit. These different constructions of the organization create a bias in interpreting any change that is introduced.

Typically, routinization is considered as successful incorporation of the innovation into regular routine practices in the organization in ways that align with the designers' intentions. More recent work, beginning with Rogers' notion of "reinvention," has acknowledged that variation in the use through adjustment by users after a period of experimentation has benefits and can be considered successful as well. In a later chapter we will consider other ways of conceptualizing outcomes of change. Here we point to the general relationships among these phases of organizational change to elaborate a different way of constructing them.

We can better represent the relationships of these concepts if we simultaneously consider the processes of environment change and an individual focal organization's change (see Figure 1.1). As is illustrated in the figure, change processes in organizations have a reciprocal impact with environmental diffusion and innovation processes. That is, a given organization's decision to adopt, its implementation process, and its

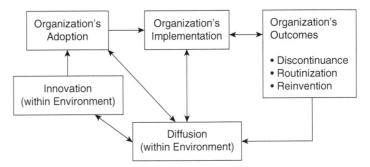

Figure 1.1   Relationships between innovation, diffusion, adoption, and implementation

"success" in implementing a change are related to diffusion of the change in the environment. A change that is more or less successful in any given organization may increase the chances of its diffusion further in the environment. So organizations that have success with an innovation are likely to be noticed by other organizations that then may base decisions to adopt and the manner of implementation, in part, on that observed experience. For example, the experience of In-N-Out Burger in implementing the drive-thru window was noticed by other organizations. Leaders of other organizations assessed the success and potential for future success with that innovation. Those observations and assessments were then useful as those leaders decided whether to incorporate the innovation into their own operations.

Further, the diffusion of a change in the environment will impact an individual organization's adoption decisions (e.g., more diffusion may make it more likely for an individual organization to adopt). So, as more and more fast-food companies added drive-thru windows, customers began to expect that option. It becomes harder to resist trends in service when competitors are all adopting the same practice.

Also, the pattern and pace of diffusion of the change within the environment may impact any given organization's manner of implementation. Other organizations' modifications to the change idea may affect the effort expended, direction of modifications, and focus of efforts in implementation within an organization. For example, if other large fast-food chains were using drive-thrus only in urban areas, but not in rural areas, that might suggest to other chains that they do likewise. However, a pattern of implementing drive-thrus across all locations would put pressure on competitors to do the same. So, the individual adoption strategies of a given organization contribute to diffusion in the environment as these are observed by other organizations. The result of this process of diffusion and the expectations that are created in organizational environments for organizations to obey is described as institutionalization. I will return to discuss this process more in Chapter 7.

This model and example illustrate a few important lessons about these key concepts related to organizational change. First, we cannot fully separate the experiences of other organizations in the environment from that of an individual organization. Where change efforts are not particular to an individual organization and there is some experience with similar change observable in the organization's environment, the ongoing diffusion and innovation related to the change elsewhere will interact with the internal change processes of any given organization. And, even if the change is original to a given organization (as in the experience of In-N-Out Burger), that change experience, once known in the environment, may well trigger sensemaking and action on the part of other organizations (e.g., drive-thru windows were copied by other restaurants when they looked like a success).

Thus, the relationships between an individual organization's process and those of other organizations as well as the environment at large are complex and ongoing. How organizational leaders make sense of and "enact" their environments (is a practice or idea "catching on" or "dying out"?), the organizations they use as important reference points (e.g., the largest organization; the longest standing leader; the trendiest organization), and the interactions that organizations have with one another and with other important stakeholders about particular experiences with changes or types of change (e.g., organizational decision makers discussions of trends in the industry; experts in various businesses processes comparison of data; market researchers sharing knowledge; advocacy organizations attempts to influence change) are critical in all these processes of innovation, diffusion, adoption, and implementation. As I argued at the beginning of this chapter, stakeholders, including leaders of organizations, influence one another's constructions of "what is really going on" in their world. The communication that occurs among them has a powerful influence on how they construct evidence for different theories of how a specific change is moving through an environment.

Second, the relationships among these processes are ongoing and often create reciprocal loops. Organizations' reaffirmation of adoption or discontinuance decisions are often considered in light of perceived outcomes. As stakeholders construct a specific organization's change as a failure to reap projected results, decision-makers may decide to reconsider an adoption decision. The same may be true if they come to the conclusion that a change isn't catching on in the environment. Thus, the adoption decision is not a single fixed point along a linear path of change. The same can be observed about implementation, in that it is an ongoing process of adjustment deriving data from observations about internal organizational outcomes; environmental diffusion; specific processes and outcomes of other organizations in the environment; and most importantly, the social interaction of decision-makers as they enact their environments and make sense of "what is going on."

We can further complicate this model if we consider that multiple change efforts will likely overlap in time with one another. As one change in a given organization is being initially adopted, another may be in a late stage of reinvention and refinement of implementation and yet another may be in a process of discontinuance due to lack of environmental diffusion. Our case study of Ingredients Inc. provides a good example of multiple change (see Case Box 1.1). As we will consider in a later chapter, these multiple change efforts have impact on one another on many levels. For now we can observe that both the reciprocality and nonlinearity among these processes as well as the interrelationship between environmental processes and organizational processes make change a highly complex dynamic.

Case Box 1.1: Ingredients Inc. Experiences Overlapping Changes

Ingredients Inc. experienced a vast array of change during a 12-month time frame: Merger, May 2006; Location or Condition changes, June 2006; Technology changes, October 2006; Responsibilities changes, October 2006; Restructuring, November 2006; Policy and Procedure changes, January 2007; new CEO, January 2007; the Acquisition, February 2007; and Pay and Bonus changes, May 2007. The lifespan of each of the changes was different, and additional changes within a change were also noted to occur (e.g., departments were restructured several times, new policies and procedures were continually released over several months).

Source: Adapted from Laster (2008).

Types of Organizational Change

There are many ways of describing types of organizational changes. Here we will review three ways to categorize and conceptualize different change types. First, we can describe change as planned or unplanned. Keeping in mind that organizing activity is constantly in flux, we can still isolate periods of discernible disruptions to patterned activity. **Planned changes** are those brought about through the purposeful efforts of organizational stakeholders who are accountable for the organization's operation. **Unplanned changes** are those brought into the organization due to environmental or uncontrollable forces (e.g., fire burns down plant, governmental shutdown of production) or emergent processes and interactions in the organization (e.g., drift in practices, erosion of skills). There is sometimes a fine distinction between planned change and planned responses to unplanned change. For example, the death of a founder CEO would count as an unplanned change but the processes involved in replacing that founder with a successor would be considered planned change. Major unplanned changes in the circumstances of organizations often require responses that are more than mere crisis intervention. In some cases lengthy and complex planned changes are necessary.

Another kind of unplanned change involves the slow evolution of organizational practice and/or structure over time. Some scholars (Hannan and Freeman, 1977, 1989) have focused their study of organizations at the level of whole communities or niches of organizations and have examined the ways in which these systems evolve over time. For some theorists, change is conceptualized as occurring gradually as an inherent part of organizing (Miller and Friesen, 1982, 1984). Life cycle theories specify standard stages of organizational development such as birth, growth, decline, and death. Others specify development of organizations as a sequence of alteration of organizational characteristics through variation, selection, retention, and variation within environments. As organizational decision-makers take note of key environmental shifts and/or alterations of the life stage of an organization, they may make planned changes to adapt to those circumstances. Often the difference between planned and unplanned change concerns the perspective from which one views the change and the triggering events for change that are relevant to the analysis.

A second way we can describe change is in terms of the *objects that are changed*. Typically, scholars refer to these objects in discrete categories of: technologies, programs, policies, processes, and person-nel. Lewis and colleagues (Lewis, 2000; Lewis and Seibold, 1998) have noted that organizational changes usually have multiple components that are difficult to describe with a single term. For example, technologi-cal changes usually have implications for new policy and new proce-dures and specify new role relationships. Making a new technology available necessitates specifying the appropriate use and users of the technology; the schedule and manner of use; and the personnel who can use and approve use. Further, the purposes of technologies are often to improve processes or products. For these reasons, it may not be useful or very accurate to describe "change type" in terms of whether they are technologies, procedures, or policies. Such theorizing is likely to be unreliable since so many changes have multiple components.

Zorn *et al.* (1999) have made the distinction between material and discursive changes. "**Discursive change**" (p. 10) often involves relabel-ing of practices as something new in order to give the appearance of changed practice without really doing things differently. They give the example of embracing the term "team" for a work group as a way of discursively altering how the organization considers the work and workers without really changing the practices or process of the work. They contrast this with "**material change**" that alters operations, prac-tices, relationships, decision-making, and the like. Although they under-score that discursive change is still consequential in organizations, it is often experienced differently from these other types of change.

I remember working in a fast-food restaurant as a high school student when the company came out with a new promotion. This was for dis-counted deals for a somewhat more modest version of a regularly priced meal and was very popular for a summer. In fact, the deals were so popular that they generated a flood of new customers – good for busi-ness, but not necessarily regarded positively by the minimum wage earners whose job it was to serve all those customers. Consequently, we nicknamed the new meal "bummers." When a customer ordered these meals, the front counter person would call back to the cooks and packaging folks "two bummers!" Once a secret shopper from the district came in to inspect and rate our performance and heard our new nick-name for the product. She was not amused. This is a good example of how an unplanned discursive change (the relabeling of the new product) can occur in organizations.

A third way to describe types of changes concerns the *size and scope* of change. This is usually described in terms of first- and second-order change (Bartunek and Moch, 1987). **First-order changes** are small, incremental predictable interruptions in normal practice. **Second-order changes** are large transformational or radical changes that depart significantly from previous practice in ways that are somewhat frame-breaking. These changes call key organizational assumptions into question. **Third-order changes** involve the preparation for continuous change.

One problem with this means of assessing the magnitude of change is that stakeholders oftentimes view changes in different ways. A change may be viewed as relatively minor and as a somewhat predictable interruption in normal practice for some, but for others considered an expansive and significant change. Individuals' experiences and tolerances for change vary and thus their perceptions of size and scope of change will vary as well. So finding an objective standard to judge size and scope may be meaningless if it does not match what stakeholders perceive.

Our individual assessments of the size and scope of change are effected by how directly the change effects us; how profound the change to our own lives may be; what we value in our organizational lives; our own history with change in our personal and organizational life; and perhaps most profoundly, the interactions we have with others about the change. In the example of Allen, the line worker in the Introduction, we see evidence that the merger represents a highly emotionally charged change for him. His reaction to the shift supervisor meeting is a gut-wrenching feeling. This might be brought on by fears that the merger could result in layoffs and put his position at risk. It might be that the way of work in his unit might change dramatically and he might not be able to maintain an acceptable quality of work. For some of his co-workers, the rumored merger might bring excitement if they think this will bring greater job security, higher wages, and more opportunities. Some may think it doesn't really change anything important for them. Each of these workers will potentially assess the size and scope of the change differently. Doubtless, they will share those assessments with one another and that is likely to trigger further sensemaking about "what is going on."

For changes that are less well defined and less understood, the assessments of the size and scope will vary even more widely. The case of Allison (the professor in the Introduction) is a good example of this. Allison felt the briefing on the expected changes taking place in higher education was a waste of her time. From the perspective of those closer to the Department of Education hearings, this was a far-reaching change that might reshape higher education. However, to Allison it seemed like another bureaucratic annoyance. Until she is convinced otherwise by trusted colleagues or influential people in her network, she would be dismissive of the change as unimportant and irrelevant.

Another complication in estimating size and scope of change is that change is sometimes not one single thing. In fact, Nicole Laster (2008) argues that changes are rarely singular. That is, changes have parts and have consequences that are in themselves changes. In her conceptualization, **multifaceted** change occurs when more than one change occurs within the same time frame. She classifies multifaceted change as either "**multiple change**" – two or more independent changes occurring at the same time – or as "**multi-dimensional change**" where one or more changes have subsequent parts. Certainly either type of multi-faceted change, especially if a larger order of change, presents a greater burden on stakeholders experiencing the change than changes more singular and/or of a smaller order. In her study, the key difference in how individual employees made sense of the size and scope of the change was how implementers talked about it at the outset. This had a huge impact on what these employees were expecting at the outset of change and colored their experiences of change in terms of setting them up for surprises, additional stress, and disappointment.

Overall, the language we have reviewed here for describing types of change help us to estimate both the size of potential ripple effects of change in an organization and the degree to which change is likely to be expected or unexpected. This language also helps us to identify the range of potential stakeholders who will experience impact from a change or set of changes. The three major cases used in this book provide examples of the types of changes from planned (merger, communication technologies) to unplanned (alteration of policy and practices in shaping higher education institutions); material (merger, communication technologies, some aspects of higher education practice) and discursive (some aspects of higher education policies); and small (communication technologies) and large scope (merger, higher education policies and practices). The contexts for these implementation efforts span from an individually newly created organization, to a closely connected interorganizational network, to a geographically dispersed set of institutions. I will rely on examples from these cases to illustrate concepts throughout the book.

We can combine these three categories (planned/unplanned; small scope/large scope; material/discursive) that describe change to construct theory about how some kinds of changes may operate differently; present unique problems; require specific strategies; and/or have differ-

	Planned	Unplanned
Smaller Scope	**Material** new copy machine	**Material** reporting procedures altered by regulatory body
	Discursive start calling staff "associates"	**Discursive** employees nickname a product/process by unwanted term
Larger Scope	**Material** merger	**Material** major funding source is cut off
	Discursive institute language of "Quality" to describe processes	**Discursive** brand becomes damaged through negative association

Figure 1.2   Types of organizational change in combination

ent implications for relationships between process and outcome. Figure 1.2 provides an example of how these different descriptors of change type can be used in concert to help us make predictions about change. With empirical work we could easily compare the eight combination types of change. For example, we might hypothesize that large-scope, material planned changes are some of the most challenging changes to carry out involving high degrees of communicative and other resources. It also may be that unplanned discursive changes are harder to explain to stakeholders than are unplanned material changes and are also more likely to lead to subsequent planned changes. Further, assessment of intended and actual outcomes from discursive changes, especially when unplanned and large, may be more difficult than assessment of material change. These are only examples of the sort of hypothesis-testing and ultimate theory building that can arise from fuller descriptions of types of change. Examination and comparison of specific real-life cases of a variety of change types will also potentially yield important insights for both scholars and practitioners from the rich detail provided in such examples.

Complexity of Change Within Organizations

Changes in complex organizations have unique characteristics by virtue of the features of interdependence, organizational structures, and politics. *Interdependence* concerns the degree to which stakeholders impact the lives of other stakeholders as they engage change. Unlike individual adoption of ideas/changes in private life (e.g., switching to HD TV, choosing a new doctor), individuals' choices to cooperate in change in organizations nearly always will have implications for others who are asked to make the same adoption choice and for others who are impacted by the ripple effects of change. So, my decision to select a given doctor over my current one may not impact my neighbor's decision (except insofar that he wants to pay attention to my choice or is socially influenced by it). However, my decision not to cooperate in a new work process could completely forestall another unit or set of workers' abilities to participate in that process as well as impact the customers of the product I help to produce. That effect is due to our interdependence.

Sequential interdependence is a special type of interdependence wherein stakeholders affect each other in sequence. An assembly line is a good example of this. As a worker toward the start of the line gets behind in her work, other workers later in the line will have the pace of their work affected too. If the later worker cannot do his part until the earlier worker does hers, they are sequentially interdependent. **Reciprocal interdependence** (Thompson, 1967) concerns the situation where one stakeholder's inputs are another stakeholder's outputs and vice versa. In this situation the work of one person is necessitated by the work of another. Further, the products of the individual work provide input back to the original propagator of the work. A good example of reciprocal interdependence is joint authorship of a report or document. As one part is written, other parts may need to be adjusted to account for the new writing. As that rewrite is completed, the original work may be adjusted again. One author cannot adjust until he/she sees what the other author has done, and those changes are the cause of the additional changes.

Where workers or other stakeholders are sequentially or reciprocally interdependent, participation in change becomes highly social and creates greater demands for coordination. Because organizational goals are often premised on interdependence among the participants, organizational leaders are unlikely to utilize an individualized choice model in introducing change. More typically, organizational leaders make the choice on behalf of units or whole organizations and then use implementation strategies to cajole, persuade or force a predesigned form of participation from internal (and sometimes external) stakeholders.

Organizations cannot always benefit from a particular change unless all, or at least most, of the stakeholders are using/participating in the change in a coordinated manner. For example, if the accounting department decides to switch to a new system for automating payroll that will be faster and more accurate, they would likely require all department supervisors to report employee work hours in the same way by the same deadline. If they let each supervisor decide independently how to report the hours and everyone was doing it differently, the benefits of the new system might not be realized. Not all changes in organizations operate in this manner. Some changes might well be adopted individually and differently. We'll return to this idea in a later chapter. The point here is that when interdependence is high, change often requires cooperative and coordinated efforts on the part of stakeholders.

Organizational structure is another component that makes organizational change especially complex and different from individual change. Organizations are made up, in part, by structures (Giddens, 1984). **Structures** are rules and resources that create organizational practices. **Rules** include simple but powerful ideas like "majority wins" or "high performers are rewarded more than lesser performers." **Resources** include ways of doing, organizational beliefs, and important possessions in an organization that can be invoked in order to move along a new idea or to make a case for staying the course on an action. Status is a powerful example of a resource in an organization. Those with powerful positions have an important resource in influencing how actions are taken. One reason people have power in organizations is by virtue of their formal (position in the organizational chart) or informal status (close connection with someone with formal status; opinion leadership; expertise, long tenure) (Stevenson, Bartunek, and Borgatti, 2003). Information is another resource. As individuals or units increase their access and control over information, especially unique information, they become potentially more powerful. Information can be used, withheld, and shared in various ways that make some individuals or units able to manipulate the decisions made in organizations, shape knowledge claims that can be made, and/or impact the ways resources are allocated.

So, organizations are made up of many structures: decision-making patterns and processes, authority and role relationships, information-sharing norms, communication networks, and reward systems among others. As change is implemented in an organization it must survive all of the potential impacts of these structures. For example, if those who hold power in the organization (even those who are not within the group that approved adoption of the change) fail to support a change effort, it is much harder to sustain the effort. In another instance a change may face challenges because it creates too many ripples in how rules operate in the organization. In another example, moving from a traditional management structure to a team concept of management may necessitate abandoning rules of hierarchy (move from those with official power making most decisions to sharing decision making); information-sharing norms (move from hoarding information to widely sharing information); and rules of division of labor (move from strict job descriptions to loosening of roles and expanding job responsibilities).

Change may involve altering much about the organization's beliefs about work as well as practices. Because structures are highly embedded in organizations, they often are resistant to change. Stakeholders become accustomed to structures as they are and their mere continued existence over time may be reason enough to maintain them. From the way a group of boys picks teammates for a recess soccer game, to the way that a church group selects its leaders for important committees, to the way that organizations cooperating in an interagency collaboration decide how much money each organization must contribute to a project, structures are often highly fixed and determinant. Change that disrupts those structures often will be resisted or derailed to some extent. Of course such resistance might be healthy for an organization and/or may end up serving the interests and stakes of more or different groups of stakeholders.

Stephen Barley (1986, 1990) has investigated the effects of the introduction of change on structure. Barley writes about the introduction of new technologies into workplaces and the resultant effects on social structure. In his 1986 study of the implementation of CT scanners in a hospital he found that the introduction of this new technology had profound effects on the social structure, specifically role relationships, of radiologists and technologists. Technologists were more expert in reading the results of the new CT scanners and now held information and knowledge that violated the normative status relationship between technologists and radiologists. Barley describes this role reversal as generating considerable discomfort for both parties. To cope with the discomfort of dealing with situations in which technologists had to explain or teach radiologists, a clear violation of status norms, they created new patterns of interaction to avoid such encounters. Radiologists retreated from the CT area and the technologists took on more independent work. The discomfort of these structural ripple effects in this hospital made the implementation of the change much more complex.

In another example, Stevenson *et al.* (2003) studied the restructuring of networks in a school. A new position, academic director, was created in order to increase coordination (and thus more direct ties) among the different academic units at the school. Administrators in the school exercised "passive resistance" against the change over a year of attempted implementation. Much of the resistance centered around overlapping authority, decision-making power, and areas of responsibility of those involved in curriculum planning. Essentially, those with high structural autonomy (e.g., those who brokered the structural holes in the organization) were opposed to a change that would deflate their influence. Stevenson *et al.* show how the "backstage" changes in the informal communication networks of this organization had profound effects on the efforts to resist this change. As the implementation effort was trying to promote increasing ties among units, informal processes were at work in increasing separation among units. Clearly, the changes to structure were challenging to accomplish and the power of informal structure, operating underneath the radar of the implementers, was so difficult to detect that they concluded that nothing had changed in the year of introducing the change.

Politics is another component of organizations that can present challenges for change efforts (Buchanan, Claydon, and Doyle, 1999; Kumar and Thibodeaux, 1990). Drory and Romm (1990) define the elements of organizational political behavior as (1) a situation conditioned by uncertainty and conflict, (2) use of covert nonjob-related means to pursue concealed motives, and (3) self-serving outcomes that are opposed to organizational goals. From their perspective, politics results from the resolution of colliding interests among sets of stakeholder groups in and around organizations through institutional or personal power bases. As Boonstra and Gravenhorst (1998) argue concerning a theory of structural power during organizational change, "power use becomes visible when different interest groups negotiate about the direction of the change process" (p. 99). In politically sensitive change episodes where multiple parties have opposing interests and a balanced power relationship, "negotiations will be needed to come to an agreement about for instance the goals of the change, the way the change is going to be implemented, and the role of the different parties in the change process" (p. 106).

Implementation of change can compete for time, energy, attention, and resources that might otherwise be devoted to other things. The potential for this competition can give rise to politicization of change. Sponsors of a change can feel threatened by the redirection of resources towards other changes or other ongoing practices. Also, change programs that are risky or highly charged with potential for reward can give rise to competitive stakes in getting credit or blame for the outcomes. These dynamics can lead to sabotage, arguments rooted in self-interest, deal-making for mutual support and the like. Buchanan and Badham (1999) conclude from their review of literature and a set of case studies that "political behavior is an accepted and pervasive dimension of the change agent's role" (p. 624). In fact, some research has found that failures of change can sometimes be traced to failure of organizational coalitions supporting the change to marshal effective political strategies (Clegg, 1993; Perrow, 1983).

In Blazejewski and Dorow's (2003) account of a privatization of the Polish company that produced the Nivea brand of personal care products in Poland, they describe how internal political barriers against organizational change inhibited its effective adaptation to new complex environmental conditions. When the company was reacquired by its former parent company, it was dramatically restructured through a coercive non-participative model of change implementation. The authors suggest that resistance to this strategy was low because it was accompanied by the investment of a number of desirable resources including new pay and benefits; changing work conditions; changes to physical environment and office technology. The commitment perceived by the takeover company facilitated tolerance for the top-down style of management during the change. A micro-level political game played out where benefits outweighed the disadvantages of the method of change. This was possible because of the power base available to the implementers – namely, huge financial resources.

The Spellings case provides another example of how politics can play a role in change (US Department of Education, 2006; see Case Box 1.2). When one of the Commissioners, a leader in an influential higher education association, decided neither to endorse nor sign the Report it served as a powerful symbol that provided both supporters and critics of the Report as a reference to rally for their side of the issues. For some this was seen as a demonstration of power that thwarted attempts to make progress outlined in the Report; for others as a useful and high profile

Case Box 1.2: Spellings Commission Political Positions Play a Role

Each of the Spellings Commission members were asked to endorse the Report and all but one did. David Ward, the president of the American Council on Education, refused to sign. This was potentially a big problem since Ward represented the association with the most global and inclusive perspective on higher education. Ward explained his position in a statement that read in part:

> I didn't oppose the Report; I just simply said I couldn't sign it. There were significant areas that I supported. But in my case, I needed to be on the record in some formal way about those areas that gave me some disquiet. … I consider [my negative vote to suggest] a qualified support of a substantial part of it, but there were some significant, important areas that I just couldn't sign on to.

David Ward's refusal to sign and explanation stimulated much sensemaking on the part of stakeholders. As one interviewee in our study said "I think it was probably, in the big scheme of things, helpful, because it did indicate that there were different points of view." Some others expressed the point of view that the withheld signature further contributed to defensiveness and a counterproductive framing that decreased possibilities of a constructive response or collaborative tone. A few felt that Ward's action had little impact since other higher education leaders did endorse the Report.

Source: Adapted from Ruben, Lewis, and Sandmeyer (2008).

means for those in higher education to stand up against the Commission's indictments against higher education. However his action was regarded by individual stakeholders, it is clear that this leader relied upon his status both in higher education and his visible role in the Commission as a means to make a symbolic statement that carried political weight with many stakeholders. The ways in which stakeholders made sense of that symbolic act influenced their own willingness to support the Report's conclusions.

The picture emerging of change in complex organizations portrays a dynamic, interdependent, power-oriented image. How stakeholders react to changes as they are introduced in organizations may certainly be based in part on assessments of costs and benefits of use/participation in the change as a stakeholder examines the features, ties, and likely consequences of the change itself. However, it is just as, if not more, likely that reactions to changes will be rooted in complex social systems, organizational structures, power relations, and other ongoing organizational dynamics. Further, as observed throughout this chapter, the sensemaking engaged in through interaction among stakeholders plays an incredibly important role in enacting the "reality" of "what is really going on" in change, environments, and organizations. Various stakes are played out in these sensemaking conversations that have tremendous implications for how interdependent stakeholders, connected through complex network relationships and power structures, come to grapple with change.

Conclusion

In summary, this chapter has introduced the concept of change and helped to define the ways we can describe change. We have noted that organizations of all types are pressured and pushed towards change for all sorts of cultural, environmental, and internal reasons, and that the ways in which stakeholders enact their environments through social interaction are highly influential in enabling change to be considered and implemented. Further, change efforts – especially large-scale changes – often are constructed by influential stakeholders as having failed. Changes come in many sizes and types. We can describe change in terms of being planned and unplanned; of different types; and of different sizes and scope. We also have much evidence to suggest that change in complex organizations is often more dynamic and potentially more problematic because of the interdependent relationships among stakeholders, the political context of change, and the nature of organizational structures. Communication plays tremendously important roles throughout change processes in serving as the means by which people construct what is happening, influence the constructions of others, and develop responses to what is being introduced to them as change. The next chapter will focus more on some of the specific ways that stakeholders communicate and the communicative roles they play during organizational change.

Notes

1. Source: http://en.wikipedia.org/wiki/Drive-through.
2. Source: http://www.pharmacy.ohio-state.edu/news/med_errors.cfm.
3. American Pharmacists Association Academy of Student Pharmacists Report of the 2008 AphA-ASP Resolutions Committee.

References

Barley, S. (1986) Technology as on occasion for structuring: Evidence from observations of CT scanners and the social order of radiology departments. *Administrative Science Quarterly*, 31, 78–108.

Barley, S. (1990) The alignment of technology and structure through roles and networks. *Administrative Science Quarterly*, 35, 61–103.

Bartunek, J. M. and Moch, M. (1987) First order, second order, and third order change and organization development interventions: A cognitive approach. *Journal of Applied Behavioral Science*, 23, 483–500.

Blazejewski, S. and Dorow, W. (2003) Managing organizational politics for radical change: The case of Beiersdorf-Lechia S.A., Poznan. *Journal of World Business*, 38, 204–223.

Boeh, K. K. and Beamish, P. W. (2006) *Mergers and Acquisitions*. Thousand Oaks, CA: Sage.

Boonstra, J. J. and Gravenhorst, K. M. B. (1998) Power dynamics and organizational change: A comparison of perspectives. *European Journal of Work and Organizational Psychology*, 7 (2), 97–120.

Buchanan, D. and Badham, R. (1999) Politics and organizational change: The lived experience. *Human Relations*, 52 (5), 609–629.

Buchanan, D., Claydon, T., and Doyle, M. (1999) Organization development and change: The legacy of the nineties. *Human Resource Management Journal*, 9 (2), 20–37.

Bush, A. J., Moore, J. B., and Rocco, R. (2005) Understanding sales force automation outcomes: A managerial perspective. *Industrial Marketing Management*, 34 (4), 369–377.

Clegg, C. (1993) Social systems that marginalize the psychological and organizational aspects of information technology. *Behaviour and Information Technology*, 12 (5), 261–266.

Drory, A. and Romm, C. T. (1990) The definition of organizational politics: A review. *Human Relations*, 43 (1), 1133–1154.

Flanagin, A. (2000) Social pressures on organizational website adoption. *Human Communication Research*, 26 (4), 618–646.

Giddens, A. (1984) *The Constitution of Society: Outline of the Theory of Structuration*. Berkeley, CA: University of California Press.

Hannan, M. T. and Freeman, J. (1977) The population ecology of organizations. *American Journal of Sociology*, 82, 929–9064.

Hannan, M. T. and Freeman, J. (1989) *Organizational Ecology*. Cambridge, MA: Harvard University Press.

In-N-Out Burger Home Page: http://www.in-n-out.com/history.asp.

Knodel, T. (2004) Preparing the organizational "soil" for measurable and sustainable change: Business value management and project governance. *Journal of Change Management*, 4, 45–62.

Kumar, K. and Thibodeaux, M. S. (1990) Organizational politics and planned organizational change. *Group and Organization Studies*, 15, 357–365.

Laster, N. M. (2008) Communicating multiple change: Understanding the impact of change messages on stakeholder perceptions. Dissertation Abstracts International (UMI No. AAT 3342339).

Lewin, K. (1951) *Field Theory in Social Science*. New York: Harper.

Lewis, L. K. (2000) "Blindsided by that one" and "I saw that one coming": The relative anticipation and occurrence of communication problems and other problems in implementers' hindsight. *Journal of Applied Communication Research*, 28, 44–67.

Lewis, L. K. and Seibold, D. R. (1998) Reconceptualizing organizational change implementation as a communication problem: A review of literature and research agenda. In M. E. Roloff (ed.), *Communication Yearbook 21* (pp. 93–151). Thousand Oaks, CA: Sage.

Marks, M. L. and Mirvis, P. H. (2001) Making mergers and acquisitions work: Strategic psychological preparation. *Academy of Management Executive*, 15, 80–92.

Meaney, M. and Pung, C. (2008) McKinsey global results: Creating organizational transformations. *The McKinsey Quarterly*, August, 1–7.

Miller, D. and Friesen, P. H. (1982) Innovation in conservative and entrepreneurial firms: Two models of strategic momentum. *Strategic Management Journal*, 3, 1–25.

Miller, D. and Friesen, P. (1984) *Organizations: A Quantum View*. Englewood Cliffs, NJ: Prentice Hall.

NASULGC (2008) National Association of State Universities and Landgrant Colleges. Retrieved 11/01/08 from http://www.nasulgc.org/NetCommunity/Page.aspx?pid=1059andsrcid=183.

Perrow, C. (1983) The organizational context of human factors engineering. *Administrative Science Quarterly*, 521–541.

Rizzuto, T. E. and Reeves, J. (2007) A multidisciplinary meta-analysis of human barriers to technology implementation. *Consulting Psychology Journal: Practice and Research*, 59 (3), 226–240.

Sickels, R. J. (2004) *The 1940s*. Greenwood Press.

Rogers, E. M. (1983) *Diffusion of Innovations* (3rd edn.). New York: Free Press.

Ruben, B. D., Lewis, L., and Sandmeyer, L. (2008) *Assessing the Impact of the Spellings Commission: The Message, the Messenger, and the Dynamics of Change in Higher Education*. Washington, DC: National Association of College and University Business Officers.

Stevenson, W. B., Bartunek, J. M., and Borgatti, S. P. (2003) Front and backstage processes of an organizational restructuring effort. *Journal of Applied Behavioral Science*, 36 (3), 243–258.

Thompson, J. D. (1967) *Organizations in Action*. New York: McGraw-Hill.

Tornatzky, L. G. and Johnson, E. C. (1982) Research on implementation: Implications for evaluation practice and evaluation policy. *Evaluation and Program Planning*, 5, 193–198.

US Department of Education (2006) *The Spellings Commission Report*.

Weick, K. E. (1979) *The Social Psychology of Organizing*. Reading, MA: Addison-Wesley.

Weick, K. E. (1995) *Sensemaking in Organizations*. Thousand Oaks, CA: Sage.

Zorn, T., Christensen, L. T., and Cheney, G. (1999) *Do We Really Want Constant Change?* San Francisco, CA: Berrett-Koehler.

2

Processes of Communication During Change

The most important thing in communication is to hear what isn't being said

Peter Drucker

Without credible communication, and a lot of it, employee hearts and minds are never captured

John P. Kotter, "Leading change"

We are drowning in information but starved for knowledge

John Naisbitt

Communication practices are tremendously important in implementation of change in organizations, partly because they can be very problematic. A study (Lewis, 2000a) conducted with an international sample of for-profit, nonprofit, and governmental organizational implementers found that implementers rated communication problems as some of the most severe. The data analyses revealed that problems

Organizational Change: Creating Change Through Strategic Communication,
First Edition. Laurie K. Lewis.
© 2011 Laurie K. Lewis. Published 2011 by Blackwell Publishing Ltd.

related to poor communication of vision, poor follow-through, lack of top management support, and communication about implementation were among those that implementers failed to anticipate at the outset of the change. It appears that communication can be significantly troublesome to implementers and that the potential for problems is not always anticipated accurately.

In this chapter we will first make the distinction between formal and informal communication and then explore three key processes in communication during planned change in organizations – dissemination of information, soliciting input, and socialization – and discuss how both implementers as well as other stakeholders make strategic decisions about how to engage in each of these processes, as well as some of the consequences of communication that each process emphasizes.

The importance of communication can be captured in both formal and informal contexts. **Formal communication** involves use of official channels; declarations and policy set down by organizational leaders; implementers' instructions about the rate, timing, and details of change; formal responses of leaders to other stakeholders' challenges; and questions about changes. For example, one critical part of formal communication is the first official announcement of change. Often the manner, timing, message, and spokesperson of such announcements can set a tone that may have implications for the entire implementation effort (Smeltzer, 1995). For example, in the Spellings Commission case (see Case Box 2.1) the foretelling of the changes that the Commission was attempting to stimulate in higher education in the US set a highly negative tone. Readers of the report reacted with a knee-jerk defensiveness for being publicly critiqued by a body they considered as "outsiders" to higher education.

Informal communication may play an even larger role in determining outcomes of change. Informal communication during change includes the spontaneous interactions of stakeholders with each other, with implementers, and with non-stakeholders. These interactions may be no less strategic than the formal communication, but they are undertaken without the force of official authority or access to official channels, and sometimes in a manner that enables participants to deny ownership of what is shared (e.g., through off-record encounters and anonymous channels). They may concern reactions to change, supportive communication, tactical discussions formed around either advancing or resisting the change efforts, or evaluating and sharing information about change. Stakeholders interact with implementers, leaders, decision-makers, and with one another in informal day-to-day interactions about

Case Box 2.1: Spellings Commission – Responses to Change Announcement

The higher education community reacted with high initial resistance and negativity toward the Commission's Report. The language of the Report produced a backlash in response to a perceived overly harsh critique of the current state of higher education. Stakeholders considered that the gaps between the present and desired state of higher education were not as wide as the Commission implied in its Report. There was also concern that the Report implied a new crisis that many in higher education did not perceive. Rather, many stakeholders considered the legitimate critiques to have been fairly long-standing, resolvable, and not reason for public panic. As one interviewee, a higher education association leader, commented, "I'd say for the most part, [the Commission] is viewed pretty negatively."

An additional initial reaction to the Report was expressed in terms of whether "outsiders" had the right or responsibility to identify "problems" and/or to suggest repairs for them. Much of the response to the Report came in the form of "don't tell us what we already know, like we don't know it." One respondent put it this way, "I don't think the federal government needs to tell us that we need to offer lifelong learning opportunities." One chief academic officer described the reaction of the higher education community as ranging "from apathy to annoyance."

Source: Adapted from Lewis, Ruben, Sandmeyer, Russ, and Smulowitz (unpublished).

the substance of change, the process of change, and the implications and reasons for change. These interactions have the potential to shape attitudes, willing participation, efforts to oppose change, and ultimately, the outcomes of change.

Increasingly, scholarly and practitioner literatures have been focused on the communicative activities surrounding implementation of change. Scholars in change management, leadership, business strategy, communication, and other disciplines have explored the reactions stakeholders have to implementer communication choices (Griffith and Northcraft, 1996; Miller, Johnson, and Grau, 1994; Sagie, Elizur, and

in the external environment? what is its future?), structural (how will this organization operate? what will its culture be like?), and job-related (how will my job, rewards, and status change?) uncertainties. In much of change scholarship, implementers are depicted as the possessors of information and their tasks as (1) appropriate dissemination of information about a change, (2) discovery of inaccurate interpretations or misunderstandings of information they disseminate, and (3) clarification of misconstrued information.

There are a few problematic assumptions built into this approach to uncertainty reduction. First, by privileging the knowledge and information possessed by implementers and top-level decision-makers we may devalue knowledge and information possessed and created by other stakeholders. In the traditional frame, uncertainty is something only non-implementers experience. Dissemination strategies that are designed around informing those outside of implementation planning groups and "correcting" their misunderstandings may certainly miss the importance of surfacing knowledge and information held and created by other stakeholders even before implementers have made decisions about how to introduce change, and perhaps even before decision-makers have made adoption decisions. Further, this limited understanding of information dissemination ignores the important circulation of and creation of information among other stakeholders.

A second assumption of this approach is that uncertainty is a less preferable state that all stakeholders attempt to avoid through a rational process of increasing access to relevant information. Although a great deal of support can be found to bolster the problematic nature of uncertainty and the general tendency for individuals to avoid it (Bordia, Hunt, Paulsen, Tourish, and DiFonzo, 2004), some argue that individuals sometimes use other coping methods to deal with uncertainty and that uncertainty is not always problematic (Brummans and Miller, 2004).

Babrow (2001) argues, following the theory of Problematic Integration, that people form two sorts of orientations to the world: probabilistic (what is this thing like? how likely is this thing to happen?) and evaluative (is this a good /bad thing?). These orientations and the associated questions they raise can give rise to uncertainties both about what we know and about what we can reliably know (i.e., whether information can be gained, trusted, and interpreted usefully). Uncertainty can arise not just from a lack of information but also from the overabundance of information that is difficult to interpret; disorganization of available information; or contradiction or paradox in available information. Babrow suggests that people may cope with uncertainty in other ways than merely increasing access to information. In fact, additional information can make uncertainty worse.

Think of the last time you researched something on the Internet. You may have done a search on a key word or phrase to learn about a new technology, locate information to provide guidance on a purchase, or diagnose a medical concern. As you clicked through the likely very lengthy list of generated "hits" on the topic, the information may have become quite overwhelming. That feeling of being overwhelmed can come not only because information volume is high but also because it can be hard to determine which sources are more credible; how to resolve conflicting information; and how to establish a level of trust or know the level of expertise of information sources. A perfect evaluation of the information would include (a) reading all of it, (b) assigning some level of credibility to each source (which would involve additional searches of information on the sources), and (c) then creating and using some system to evaluate all the information provided by each source to maximize a rational sorting of the information and come to a conclusion. Few of us have that much time or can even know exactly when we've evaluated every source of information on any topic. Therefore, high levels of information can sometimes increase our uncertainty.

Another way people cope with uncertainty, aside from increasing the amount of information they have, is to reevaluate the object and decide it is not important. That reevaluation makes uncertainty about the object less troublesome. In another strategy, the person may reframe the object as merely "the way things are" within a larger social context where ideological forces may determine the frames to use to interpret objects (e.g., layoffs are a fact of business; the CEO gets to make decisions about how work is done; changes come and go and so will this one). Sometimes, we may be able to tolerate "mysteries" as simply unexplainable objects that "everyone" understands as unexplainable. Also, some cultures may not be as dominated by probabilistic and/or evaluative orientations. For some cultures there may be what Babrow calls "habitual certainty" where members cling strongly to a clear and compelling understanding of the world and objects in it. Every event and object can be easily explained within that understanding and uncertainty is rare. In sum, uncertainty is not a problem for everyone in every situation of change and is not always resolved through accrual of additional information.

Organizational communication scholars (McPhee and Zaug, 2001; Weick, 1995) have examined how *uncertainty* (too few available interpretations of events or objects) and **equivocality** (ambiguous meanings and too many available interpretations of events or objects) lead to social sensemaking processes in organizations. When people are overwhelmed by many possible interpretations of messages, objects, and events they do not just need more information. They need values, priorities, and preferences that help clarify what matters (McPhee and Zaug, 2001). They also use these values, priorities, and preferences to reframe problematic situations (Kuhn and Jackson, 2009). Reduction of uncertainty and equivocality may arise from the four main processes of interpretation construction that Karl Weick (1979) lays out: arguing, expecting, committing, and manipulating. These are ways of resolving uncertainty and equivocality problems without necessarily obtaining new information.

Kramer, Dougherty, and Pierce (2004) provide an example of this in their investigation of uncertainty in the context of an airline acquisition. They note that in previous research of mergers and acquisitions employees have generally been shown to seek information. However, they tend to feel the need for more information no matter how much information they accrue. Kramer (1999) suggests that individuals may (1) use alternatives to seeking information, (2) have competing motives that inhibit information seeking, and (3) gain information that increases uncertainty. Kramer *et al.*'s study of airline pilots' reactions to the acquisition found that levels of uncertainty changed over time in some cases and that the value of certain sources of information changed over time as well. The study also found that individuals differed in the degrees to which they sought out information. Seventy-one percent of the sample actively sought out more information; 29% of respondents were far less active in information seeking. These latter managed uncertainty internally and discounted the available information that they could have sought out as likely to be inaccurate, misleading, or unavailable and therefore not worth the effort to gather. This study also found that a large percentage of the sample (79%) reported seeking information not just to reduce uncertainty but also to create a sense of comfort with peers. Even gossip and rumor communication was embraced for this function even though the participants believed it lacked any useful or reliable information. Interaction of this nature provided supportive communication and helped employees to feel bonded by a common experience.

Another interesting conclusion of the Kramer *et al.* study concerns the ways in which high uncertainty impacted outcomes of job satisfaction, commitment, and stress. "Despite their uncertainty and declining attitudes, the pilots continued to like their work and to be committed to it ... This appears to be a situation of high uncertainty in which employees adopt a professional or occupational orientation instead of an organizational [one]" (p. 97). Pilots in this study appear to have allowed priorities for professional affiliation help them to reframe the importance of uncertainty about the employing organization. Rather than seek information to evaluate the new acquiring company, they reevaluated the organizational ownership as less important than their professional identities – I'm a pilot, and that matters more than the company that employs me. In this way uncertainty about the acquisition became less troublesome and thus for some may have lessened the felt need to seek information to reduce uncertainty about it.

Although there are many complex processes and relationships surrounding uncertainty reduction during organizational change, it is also likely true that a great deal of effort is put forth by implementers, and other stakeholders, to facilitate information flow and reduction of uncertainty. It is also likely that most stakeholders engage in some information-seeking as means to reduce uncertainty about change and that the attention to their informational needs is beneficial. A rare field experiment (Schweiger and DeNisi, 1991) examined extensive realistic previews in the case of a merger. In the experimental plant, the plant manager met frequently with employees, listened to and answered questions, and provided information about rationale, expected layoffs, detailed implications of the merger, and background. The control plant received only notification that the merger would take place. The researchers found that providing early previews of the details of the merger and its process in the experimental plant significantly lowered uncertainty and increased job satisfaction, commitment, perceived trustworthiness, honesty, caring, and self-reported performance. These effects endured over time as the merger progressed. Clearly, this study would suggest the potential power of high-quality dissemination of information.

Information dissemination has received a good deal of attention within the practitioner advice books and articles about change implementation. It involves the spreading of facts, clarifications, notices, details, rationale, and the like for the purpose of increasing the knowledge about a change initiative. Advice books frequently advocate that implementers provide information that will clarify roles, tasks, responsibilities, and procedures as well as remind stakeholders of the rationale and goals of change. Widespread dissemination of information to multiple stakeholders, repetition of messages, and making use of opportunities to communicate in everyday activities is also common advice. For example, Kotter (1998) suggests that references to the change be raised in routine work discussions. Duck (2001) says, "It's important to provide regular updates, even when there isn't any 'hard' news to deliver" (p. 212).

An organization that I worked with a number of years ago serves as a good example of these practices. PACT (Progress through Action, Communication and Teamwork) was a change program at a university (Lewis, 2000b) aimed at identifying and proactively seeking solutions to problems affecting a number of university service departments (e.g., mail services, financial services, printing and reprographics). In order to keep the employees up to date on the latest accomplishments and activities of PACT, the lead implementer created a newsletter called the PACT FLASH. The editor of the FLASH attempted to use this channel not only to disseminate information about the various training, social, and other activities of PACT but also as a method to establish the legitimacy of PACT.

PACT was established in response, for the most part, to a dire financial crisis that had resulted in job losses, pay and budget cuts, and staffing shortages. Although PACT was not really empowered to cope directly with any of these problems, the implementer wanted to create the sense that PACT was relevant in pushing for effective solutions to problems. In an attempt to build the legitimacy of PACT, the FLASH editor published a set of letters to the editor complaining about the university's lack of responsiveness to the dire problems and the frustrations of staff. In an ironic twist, the Vice Chancellor wrote a response letter to be published in FLASH that made no mention of the role PACT played in aiding University Services weathering the fiscal storm. In this case, the major channel for dissemination of information worked more against promoting the change than it did for it.

Other more typical approaches to information dissemination include what amount to marketing campaigns in which the implementers create an atmosphere where their key messages about the change are hard to miss and are emphasized through repetition and forcefulness as the new reality of the organization or unit. Glen H. Hiner, Chairman and CEO of Owens-Corning, suggests that the key to changing companies is "consistent, persistent, and repetitive communications" (Richardson and Denton, 1996, p. 203). He argues that a good indicator of how much to talk about a change is to do so until you cannot stand to do it again – then you are probably about half way there.

In some cases of large-scale change, communication commences in stages. The Ingredients Inc. merger case (see Case Box 2.2) is a good example of this strategy of information dissemination. Both of the legacy organizations announced and managed initial communication about the merger internally and differently. Once the merger became a legal and practical reality, the information was coordinated more centrally. The communication campaign included the use of various channels and the timing of important announcements of key events. In another example, Delta Airlines' major restructuring effort involved the establishment of a special 800 number to accept comments and questions and provide updates on the change; the use of the company newspaper; senior management open forums on job sites around the country; a system- wide management conference; and a video that could be shared with all Delta personnel (Richardson and Denton, 1996).

Case Box 2.2: Ingredients Inc. – Information Dissemination Campaigns

There were rumors about the possible merger for over a year in both organizations. A formal announcement was made in one of the two organizations (EC) on May 2. This information was disseminated electronically, conducted over the phone and also shared face-to-face in a series of town hall meetings. The CEO of the other organization (MC) managed this dissemination with fewer channels and with more communication links. He first shared details of the merger with his executive team. They then shared this information through direct reports. Employees in both organizations also received memos about the change. The MC managers held small group meetings with their teams or with their laborers. Employees at both organizations were given a FAQ (Frequently Asked Questions) sheet that asked and answered specific questions about the reasons and goals for the merger. It was disseminated to the employees through email, in paychecks, and posted in break rooms for hourly workers.

The FAQ document highlighted general concerns and provided reasons and goals for the merger as well as detailed many next steps and a general timeline. The CEO of the merged company believed that his communication campaign was managed professionally and provided a comprehensive communication approach.

Employees' recollections suggested otherwise. Few of the employees mentioned receiving the memo and/or attending individual or town hall meetings, and only one of the 46 respondents in the case study referenced receiving the FAQ document.

Follow-up communication occurred about 90 days after the first announcement. Several weeks later the internal and external stakeholders were informed of the official name change to Ingredients Inc. Employees were also provided details about the new corporate office located in MC. Following those announcements the CEO of MC announced his resignation to the new executive team. A formal memo was circulated to all employees noting the resignation and naming Ingredients Inc.'s new CEO, the former president of EC.

Following the merger, an acquisition occurred a few months later. For legal reasons, management was unable to release any information about this change until it occurred. This change was sent out to the employees via a memo. However, implementation of this change occurred prior to formal notice. The plants began producing new materials before the memo was circulated.

A series of memos were released in the next months outlining new changes. For example, employees of Ingredients Inc. were instructed about new rules for office décor (e.g., no real plants in offices) and general conduct (use of "library voices" in hallways). A new point system for attendance and tardiness was explained to laborers. In each of these cases, employee information was shared via formal and informal communication channels. Employees discussed these changes occasionally with direct supervisors and almost always with coworkers. Changes related to the merger continue today. Communication about these changes continues using systematic memo and random informal channels.

Source: Adapted from Laster (2008).

Organizations sometimes create new channels to disseminate information, such as the PACT FLASH and Delta's 800-number, but often they rely on routine channels for disseminating information. In a study (Lewis, 1999) involving an international sample of implementation efforts in 24 US states and 11 countries (Argentina, Belgium, Canada, Egypt, Germany, Japan, Mexico, Singapore, Taiwan, United Kingdom, and the US) the two most commonly used channels reported for disseminating information about change were small informal discussions and general informational meetings. The use of wikis and other more advanced communication technologies in organizations today has no doubt changed this landscape (although we have little data on which to draw conclusions).

Erik Timmerman (2003) proposes that a set of source, organizational, media, message/task, receiver, and strategic factors will influence the choices of media that implementers use to disseminate information. For example, Timmerman suggests that a preplanned, top-down programmatic approach to implementation is likely to be associated with "official" media that emphasize one-way communication. An adaptive approach that is more emergent and responsive to stakeholders as conditions and reactions are altered during the course of an implementation effort will see different media choices. Such an approach is more likely to involve use of both formal and informal media as well as channels that are more interactive and that will accommodate feedback about the implementation effort. Timmerman also proposes that different kinds of media will be used at different phases of the change process as needs for information and feedback change.

Formal information dissemination is a critical process during change implementation because it has the potential to help implementers clarify and explain the purpose and process of change; to create a common level of understanding about a change effort; and to help dispel inaccurate rumors. A less understood aspect of information dissemination during change concerns informal efforts by non-implementers to disseminate information. Very little attention, if any, has been paid to the informational campaigns of non-implementer stakeholders during change. Stakeholders with no formal role in implementation also hold and/or create information about change. In the Spellings Case (see Case Box 2.3) the informal information dissemination campaign launched by those with negative reactions to the Commission report reframed and challenged much of the communication disseminated by the Commission's official documents and website.

Dissemination of information in organizations is purportedly done for the purpose of increasing the knowledge of stakeholders. Kuhn and Jackson (2009) make an important distinction between "**knowledge**" (a noun: stable facts, objects, and dispositions) and "**knowing**" (a verb: an active and ongoing accomplishment of problem solving). These authors argue that knowledge is emergent, constantly in flux, and negotiated among stakeholders. That is, what is knowledge changes through interaction and by communities. Further, Contractor and Monge (2002) make the case that knowledge does not reside within individual "nodes" (people, units, groups, websites) but is a product of the network itself.

Case Box 2.3: Spellings Commission – Stakeholders' Informational Campaign

Efforts by the Department of Education to use the report as a spring-board to create change on the ground in higher education was met with intensified communication and advocacy efforts by some stake-holder groups. Stakeholders' serious concerns about the Commission's goals and the likely outcomes of its change efforts prompted use of website publications, as well as use of coordinated and well-orchestrated communication campaigns that stressed similar themes and "talking points." Nearly all of the higher education association and accrediting agency members interviewed for the case study indicated that they had initiated or participated in such efforts.

These lobbying efforts were viewed by some as providing the higher education stakeholders with what one member described as "an oppor-tunity to strengthen our leadership role with the community." Others who saw the resistance intensify as a consequence of some of these informal communication campaigns suggested that unsubstantiated fear was being created. As one interviewee from the Department of Education said, "... even though this was not [a] fact-based [concern], it created fear. ... If you look at ... all these alert letters [sent out by] the associations ... to their members, [you would conclude that] this was a 'very calculated strategy.'"

The presumed goal of some of this strategic campaigning on the part of some higher education associations was to create anxiety about the Department of Education's intentions. Whether by design or default, concerns about a one-size-fits-all approach were great for many stake-holders. Public statements by the Department of Education, the Secretary, and some Commissioners belied the notion that such a model was being proposed. However, interactions among stakeholders on this issue were so strong that the denials seemed to have negligible impact on reactions and public rhetoric within higher education. Tensions over the one-size solution continued to rise.

Source: Adapted from Lewis *et al.* (unpublished).

Various explanations have been offered for what motivates individuals to participate in knowledge networks (self-interest, social exchange, attraction to similar others). Contractor and Monge argue that three major mechanisms account for how and from whom individuals forge ties for information sharing/retrieval:

> Individuals tend to retrieve information from those who they think are knowledgeable; they also tend to retrieve information from those to whom they can offer expertise in another area in exchange, and finally they seek information from others who are in close proximity, irrespective of whether they may be considered an expert. (p. 253)

We can also distinguish between different kinds of "knowledge." Cooney and Sewell (2008), on the basis of the work of Marglin (1990), distinguish between "techne," a personal nonrationalized way of knowing (e.g., from doing a task over and over again) and "episteme," a universal and rule-based way of knowing (e.g., the official organizational facts, understandings, and procedures). Sometimes in organizations "knowledge" isn't considered "expert" until it rises to the level of "episteme." Employees' and other stakeholders' informal knowledge isn't considered valid or legitimate until an "expert" manager embraces and endorses that knowledge.

However, some scholars (Riesbeck and Schank, 1989) would argue that case-based knowledge where those involved in knowledge creation spend a great deal of time analyzing specific problems, gaining various perspectives, and pulling apart specific dynamics unique to the situation will rise to the level of expert knowledge. This may be a more effective strategy to accumulate useful and practical knowledge that can be applied in real-life organizations as new situations present themselves.

Understanding how knowledge is created and shared within and across stakeholders of change is a key to understanding how "knowing" is accomplished in this context. We also must appreciate that different levels of legitimacy and power can be attached to different types of knowledge in organizations. The interaction among stakeholders, both implementers and non-implementers, is where knowledge about change is created and held and where legitimacy for some knowledge is granted or denied.

Soliciting Input

Soliciting input from stakeholders during change is a notion that has been called by many names: participation, participation in decision-making, empowerment, positive climate, feedback, upward communication, and voice. Asking for opinions, feedback, reactions, and the like is encouraged by experts so that implementers can actively engage and empower stakeholders and manage feelings and concerns about change. Evidence suggests that soliciting input, especially in the context of a general philosophy of stakeholder participation in decision-making about change, can reap a number of benefits desired by implementers, including lowering resistance to change; increasing satisfaction of participants; and increasing stakeholders' feelings of control (cf. Bordia *et al.*, 2004; Sagie and Koslowsky, 1994; Sagie *et al.*, 2001). Ironically, evidence also suggests that participative approaches to communication are the least utilized since most implementers emphasize downward dissemination about change programs over soliciting input of stakeholders (Lewis, 1999, 2006; Lewis, Richardson, and Hamel, 2003). Doyle, Claydon, and Buchanan's study (2000) of UK managers' reflections on past change efforts in their own organizations found that only 50% of respondents agreed that "we have remained faithful to the principle of participative change implementation" (p. S65).

Advice varies on the form and function of soliciting input. For some experts, it can involve therapy-like sessions where venting can take place. In a workshop on change I recently did for mid-level managers, a nurse manager asked me at what point she should call an end to venting since it reaches a point where it is "counter-productive." Her question implies the purpose of the activity for her – to truly let the feelings and concerns "vent," but not to attempt to capture the concerns for future consideration during decision-making. My response to her question was to suggest that she could never stop the venting since she did not have control over it. She could only limit her own access to it by not listening any longer. To put it more metaphorically, if smoke was filling your kitchen due to something that had burned in the oven, when would you stop venting it out of doors and windows? – when the smoke was gone or when you were tired of dealing with it? And, more importantly, would you use the "venting" as a signal to solve a potential problem with the functioning of your oven and/or your cooking methods or would you merely vent and repeat the same practices that led to the smoke in the first place?

Venting sessions, and other more systematic attempts to access feedback and monitor reactions of lower level employees and other stakeholders, are not often well designed to make use of the knowledge that is gathered or created. Input is often conceptualized as monitoring reactions to change in order to correct course by emphasizing more or different information or to respond to or correct misinterpretations evidenced in feedback. In other words, the "smoke" is often considered a signal of a problem in the perceiver /stakeholder not a signal of a problem in the change effort.

There has been a good deal of recent work that reconceptualizes "participation" in organizational contexts in richer ways. Kuhn and Deetz (2008) suggest (pp. 188–189) that an "ideal speech situation" that would involve stakeholders in important decision-making would include: (1) reciprocity for expression, (2) some equality in expression skills, (3) setting aside of authority relations, (4) open investigation of stakeholder positions and "wants" to more freely ascertain their interests, (5) open sharing of information and transparency of decision processes, and (6) the opening of fact and knowledge claims to re-determinization based on contestation of claims and advantaged modes of knowledge creation.

These authors argue (p. 188) that "managerial-driven" forms of participation are usually lacking these markers and are more likely driven by strategic attempts to increase loyalty and commitment and decrease resistance rather than seek genuine decisional input. For Kuhn (2008) and Kuhn and Deetz (2008), just giving stakeholders a say or a seat at the table is not enough to create the ideal speech situation that truly empowers stakeholders, engages conflicts, and produces creative solutions to problems. Additionally, as Neumann (1989) argues regarding her research concerning factors that militate against employees' participation during change implementation efforts, "frequently, primary organizational decision-making processes have little connection with an enterprise's participative efforts. Most participative schemes run parallel to the decision-making process of the organization" (p. 185). This parallel structure that runs alongside the formal bureaucracy may discourage some stakeholders from participation, "as long as the real decisions of the organization get made via the chain-of-command, then the participative effort will be perceived as less important than daily operations" (p. 186).

Clearly, there are important differences to various possible levels and types of participation. Figure 2.1 presents one possible arrangement of a limited set of models of stakeholder participation during change implementation. This model illustrates a range of ways in which implementers can treat stakeholder participation: *as symbol* (merely create an appearance of participation) or *as resource* in the implementation effort (empowering stakeholders to have impact on the manner, rate, timing, and possibly even the wisdom of implementing a change at all).

Symbol

- Stakeholders are told they are considered important participants in change

- Stakeholders are provided input channels in order to make them feel more involved

- Stakeholders are provided input channels so their complaints, concerns, and ideas can be vented

- Stakeholders are asked to provide perspectives on change so that implementers can correct misinterpretations of disseminated information and stop or correct rumors

- Stakeholders are encouraged to put forward ideas and suggest improvements in the process of implementing change that are then used to alter the implementation

- Stakeholders are asked to provide initial guidance and render opinions about change adoption and implementation that is heavily influential in decision-making

- Stakeholders are given decision-making power and resource control over whether to adopt change and how to implement it

Resource

Select Stakeholders

Diverse Stakeholders

Figure 2.1 Array of implementers' approaches to stakeholder participation

Zorn, Page, and Cheney (2000) provide an example of the more symbolic form of participation. Their study of a New Zealand government organization's attempt to emulate Southwest Airline's change of culture as exemplified by the NUTS! book illustrates how employees were involved in ritual ways. The CEO Ken "scheduled several weekend activities focused on improving teamwork and learning best practices for customer service. Among these were 'experience days,' or benchmarking visits to other organizations with reputations for excellent customer service" (p. 531). Ken also asked the employees to read NUTS! and to make regular presentations based on the book's lessons. Each week at the departmental team briefing, one of the eight women in his department was asked to present a short extract from NUTS! that she "personally found meaningful"(p. 530).These means of "involvement" of employees in the change effort were constructed in ways to ensure the predetermined outcome of acceptance of Ken's vision. Their input was neither course-correcting nor empowering in the sense that it could alter original plans. In this way their participation was merely symbolic.

In contrast, Edmondson, Bohmer, and Pisano (2001) provide a strong example of use of a resource approach to soliciting input in their study of the implementation of an innovative technology for cardiac surgery:

> An OR nurse at Mountain described the team preparation step in detail, ...
> We talked about how the communication would be important, and every-
> one was involved in [this] conversation – nurses, surgeons, everyone. ...
> The practice session then reinforced the message that teamwork was
> critical to success and that the surgeon would be playing a new, more
> interdependent role, with other members speaking up with ideas and
> observations. (p. 702)

Edmondson *et al.* describe how success was an outcome in hospitals that adopted these more teamwork and participatory communication practices that enabled psychological safety (where it was safe to make public mistakes as learning was ongoing) and where status differences were minimized or ignored. In cases where the implementation was less successful, traditional modes of communication, with high attention to established status differences, were observed:

> At Chelsea, team members said that communication in the OR did not
> change for MICS, and as a result, ... there is a painful process of finding
> out what didn't work. ... We are reactive. ... Team members reported being
> uncomfortable speaking up about problems. The team at Decorum simi-
> larly remained entrenched in old communication routines during trials.
> (p. 704)

Kuhn and Deetz (2008) point out that even if managers wish to engage stakeholders as a resource they may lack the skills and knowledge to do so. Additionally, methods of disclosing information, sharing power, and granting autonomy have serious implications for organizational structure that can cause many ripple effects in the organization. It is not so simple as to "engage in dialogue" as some practitioner advice books suggest. Techniques that are useful in facilitating interaction that leads to creative and mutually satisfying outcomes nearly always require training and practice. Further, when we assume that good participatory attitudes are sufficient for quality participation to take place, we oversimplify these complex processes that require sophisticated skill sets.

It is also not easy to determine how much participation is necessary or beneficial to a specific change effort. Miller and Monge (1985) caution against assuming that more participation is always better: "like theorists advocating contingency models of participation, we should look carefully at the situations and individuals for which participation is most appropriate" (p. 224). Leonard-Barton and Sinha (1993) found in their study of the relationship between user involvement in the design stage of change programs and subsequent user satisfaction, that there is not a strict linear relationship between involvement and satisfaction. While they found that very low levels of involvement predicted lower user satisfaction, they also found that extensive user involvement was not always predictive of user satisfaction.

Participation can be accomplished in many ways. It can be direct (individuals represent themselves) or indirect (a representative stands in for a group of stakeholders); forced (as when line supervisors are required to represent their subordinates' reactions to change) or voluntary (which may come at some perceived or real political risk); formal (committees or task forces) or informal (water-cooler moments where leaders question other stakeholders about change); and with varying degrees of intentions (as the previous examples illustrate). The timing and duration of the participation (e.g., before or after major decision-making or major problems occur) also may have important effects on how participation is received and what outcomes are reaped from it.

It is also true that participation opportunities for stakeholders may not be equivalent. In some earlier work with my colleagues Brian Richardson and Stephanie Hamel (Lewis et al., 2003), we found that in the context of nonprofit initiation of change, those who were more "internal" (e.g., paid staff, board members, members) to the organization received the "lion's share" of opportunities to communicate with implementers as opposed to boundary stakeholders (e.g., volunteers, clients/customers) or more external stakeholders (e.g., government agencies, partner organizations) who received significantly less communicative attention. It is clear that due to both efficiency and effectiveness reasons, implementers pick and choose from whom to solicit input. We will discuss attention to stakeholder groups more in Chapter 3, but for now we note that a part of understanding solicitation of input during change is attending to who gets attention and opportunities for voice.

Table 2.1   Implementers' styles of participation

	Symbol	*Resource*
Select Stakeholder Involvement	Bankrupt Participation	Privileged Empowerment
Diverse Stakeholder Involvement	Ritualistic Participation	Widespread Empowerment

The combination of the degree of involvement (many or few stakeholders) and the symbolic or resource approach to participation results in a description of four styles of participation during change. Table 2.1 depicts these four styles. **Widespread Empowerment** exists where solicitation of input is done in a manner consistent with a resource approach and is widespread. This is the situation most closely associated with Kuhn and Deetz's notion of the ideal speech situation. **Privileged Empowerment** is the implementer style wherein select stakeholders are approached for input in a resource-based way. In this case, perhaps like some of those cases that my co-authors and I found in our study of nonprofits, select stakeholders or groups of stakeholders were used as a resource to help guide and direct the change, but many other stakeholders were not provided those same opportunities. In the two cases of symbolic solicitation of input we observe implementer participation styles where stakeholders are manipulated into thinking their input is desired and will be useful to the change when indeed it is no more than a show of involvement. **Ritualistic Participation** describes the case of diverse stakeholder symbolic involvement where many different types of stakeholders may be asked to provide input, but are routinely ignored in most or all cases. **Bankrupt Participation** describes the case where even symbolic involvement is available for only a few representative stakeholders. I use the pejorative term "bankrupt" here purposefully. Putting on a show of soliciting input is misleading and can lead to real dysfunction in change processes. When stakeholders detect insincerity it can erode trust and credibility in implementers and break down possibilities for functional exchange of information and comment on the change process. Evidence suggests that change that is forced without any consultation is likely to be viewed negatively and more often reported as a failure by stakeholders (Lewis, 2006; Lines, 2007). However, it is also true that stakeholders need to feel the attempt to solicit their input is sincere.

An example in the political realm comes to mind here. Soon after President Obama took office in 2009, he began to work to get a major piece of legislation through Congress that would, hopefully, put the country's economy back on course. During a series of meetings held by President Obama with senators and representatives, he invited those who were opposed to his initial plans to come and make their case and suggest alternatives. He presented these opportunities as genuine solicitations of input. When one opposition congressman was asked by a reporter about whether he would attend the meeting with the President, he replied, "you mean the photo op?" Clearly, this congressman doubted the sincerity of the President's desire to really gather input. Or, at least he was portraying the solicitation as insincere. The belief that such an invitation is merely symbolic would certainly decrease a participant's desire or willingness to provide quality input. Further, it is also interesting to note that even sincere attempts to gather input might be publicly ridiculed as insincere by stakeholders who might feel they would not be able to negotiate an acceptable outcome.

It is also important to consider that styles of participation may change over time and that implementers may feel that one style is appropriate at the start of the change effort but that something else is more appropriate at a later stage. This may be planned from the start of change efforts or may reflect alteration of a nonproductive result or course-correction based on negative feedback as the change progresses.

Stakeholders solicit input, as do implementers. Nearly all the work on participation in implementation of change assumes that this is an activity designed by implementers who invite, to some extent or another, input from stakeholders. Those approaches ignore the important bids of stakeholders to solicit input from each other. The Spellings case is a wonderful example of this (see Case Box 2.4). The Higher Education community used published outlets as a channel for a national conversation about the Spellings Report. Stakeholders wrote articles for *Inside Higher Education* and *Chronicle of Higher Education* and then other stakeholders wrote online responses, published on the websites of these publications. In a content analysis of those posts, we see a good deal of evidence of stakeholders soliciting input from one another. The Spellings Report and the interactions that followed served as a "wake-up call" that stirred much reaction by various stakeholders encouraging sharing of perspectives and contrasts of opinion. As one respondent put it, "Well, I think it's promoted a structured dialogue on some of these issues in a way that ... hadn't [happened] before." A Commission member indicated "the meetings raised the dialogue and got things in the press and

Case Box 2.4: Spellings Stakeholders Solicit Input From One Another

Partly owing to the style of the Commissioners and the Secretary of the Department of Education, and partly to the confrontational stance of the Report as it was perceived by many in higher education, many of the stakeholders felt "backed up against the wall … and were defensive, or sounding defensive."

These concerns drove not only initial responses to proposed change but, perhaps more importantly, dialogue among stakeholders as they attempted to influence one another and to discuss what actions ought to result.

Preoccupation with the "right" of government to lead the change militated against serious discussion of some even uncontroversial changes that were proposed in the Commission's Report. Fear (or even paranoia) about losing autonomy may have distracted higher education stakeholders from being more proactive and collaborative in attempting to develop innovative solutions to problems that had long been known and acknowledged. However, that paranoia may have been what drove many of the voluntary change initiatives. In a sense, many stakeholders came to believe that if they didn't do this voluntarily within the higher education community, change would be mandated by government. The sensemaking that took place largely within the sphere of the articles and responses published in higher education professional journals, helped shape the action steps that followed initial reactions.

Source: Adapted from Lewis *et al.* (unpublished).

put the spotlight on them. … Now … accreditation is … out of the dark … over time we'll probably do something good about it."

Implementers often discourage the informal soliciting of input among stakeholders who are not part of the official implementation team. Exchange of opinions, predictions, explanations, and similar activities are often denigrated as "rumor mills" by implementers. Implementers prefer to be the source of information on change and are uncomfortable with other stakeholders' exchanges of evaluations of change initiatives. In the same international study noted earlier, 30% of the sample of implementers reported that the primary source of information about the change was the implementation team, followed by top management (27%) and middle management (17%). However, when in another study I asked non-implementer stakeholders about primary sources for receiving information and providing input about change, they reported that they received the most information about change "word of mouth (employee to employee)" and from small informal discussions. They reported that they used line supervisors and small informal discussions as the most likely channels to provide input. These data are consistent with our understanding of the powerful influence of peer relationships in organizations in general. We repeatedly find evidence that individuals tend to seek knowledge and opportunities to create knowledge from those who are closest in proximity and who are likely to have information that is useful to us (e.g., from those who can translate into our real experiences in organizations). However, implementers' strong preferences to control information (both dissemination and input) are contrary to this normative preference.

Socialization

Another communication process that plays a major role during organizational change, *Socialization* concerns how organizations shape the understandings its members have to the values, priorities, procedures, job tasks, culture, and formal and informal expectations. Socialization has typically been examined in the context of newcomers to organizations, usually early in their careers. However, even the first writers in this literature acknowledged that socialization (or resocialization) occurs for those who change roles in organizations (Ashford and Taylor, 1990; Van Maanen, 1978). Writers in the socialization literature have described the process of altering roles or orientation to roles in stages, through various tactics of the organization, and through strategies individuals use to self-socialize (Jablin and Kramer, 1998; Louis, 1980; Miller and Jablin, 1991). There is evidence that suggests that change events in organizations provide important opportunities for resocialization of stakeholders. For example, Caldwell, Heold, and Fedor (2004) examined how individuals' perceptions of person-environment (P-E) fit (the degree to which they fit in with their organization) are altered during organizational change. They found that "in the face of change, individuals may very well perceive important shifts in aspects of their P-E fit" (p. 876). As a result of organizational change, people may no longer see themselves fitting in or may perceive enhanced fit that triggers a reassessment of how they read an organization's culture, values, and practices. Implementation often involves attempts to influence that reassessment process.

Nicholson (1984) argues in his Theory of Work Role Transitions that a person's adjustment to a role transition can be considered in terms of degrees of **personal development** (in which the person alters his or her frame of reference, values, or other attributes) and/or **role development** (in which the person tries to change the role requirements so that they better match his or her needs, abilities, and identity). In taking combinations of these two adjustment strategies, Nicholson creates four adjustment modes: **Replication** (minimal adjustment to personal or role systems – repeat what you did before); **Absorption** (person adjusts self to fit role demands); **Determination** (person adjusts the role to suit self); and **Exploration** (there is simultaneous adjustment of role and person). Nicholson hypothesizes that individuals' choices of modes will depend on (1) discretion available to them (their opportunities to alter these components that is largely built upon status and resources) and (2) novelty of job demands (the degree to which the role permits the exercise of prior knowledge, practiced skills, and established habits). As implementers consider the amount of role adjustment required of some stakeholders during change, they may also consider how much influence and choice they want stakeholders to have in their process of reinventing their roles. In some cases during change implementers want full control over changing roles and this can result in the fracturing of implied "contracts" with stakeholders.

Denise Rousseau (1996) describes **psychological contracts as** the "good-faith" relationships between stakeholders and organizations that stipulate an understanding of what is expected of each party. When circumstances in those relationships are altered, as they often are during organizational change, psychological contracts can be broken. Sometimes stakeholders may feel that they were cheated or misled or that what was promised has been unfairly withdrawn. Organizational decision-makers often feel, as Edward Ridolfi (1996) from McGraw-Hill wrote in his executive commentary to Rousseau's article:

> Employees [stakeholders] must accept those events which have occurred over which their companies had little control. They need to reframe their relationships with the organization in ways that parallel the company's response to its environment by demonstrating flexibility and adaptability. The "used-to-be's" must give way to the realities of "what is and what will be." Finally, employees must be willing to move into uncharted areas in

their relationships with employers. They need to see such movement as opportunity rather than obstacle. (p. 59)

Essentially, managers of organizations can often feel that psychological contracts must be remade and stakeholders need to become flexible when environmental changes demand it. There is some evidence to suggest that individuals don't always receive much support in efforts to reinvent roles after transitions brought about by organizational change. In a study of British managers, West, Nicholson, and Rees (1987) found that those entering newly-created jobs tend to receive less help in learning about their jobs. The socialization pattern tended to be more individual, informal, random, and disjunctive, without continuity to previous role models.

In a study of "broken promises" in the context of radical organizational change, Kickul, Lester, and Finkl (2002) found that both the perceived fairness of procedures (procedural fairness) as well as the respect and dignity communicated in interaction with stakeholders (interactional fairness) were able to mitigate the negative results of psychological contract breaches.

There are complex factors that shape the ways in which individual stakeholders perceive roles built upon not only the organization's views but also on self-concepts and societal models of roles. Neale and Griffin (2006) have argued that roles are understood as a product of **system requirements** (organizational expectations), **role schemas** (individual beliefs about what such a role typically requires/looks like), and **self-concept** (how the individual views him/herself). Any specific behavior that could be a part of role performance could align with one or more of these sources of role perceptions. For example, a behavior might be congruent with one's role schema (e.g., what I think society generally expects of this role) but at odds with one's self-concept (e.g., things I might feel comfortable doing). A given secretary might think society would expect her to get a cup of coffee for her boss, but might find the behavior to be beneath her own self-concept of her professional status. In the context of organizational change, system requirements may alter the expectations for a role, suggesting some behaviors are either newly expected or newly undesired or disallowed. Behaviors that are key to the individual's self-concept which are then disallowed by change initiatives might cause concern, as will new expectations that are at odds with the self-concept. Reactions to role changes that are at odds with role schema could either be perceived as new opportunities (e.g., a low-level employee given unusual job autonomy) or as objectionable requests (e.g., professional asked to do tasks typically reserved for less trained employees).

I experienced a change of system requirements in my role as a customer of my local grocery store that was at odds with my role schema for "customer." My grocery asks customers to bag their own groceries. To encourage this behavior, check-out clerks do not bag any of the groceries until all have been scanned for price. So, if customers don't start the bagging process themselves, they must endure the annoyed looks of other customers who are waiting in line watching the groceries pile up on the counter. I personally consider this task out of my normative experience for the role of customer and thus objectionable. However, it is part of my self-concept to be a "helper," so I grin and bear it.

Another example, the Homeless Net case (see Case Box 2.5) presents a situation where stakeholders had a difficult time incorporating new behaviors into their repertoire for communication because of discomfort with how they saw technology fitting into their role as social workers. The perceived a mismatch between what they described as a "high touch" role and the cool technology, which caused concern over how embracing these new technologies would change their role schema for social worker.

Individuals have options about how they shape these three components to accommodate changes in roles. At a very basic level, individuals can (a) tolerate misalignments of system requirements with self-concept and/or role schemas (ignoring the ill-fitting components), (b) challenge the new system requirements so that alteration of behavior is unnecessary, or (c) re-evaluate their self-concept or role schema to embrace the new behavior. For example, if getting coffee for the boss seems beneath me as a secretary, I could redefine my self-concept as different on the job than off the job. Some socialization strategies (especially divestiture and investiture) target the shaping of an individual's self-concept. They prop up new versions of self and discourage or break down others. Hazing in sororities and fraternities are socialization strategies designed to make one feel more attached and like those in the organization. In the context of change, such strategies might be employed to redefine the context of the change and the need for stakeholders to think of themselves differently. Change in the midst of crisis is an example of this. Managers' insistence that "desperate times call for desperate measures" might be an example.

Changing stakeholders' role schema may be more difficult if they are very experienced and familiar with a particular role. Such individuals are likely to have very fixed understandings of the role, as we saw in

Case Box 2.5: Homeless Net Resists Altering Role Schema

Monica and Trevor agreed that this community of service providers might benefit from better tools for coordination, collaboration, and communication. Each of the approximately 25 nonprofit and government organizations involved were equipped with the appropriate infrastructure (high speed Internet connections, powerful desktop computers, collaborative software, community listserv). They were also provided with training and ongoing technical support.

However, despite thorough training, some technologies just never caught on. The instant messaging tool that automatically launched on the provided computer rarely saw any activity. Follow-up surveys with community members reported no use of the file-sharing. Even the access to extensive electronic meeting software was all but ignored by the group.

As one agency head explained to them, "life is about who shows up. People are just not ready for the disconnect technology creates. We are in a high touch business. A lot of what we do is consensus work; not a lot of formal voting."

Trevor and Derek were frustrated. As the homeless service coordinator for the city explained to Monica:

> Among providers, people in homeless services are the least apt to jump into new technology, because we are so used to working with people who don't have access to a lot of technology, that everything we do is so paper and pencil or here's a phone number, you know, just call them or actually just go over and visit them you know. It is much less computer-oriented work that we do. And part of it is, again, because our clients don't have access to that kind of thing, so we don't get in the habit of really using this either.

Source: Adapted from Scott, Lewis, Davis, and D'Urso (2009).

the Homeless Net case. However, change implementers may be able to encourage alteration of role schema if they can point to other examples where the role has changed in similar organizational settings. Counternarratives of role schema can also be presented by other stakeholders who may wish to resist implementers' interpretations. Those who wish to create a stakeholder revolt against a change might do so by raising the issue of "atypical" behaviors being asked in the context of changing system requirements.

Challenging system requirements is likely at the foundation of much of change resistance (a topic we will return to in a later chapter). Stakeholders in this category will resist the change in behaviors being asked of them through ignoring, self-handicapping, argument or other means.

Conclusion

In summary, this chapter has introduced three processes of communication that play important roles in the implementation of organizational change. We have noted that communication is not "everything" in change because other material, political, and emotional realities also have impact in change. However, communication does have a critical role as well. Key communication processes involved in dissemination of information, soliciting input, and socialization aid or hinder the reduction or management of uncertainty; the increased access to decision-making; and the development of roles within organizations during change. These communication processes are steered by implementers as well as other stakeholders. They may be formal, strategic, and planned, or emergent in interaction. In the next chapter we will consider these processes in the larger context of stakeholder relationships and a model of stakeholder communication during implementation of change.

References

Ashford, S. J. and Taylor, M. S. (1990) Adaptation to work transitions: An integrative approach. In K. M. Rowland and G. R. Ferris (eds.), *Research in Personnel and Human Resources Management* (Vol. 8, pp. 1–39). Stamford, CT: JAI.

Babrow, A. S. (2001) Uncertainty, value, communication, and problematic integration. *Journal of Communication*, 51 (3), 553–573.

Bordia, P., Hobman, E., Jones, E., Gallois, C., and Callan, V. (2004) Uncertainty during organizational change: Types, consequences, and management strategies. *Journal of Business and Psychology*, 18 (4), 507–532.

Bordia, P., Hunt, L., Paulsen, N., Tourish, D., and DiFonzo, N. (2004) Communication and uncertainty during organizational change: It is all about control. *European Journal of Work and Organizational Psychology*, 13 (3), 345–365.

Brummans, B. and Miller, K. I. (2004) The effect of ambiguity on the implementation of a social change initiative. *Communication Research Reports*, 21 (1), 1–10.

Caldwell, S. D., Heold, D. M., and Fedor, D. B. (2004) Toward an understanding of the relationships among organizational change, individual differences, and changes in person-environment fit: A cross-level study. *Journal of Applied Psychology*, 89 (5), 868–882.

Collins, J. (2001) *From Good to Great*. New York: HarperCollins.

Contractor, N. and Monge, P. (2002) Managing knowledge networks. *Management Communication Quarterly*, 16 (2), 249–258.

Cooney, R. and Sewell, G. (2008) Shaping the other: Maintaining expert managerial status in a complex change management program. *Group and Organization Management*, 33 (6), 685–711.

Davidson, J. (2002) *The Complete Idiot's Guide to Change Management*. Indianapolis: Alpha Books.

Doyle, M., Claydon, T., and Buchanan, D. (2000) Mixed results, lousy process: The management experience of organizational change. *British Journal of Management*, 11, S59–S80.

Duck, J. (2001) *The Change Monster*. New York: Crown Business.

Edmondson, A. C., Bohmer, R. M., and Pisano, G. P. (2001) Disrupted routines: Team learning and new technology implementation in hospitals. *Administrative Science Quarterly*, 46, 685–716.

Griffith, T. L. and Northcraft, G. B. (1996) Cognitive elements in the implementation of new technology: Can less information provide more benefits? *MIS Quarterly*, 20, 99–110.

Jablin, F. M. and Kramer, M. W. (1998) Communication-related sense-making and adjustment during job transfers. *Management Communication Quarterly*, 12 (2), 155–183.

Kickul, J., Lester, S. W., and Finkl, J. (2002) Promise breaking during radical organizational change: Do justice interventions make a difference? *Journal of Organizational Behavior*, 23, 469–488.

Kotter, J. P. (1998) Leading change: Why transformation efforts fail. In *Harvard Business Review on Change* (pp. 1–21). Boston: Harvard Business School.

Kotter, J. (2005) *Our Iceberg is Melting: Changing and Succeeding Under Any Conditions*. New York: St. Martin's Press.

Kramer, M. (1999) Motivation to reduce uncertainty: Reconceptualizing uncertainty reduction theory. *Management Communication Quarterly*, 13, 305–316.

Kramer, M., Dougherty, D. S., and Pierce, T. A., (2004) Managing uncertainty during a corporate acquisition: A longitudinal study of communication during an airline acquisition. *Human Communication Research*, 30 (1), 71–101.

Kuhn, T. (2008) A communicative theory of the firm: Developing an alternative perspective on intra-organizational power and stakeholder relationships. *Organization Studies*, 29, 1197–1224.

Kuhn, T. and Deetz, S. A. (2008) Critical theory and corporate social responsibility: Can/should we get beyond cynical reasoning? In *A. Crane, A. McWilliams*,

D. Matten, J. Moon, and D. Siegel (eds.), *The Oxford Handbook of Corporate Social Responsibility* (pp. 173–196). Oxford: Oxford University Press.

Kuhn, T. and Jackson, M. (2009) Accomplishing knowledge: A framework for investigating knowing in organizations. *Management Communication Quarterly*, 21 (4), 454–485.

Laster, N. M. (2008) Communicating multiple change: Understanding the impact of change messages on stakeholder perceptions. Dissertation Abstracts International (UMI No. AAT 3342339).

Leonard-Barton, D. and Sinha, D. K. (1993) Developer–user interaction and user satisfaction in internal technology transfer. *Academy of Management Journal*, 36, 1125–1139.

Lewis, L. K. (1997) Users' individual communicative responses to intraorganizationally implemented innovations and other planned changes. *Management Communication Quarterly*, 10 (4), 455–490.

Lewis, L. K. (1999) Disseminating information and soliciting input during planned organizational change: Implementers' targets, sources, and channels for communicating. *Management Communication Quarterly*, 13, 43–75.

Lewis, L. K. (2000a) "Blindsided by that one" and "I saw that one coming": The relative anticipation and occurrence of communication problems and other problems in implementers' hindsight. *Journal of Applied Communication Research*, 28 (1), 44–67.

Lewis, L. K. (2000b) Communicating change: Four cases of quality programs. *Journal of Business Communication*, 37, 128–155.

Lewis, L. K. (2006) Employee perspectives on implementation communication as predictors of perceptions of success and resistance. *Western Journal of Communication*, 70 (1), 23–46.

Lewis, L. K. and Seibold, D. R. (1996) Communication during intraorganizational innovation adoption: Predicting users' behavioral coping responses to innovations in organizations. *Communication Monographs*, 63 (2), 131–157.

Lewis, L. K., Hamel, S. A., and Richardson, B. K. (2001) Communicating change to nonprofit stakeholders: Models and predictors of implementers' approaches. *Management Communication Quarterly*, 15, 5–41.

Lewis, L. K., Richardson, B. K., and Hamel, S. A. (2003) When the stakes are communicative: The lamb's and the lion's share during nonprofit planned change. *Human Communication Research*, 29 (3), 400–430.

Lewis, L. K., Ruben, B., Sandmeyer, L., Russ, T., and Smulowitz, S. (unpublished) Sensemaking interaction during change: A longitudinal analysis of stakeholders' communication about Spellings Commission's efforts to change US higher education.

Lewis, L. K., Schmisseur, A., Stephens, K., and Weir, K. (2006) Advice on communicating during organizational change: The content of popular press books. *Journal of Business Communication*, 43 (2), 113–137.

Lines, R. (2007) Using power to install strategy: The relationships between expert power, position power, influence tactics and implementation success. *Journal of Change Management*, 7 (2), 143–170.

Louis, M. R. (1980) Surprise and sense making: What newcomers experience in entering unfamiliar organizational settings. *Administrative Science Quarterly*, 25 (2), 226–251.

Marglin, S. A. (1990) Losing touch: the cultural conditions of worker accommodation and resistance. In F. Apffel Marglin and S. A. Marglin (eds.), *Dominating Knowledge: Development, Culture, Resistance* (pp. 185–216). Oxford: Clarendon Press.

McPhee, R. D. and Zaug, P. (2001) Organizational theory, organizational communication, organizational knowledge, and problematic integration. *Journal of Communication*, 51 (3), 574–591.

Miller, K. I. and Monge, P. R. (1985) Social information and employee anxiety about organizational change. *Human Communication Research*, 11, 365–386.

Miller, V. D. and Jablin, F. M. (1991) Information seeking during organizational entry: Influences, tactics, and a model of the process. *Academy of Management Review*, 16 (1), 92–120.

Miller, V. D., Johnson, J. R., and Grau, J. (1994) Antecedents to willingness to participate in a planned organizational change. *Journal of Applied Communication Research*, 22, 59–80.

Neale, M. and Griffin, M. A. (2006) A model of self-held work roles and role transitions. *Human Performance*, 19 (1), 23–41.

Nicholson, N. (1984) A theory of work role transitions. *Administrative Science Quarterly*, 29, 172–191.

Neumann, J. E. (1989) Why people don't participate in organizational change. In R. W. Woodman and W. A. Pasmore (eds.), *Research in Organizational Change and Development* (Vol. 3, pp. 181–212). Greenwich, CT: JAI Press.

Nutt, P. C. (1987) Identifying and appraising how managers install strategy. *Strategic Management Journal*, 8, 1–14.

Richardson, P. and Denton, K. (1996) Communicating change. *Human Resource Management*, 35 (2), 203–216.

Ridolfi, E. (1996) Executive commentary. *Academy of Management Executive*, 10 (1), 59.

Riesbeck, C. K. and Schank, R. C. (1989) *Inside Case-based Reasoning*. Hillsdale, NJ: Lawrence Erlbaum.

Rousseau, D. M. (1996) Changing the deal while keeping the people. *Academy of Management Executive*, 10 (1), 50–59.

Sagie, A. and Koslowsky, M. (1994) Organizational attitudes and behaviors as a function of participation in strategic and tactical change decisions: An application of path–goal theory. *Journal of Organizational Behavior*, 15, 37–47.

Sagie, A., Elizur, D., and Koslowsky, M. (2001) Effect of participation in strategic and tactical decisions on acceptance of planned change. *Journal of Social Psychology*, 130 (4), 459–465.

Schweiger, D. M. and DeNisi, A. S. (1991) Communication with employees following a merger: A longitudinal field experiment. *Academy of Management Journal*, 34 (1), 110–135.

Scott, C. R., Lewis, L. K., Davis, J. D., and D'Urso, S. C. (2009) Finding a home for communication technologies. In J. Keyton and P. Shockley-Zalabak (eds.), *Case Studies for Organizational Communication: Understanding Communication Processes* (2nd edn.). Los Angeles, CA: Roxbury.

Smeltzer, L. R. (1995) Organization-wide change: Planning for an effective announcement. *Journal of General Management*, 20, 31–43.

Timmerman, C. E. (2003) Media selection during the implementation of planned organizational change. *Management Communication Quarterly*, 15 (3), 301–340.

Van Maanen, J. (1978) People processing: Strategies of organizational socialization. *Organizational Dynamics*, 7, 19–36.

Weick, K. (1979) *The Social Psychology of Organizing* (2nd edn.) Reading, MA: Addison-Wesley.

Weick, K. (1995) *Sensemaking in Organizations*. London: Sage.

West, M. A., Nicholson, N., and Rees, A. (1987) Transitions into newly created jobs. *Journal of Occupational Psychology*, 60, 97–113.

Zorn, T. E., Page, D. J., and Cheney, G. (2000) Nuts about change: Multiple perspectives on change-oriented communication in a public sector organization. *Management Communication Quarterly*, 13 (4), 515–566.

Further Reading

Armenakis, A. A., Harris, S. G., and Mossholder, K. W. (1993) Creating readiness for organizational change. *Human Relations*, 46 (3), 681–703.

Ashford, S. J. (1988) Individual strategies for coping with stress during organizational transitions. *Journal of Applied Behavioral Science*, 24, 19–36.

Basinger, N. W. and Peterson, J. R. (2008) Where you stand depends on where you sit: Participation and reactions to change. *Nonprofit Management and Leadership*, 19 (2), 243–257.

Coyle-Shapiro, J. A. M. (1999) Employee participation and assessment of an organizational change intervention: A three-way study of total quality management. *Journal of Applied Behavioral Science*, 35 (4), 439–456.

Dutton, J. E., Ashford, S. J., O'Neill, R. M., and Lawrence, K. A. (2001) Moves that matter: Issue selling and organizational change. *Academy of Management Journal*, 44 (4), 716–736.

Wanous, J. P., Reichers, A. E., and Malik, S. D. (1984) Organizational socialization and group development: Toward an integrative perspective. *Academy of Management Review*, 9 (4), 670–683.

3

A Stakeholder Communication Model of Change

People do not always argue because they misunderstand one another, they argue because they hold different goals
William H. Shyte, Jr.

Would you persuade, speak of interest, not of reason
Benjamin Franklin

If you would win a man to your cause, first convince him that you are his sincere friend
Abraham Lincoln

We all have stakes in organizations. Only someone living a Thoreau-like existence on Walden's Pond with no contact with resource providers, social groups, political affiliations, or proximity to government, business or any vestige of society could claim no stakes in organizations. As shown in the examples already presented in this book, organizations often have diverse stakeholders both within and without the identifiable

Organizational Change: Creating Change Through Strategic Communication,
First Edition. Laurie K. Lewis.
© 2011 Laurie K. Lewis. Published 2011 by Blackwell Publishing Ltd.

boundary of operation. Employees, customers, suppliers, governments, competitors are obvious types of stakeholders who demand things from organizations; depend on or are effected by organizational operations; and often provide comment on what organizations do. However, the picture of a given organization's stakeholders can be much more complex than this since stakeholders are not always obvious to or acknowledged by organizations. Further, how we are perceived or self-perceive our stakes and stakeholder status for a given organization can be complex. We may play more than one role in an organization simultaneously (e.g., customer and employee; community member and volunteer) making the relative demands of groups of stakeholders quite dynamic and potentially difficult to manage both for organizations and for stakeholders.

In this chapter we will explore a model (see Figure 3.1) of change processes in the context of stakeholder communication that frames this book. We will first discuss the importance of Stakeholder Theory and introduce its basic tenets as well as some novel ways to view the "map" of stakeholders relevant to any given change effort. Second, we will explore key roles that stakeholders play during change, pointing to both formal and informal roles that stakeholders may play in the processes of change. Third, we will briefly tour the model. Each of the major parts of the model including components and relationships among the components will be developed in later chapters.

Stakeholder Theory

Stakeholder Theory is aimed at explaining how organizations map the field of potential stakeholders and then decide strategic action in managing relationships with various groups of stakeholders. These relationships are usually conceptualized as a hub and spokes (see Figure 3.2). Organizations are portrayed as having independent relationships with each of a set of definable stakeholder groups. Stakeholder Theory can be thought of as a family of perspectives launched by Edward Freeman in his now classic book, *Strategic Management: A Stakeholder Approach* (1984). Three main branches of this perspective have developed in the literature. The *descriptive approach* depicts existing relationships with stakeholders. In the *instrumental approach* scholars test claims about how organizational actions shape stakeholder relationships (e.g., certain strategies with stakeholders are associated with certain outcomes: Jones and Wicks, 1999). In the *normative approach*, scholars focus on

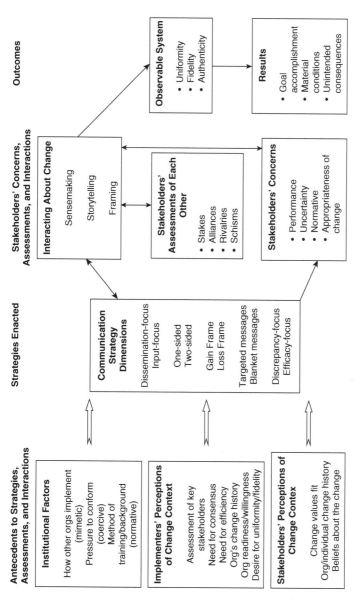

Figure 3.1 Change process in context of stakeholder communication

Antecedents to Strategies, Assessments, and Interactions

Strategies Enacted

Stakeholders' Concerns, Assessments, and Interactions

Outcomes

Institutional Factors

How other orgs implement (mimetic)
Pressure to conform (coercive)
Method of training/background (normative)

Implementers' Perceptions of Change Context

Assessment of key stakeholders
Need for consensus
Need for efficiency
Org's change history
Org readiness/willingness
Desire for uniformity/fidelity

Stakeholders' Perceptions of Change Context

Change values fit
Org/individual change history
Beliefs about the change

Communication Strategy Dimensions

Dissemination-focus
Input-focus

One-sided
Two-sided

Gain Frame
Loss Frame

Targeted messages
Blanket messages

Discrepancy-focus
Efficacy-focus

Interacting About Change

Sensemaking

Storytelling

Framing

Stakeholders' Assessments of Each Other

• Stakes
• Alliances
• Rivalries
• Schisms

Stakeholders' Concerns

• Performance
• Uncertainty
• Normative
• Appropriateness of change

Observable System

• Uniformity
• Fidelity
• Authenticity

Results

• Goal accomplishment
• Material conditions
• Unintended consequences

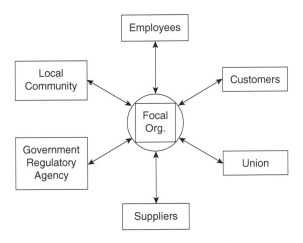

Figure 3.2   Hub and spokes model of stakeholder relationships

moral and ethical obligations of managers to various stakeholders. Scholarship in this vein is exemplified in **corporate social responsibility** (CSR) literature (cf. Donaldson and Preston, 1995; Jennings and Zandbergen, 1995).

Stakeholder Theory is centrally concerned with how organizations allocate stakes and attention to various recognized stakeholders. Identifying "important" or "critical" stakeholders is an important part of that calculus. Theorizing from an instrumental perspective of Stakeholder Theory, Mitchell, Agle, and Wood (1997) suggest that stakeholders be defined according to three attributes: (a) power (ability of a stakeholder to impose will), (b) legitimacy (generalized assessment that a stakeholder's actions are desirable, proper, or appropriate), and (c) urgency (degree to which a stakeholder's claims are time-sensitive, pressing, and/or critical to the stakeholder). Those stakeholder groups that are perceived to possess all three characteristics are labeled "**definitive stakeholders**." These authors argue that organizational leaders have a clear and immediate requirement to focus their attention and resources on definitive stakeholders' needs. An example of a definitive stakeholder for those organizations that are part of Homeless Net might be the US Department of Housing and Urban Development (HUD) (see Highlight Box 3.1). HUD provides a large amount of funding for municipalities to spend on affordable housing and shelter. Without HUD funding, many cities and counties could not afford to execute their missions to serve homeless persons. In order to secure the funding, applicants must abide

Highlight Box 3.1: HUD as a Definitive Stakeholder for Agencies Serving Homeless Populations

Created in 1965, HUD's mission is to increase homeownership, support community development, and increase access to affordable housing free from discrimination. To fulfill this mission, HUD will embrace high standards of ethics, management, and accountability and forge new partnerships – particularly with faith-based and community organizations – that leverage resources and improve HUD's ability to be effective on the community level.

When HUD publishes a Notice of Funding Availability (NOFA) for Continuum of Care Homeless Assistance in the Federal Register, applicants must submit specific information about a proposed project, along with their Continuum of Care application. Each application must include a certification that the project is consistent with the Consolidated Plan of the jurisdiction where each proposed project is found.

Eligible applicants include States, local governments, other government agencies (such as public housing agencies), private nonprofit organizations, and community mental health associations that are public nonprofit organizations.

Source: www.hud.gov.

by the time schedule, eligibility requirements, reporting requirements, guidelines, and procedures that HUD lays out. HUD fulfills all of Mitchell *et al.*'s requirements to be a definitive stakeholder for this group of agencies because it has legitimacy as a federal agency; power, as a major source of funding; and urgency, in that it demands timely application and reporting in order for the provider agencies to earn funding. HUD cannot be ignored or put off, given this status.

Stakeholders may also possess only one or two of Mitchell *et al.*'s attributes. So, they may be perceived to have legitimacy but not urgency or power; or power and urgency but not legitimacy. Lacking one or two of the critical attributes of definitive stakeholders in the eyes of organizational leaders may make them less "important" in the assessment of stakes or the attention paid by organizational decision-makers. However, stakeholders who hold even one of these characteristics might make it hard for organizations to ignore them. For example, even if a stakeholder lacks legitimacy and urgency, organizations may have to attend to them if they have significant power. A prime example is the power of unions to strike. Even if organizations consider employee complaints to be illegitimate, the power of striking the company and ceasing operation is one that is hard to ignore. Mitchell *et al.*'s approach to determining more or less important stakeholders puts organizational decision-makers at the center of the picture. Managers of organizations survey stakeholders that they perceive, and rely upon their own perspectives to determine stakeholders' claims on the organization.

As we have observed in earlier examples, stakeholders do not always reside outside of an organization. Employees, volunteers, members, etc. are part of "focal organizations" and are also important stakeholders. Not all stakeholder groups are easy for organizations to identify and in some cases, the introduction of change makes some stakeholders more obvious. Homeless Net provides a good example of how the introduction of change can actually alter the visible landscape of important stakeholders (see Case Box 3.1). As the network participants increased their use of the listserv set for the community of providers they discovered a widening of the boundary of who was part of the community. New agencies were discovered by members of the listserv that were previously unknown to many of the organizations in the network. The active use of and participation in the listserv actually elevated the status of some agencies in the network as it increased their profile among other stakeholders.

In the Corporate Social Responsibility (CSR) approach, which operates from a normative perspective of Stakeholder Theory, scholars are concerned with describing how organizations attend to stakes of stakeholders who have claims on the organization that are not related to the bottom line. McWilliams and Siegel (2001) define CSR as "actions that appear to further some social good beyond the interests of the firm and that which is required by law" (p. 117). Examples of CSR include creation of environmentally friendly products and processes; adoption of progressive human resource management practices; and aiding the advancement of community goals and those of community-serving non-profits. Some scholars argue that these activities ought to be engaged in for the good of the organization and others argue they should be entered into because it is right to do so. A number of companies have extensive records in CSR including General Electric, Target, Starbucks, UPS, Walt Disney, Johnson and Johnson, and Whole Foods. For example, the Starbucks website claims the following:

Case Box 3.1: Homeless Net Implementation of Listserv Increases Awareness of Stakeholders

Some CTOSH organizations benefited from CTOSH tools by creating more of a presence in the network. The email list usage grew over the three years in which the consultants were formally involved with this project. Even though the list was started with approximately 60 individuals it eventually grew to twice that size, incorporating a much wider range of organizations and concerned individuals. Over the course of the project there was a clear growth in the number of posts: 234 in the first year, 314 in the second year, and 438 in the third year.

In an interview, a participant indicated that he learned about a lot of the "little small niche mom and pop" organizations and programs. He said, "they offer something and you want to know about those, and so that has been good." One interviewee speculated that the smaller providers might not have been noticed without CTOSH's attention, "maybe those would have been found other ways, maybe not." CTOSH tools defined the boundaries of the network in new ways and the feeling of being included appears to have expanded as a result.

Other interviewees made similar comments. "People are more connected. There is probably much more understanding of what is happening on a macro level. Before people operated more in their silos. So CTOSH has brought people together." "It [the listserv] provides more cohesion to our community of service providers." "When I open up an email and it is from CTOSH partners, there is no question that I found it valuable. Whether it is going to work for me or not, I have a lot of respect and value for it coming through CTOSH."

Source: Adapted from Scott, Lewis, and D'Urso (2010) and Lewis, Scott, and D'Urso (unpublished).

Our Commitment to Being a Deeply Responsible Company. Contributing positively to our communities and environment is so important to Starbucks that it's one of the six guiding principles of our mission statement. We work together on a daily basis with partners (employees), suppliers, farmers and others to help create a more sustainable approach to high-quality coffee production, to help build stronger local communities, to minimize our environmental footprint, to create a great workplace, to promote diversity and to be responsive to our customers' health and wellness needs.

Whole Foods' website describes their efforts to increase accountability with involvement of stakeholders:

> In conjunction to working with farmers on alternatives and educating our consumers about the harmful effects of some pesticides, we are the only retailer that participated in the joint EPA/USDA Tolerance Reassessment Advisory Committee. The task of this multi-stakeholder advisory board was to advise those agencies how they should fairly reassess all the pesticides that had previously been approved, taking into consideration their effect on the delicate immune systems of infants and children, as well as cumulative effects of their use.

Some scholars have been critical of the CSR branch of scholarship as it may obscure an understanding of the value-laden decisional processes of organizations that have important repercussions for many stakeholders regardless of attempts to appear inclusive and responsive. In other words, organizations may engage in CSR activities in order to create an impression of listening to and engaging stakeholders who have little impact on the bottom line. As Kuhn and Deetz (2008) argue, such practices "actually prevent the creation of a democratic society because they mollify citizens who might otherwise demand systemic change" (p. 174). Further, some CSR strategies are used in order to attract socially responsible consumers (Barron, 2001), or build employee loyalty. In such cases, the organization's strategic goals supersede any direct benefits of actions to community or other stakeholders.

Complicating Stakeholder Relationships

There has been scant acknowledgment of the relationships that stakeholders have with one another in the Stakeholder Theory literature. However, a few scholars (Hendry, 2005; Post, Preston, and Sachs, 2002; Rowley, 1997) have argued that not only do stakeholders recognize one another; they also assess the degree to which their stakes are competitive or complimentary with other stakeholders. For example, Mitchell *et al.* (1997) have noted that stakeholders who form alliances in advocating some stake or preferred action on the part of a focal organization can increase chances of the focal organization's compliance. Thus, a

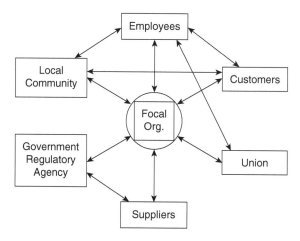

Figure 3.3   Complex stakeholder relationships

union might seek the sympathies of the community at large and/or specific customers of an organization in order to have greater leverage over the organization. Given this more complex picture, Figure 3.3 is a better representation of the actual map of such relationships in that it illustrates the reality that stakeholder groups have awareness of and relationships with each other.

Rowley (1997) argues that *dense networks* (where there are many shared norms, values, information, and agreed behavioral constraints) of stakeholders will create a challenging environment for a given focal organization to force its will. In such cases an organization would have "more difficulty playing one group against another or finding a sympathetic group of stakeholders with whom it could form an alliance" (p. 897). Rowley also argues that *centrality* is another essential characteristic of the focal organization's network position. If for example the focal organization played a very critical gatekeeper role, influencing behavior expectations and managing information flows, it would have a better power resource to manage stakeholders. In Rowley's conceptualization, being highly centralized in a less dense network is the ideal situation to exert maximum influence. As one's own centrality decreases or the density of the stakeholder network increases, more compromising or subordinate roles must be adopted.

Some scholars (Rowley and Moldoveaunu, 2003) have also argued that mere identification among stakeholder groups will motivate reaction related to an organization's actions. A feeling of solidarity may act as a powerful catalyst for collective action. As Fireman and Gamson (1979) argue, groups may participate in group action because they become "linked together in a number of ways that generate a sense of common identity, shared fate, and general commitment to defend the group" (p. 21).

Another important concept related to the network relationships within stakeholder networks concerns the gaps between stakeholders. These "structural holes" (Burt, 1992) where stakeholders are not connected directly open up opportunities to those who "broker" the different parties. Spanners who bridge these gaps are well positioned to hold a good deal of power since the separated parties need to go through the middle node in order to effectively interact, share information, and share resources. When links between the parties form directly, the spanner is not as necessary or powerful.

We can translate these predictions into a simple personal example if we consider the same principles in a friendship network. If Sally has ten close friends and wants to have a good deal of influence with each of them, she will probably have the best luck if she is the one with lots of "between links" in the network. That is, if the friends mostly only know one another through her (and don't directly interact without Sally), she will have the most influence. If the friends start having lots of social ties directly with one another without Sally, that equalizes or minimizes Sally's influence with the other people in the network. Sally would be less able to manipulate opinions, control gossip, influence decision-making in such a situation.

We can complicate this model even further if we acknowledge that organizations do not speak with one disembodied voice. In fact, stakeholders interact with various boundary-spanners that represent organizations (e.g., customer service representatives, immediate supervisors, salespersons, lawyers). **Boundary-spanners** are individuals who connect an organization with external environments (Adams, 1980; Leifer and Delbecq, 1978). Boundary-spanners don't always present the same "face" to stakeholders, aren't always consistent with one another, and may create widely varying levels of trust, credibility, and integrity with different stakeholders. Figure 3.4 is an even better depiction of stakeholder relationships in acknowledging this multi-voice aspect of boundary interactions. An even truer representation of these relationships would include the same level of complexity for each stakeholder group (depicting multiple boundary-spanners within each of the stakeholder groups).

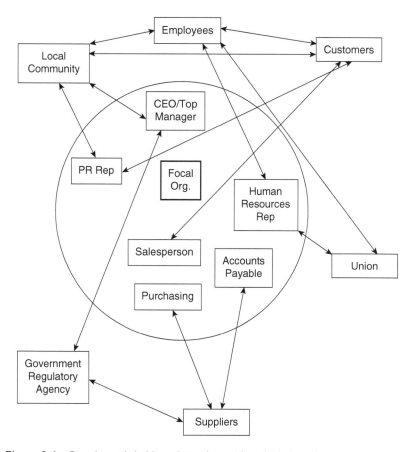

Figure 3.4 Complex stakeholder relationships with multiple boundary-spanners

Multiple Stakeholder Identities

Stakeholders do not always have singular identities with regard to a focal organization. That is, some stakeholders play multiple roles regarding the organization and therefore may occupy overlapping stakeholder identities (Rowley and Moldoveaunu, 2003). A customer might be an employee (e.g., I might take an evening course at the university where I am on faculty); a volunteer may also be a client (e.g., Red Cross volunteers may find themselves in need of emergency aid during a disaster); a community member may also be an employee, and so forth. There are many such overlapping stakeholder identities. We can also see that individuals may identify with various subgroups within or relative to an organization. Scott (1997; 1999) refers to these as multiple **targets of identification**. Our targets can include multitudes of identities that are salient for us including: cohorts (e.g., employees who were hired at the same time; groups of clients in the same age range; volunteers who were trained together), workgroups, professional affiliations, and areas of expertise among many others. This makes the mapping of stakeholders during change a much more challenging task because you cannot necessarily peg any one individual or group to a single perspective that they represent or with which they affiliate.

Targets of identification for stakeholders may be altered or highlighted by the nature of the change being undertaken. This is true because change often makes some identities more salient. Introduction of a parental leave policy will make our status as parents or potential parents more salient. For the childless person, it may highlight that status and raise issues of fairness. The implementation of an idea that an individual helped create would likely make salient her identity as part of the design team. The introduction of complex new technologies in a workplace previously lacking such an innovation, might raise salience of identities related to expertise or technological qualifications (e.g., those who self-perceive as "techies" versus those who are uncomfortable with technology).

Our connections and identifications with different "targets" within and around organizations may have a profound influence on how we view any given change initiative and the likelihood we will join efforts to act in support or against a change. In an effort to examine these sorts of influences, Michael Gallivan (2001) examined how different stakeholder groups viewed a technology change in different ways. He uses Orlikowski and Gash's (1994) definition of "technology frames" as "the assumptions, expectations, and knowledge [that people] use to understand technology in organizations" (p. 178). Gallivan examined a company's efforts in reskilling (upgrading employee skills in replacement of outmoded practices and equipment) of computer programmers, systems analysts, and other IT professionals in the 1990s. Gallivan suspected that various stakeholders by virtue of different memberships in occupational groups, hierarchical levels, and socialization into specific jobs would have different bases of experience and awareness that would shape their assumptions about organizational change and cause them to observe the same events or receive the same messages about change in very different and even contradictory ways. He observed three groups of stakeholders – change managers; IT managers and employees; those who interacted with IT but who were not target of reskilling – all making sense of the size, scope, and purpose of the change in vastly different ways (see Highlight Box 3.2). We will return to this discussion in Chapter 8 where we consider how the interaction among stakeholders further complicates this picture. That is, even though stakeholders share interests and stakes, they may not hold the same understanding of a change effort. Their interactions with other stakeholders will be a major determinant of how they view it. For now, it is important to recognize that identification with a specific group of stakeholders can influence our initial read on a change as well as our motivation to act in support or against the change.

Highlight Box 3.2: IT Reskilling Case Study – How Stakeholder Groups View Change Differently

The change managers – described a vision for reskilling that relied on a partnership among themselves, the IT managers, and the IT employees. This vision implied major transformation in programmers' roles and skill sets, and significant change in the organizational culture. This group envisioned mentoring and career development as key as well.

The IT managers and IT Employees – viewed the goals of the change as a narrow focus on updating technical skills of IT employees and did not acknowledge or recognize any broad change to their level of business knowledge, job roles, culture, or interaction with customers. These stakeholders expected incremental and mostly autonomous change efforts that would be conducted through trial and error experiments to reskill.

Those who worked with IT – viewed the change as a radical one that would be achieved mostly through the efforts of outside consultants. They expected dramatic layoffs and new deskilled IT roles.

Source: Adapted from Gallivan (2001).

The possibility that multiple targets of identification are simultaneously salient for any given individual raises the possibility that our different "selves" will have conflicting points of view on a change. As a parent, I may really like the new parental leave policy since it provides a means for me to take time off with my newborn. As a supervisor, I may think the policy is overly generous in that it will create havoc for me when my subordinates begin to disappear for months at a time to have their children. The push and pull of our various salient targets of identification can create internal turmoil as we consider change. It also creates a more challenging picture for implementers of change to manage since it may be hard to predict which of stakeholders' multiple "identities" will have more influence in their reactions.

Identification with different stakeholder groups with different positions on a change initiative can also drive us to debate our viewpoint. For example, friendship with a group of workers who are being laid off during a merger may get in the way of support for a change that otherwise may be acceptable to an individual. Implementers who are strategic in their approach to communication will likely attempt to make certain identities more salient if they think it will result in stronger compliance and cooperation from stakeholders. For example, a manager in the case of a layoff might appeal to the "good of the company," heightening identification with the survival of the company over identification with friends who have to go. Similarly, those opposed to the change may highlight other stakeholder identities to urge individuals to make different commitments.

In my own university, there are currently some dire budgetary discussions. The president sent an email to all employees highlighting the "university community" as a target of identification. On the heels of that email I received one from the union leadership reminding its membership of union loyalties – highlighting that community as a target of identification. Neither email specifically requested anything at this point, but clearly both are attempting to make some targets of identification more salient than others. We will return to the topic of strategic communication in Chapter 5.

Stakeholder Interactions

Partly as a result of attempts to highlight or make some identities more salient, stakeholders negotiate with one another (Allen and Callouet, 1994; Kuhn, 2008). Stakeholders may spend as much time and energy

Highlight Box 3.3: Upton Sinclair Sets Off Stakeholder Advocacy to Clean Up Meat Packing Factories

Upton Sinclair became involved in the growing socialist movement in America and wrote books advocating change through investigative journalism; this practice was called "muckraking." Sinclair moved to Chicago to investigate the meat-packing industry in order to document the poor conditions of workers. His findings were published in *The Jungle*, a novel depicting an immigrant who worked in one of plants.

An instant best-seller, Sinclair's book exposed sickening practices in the meat-packing industry. He told how dead rats were shoveled into sausage-grinding machines, how bribed inspectors looked the other way when diseased cows were slaughtered for beef, and how filth and guts were swept off the floor and packaged as "potted ham." In short, *The Jungle* came close to converting a lot of readers into vegetarians! When it was published, the public reaction was instantaneous.

Working from a New York City hotel room Sinclair launched a publicity campaign. He wrote articles with titles like "Campaign against the wholesale poisoners of the nation's food," and released more stomach-churning details. He claimed that Armour made its potted hams by taking nubs of smoked beef, "moldy and full of maggots," and grinding them with ham trimmings. In a newspaper letter, he dared J. Ogden Armour, the meat-packing magnate, to sue for libel.

Within months, the aroused public demanded sweeping reforms in the meat industry and deluged President Theodore Roosevelt with letters. The President sent his own agents to Chicago to investigate whether meat-packing was as bad as Sinclair described. He also invited Sinclair to the White House and solicited his advice on how to make inspections safer. As a result of Sinclair's crusade, Congress passed the Pure Food and Drug Act, which up to that point had been effectively blocked by industry. To this day, our hamburgers, chicken patties, and other meats are safeguarded by the same law.

Source: Adapted from http://teachingamericanhistorymd.net/000001/000000/000167/html/t167.html, http://www.capitalcentury.com/1906.html, and http://www.nytimes.com/2007/01/02/opinion/02tue4.html (A. Cohen, "100 years later, the food industry is still 'the jungle'").

negotiating stakes with one another as they do with the organization. As Deetz (2001) argues, "interaction among stakeholders can be conceived as a negotiative process aiding mutual goal accomplishment. Communication is the means by which such negotiation takes place" (p. 39). As stakeholders become aware of mutual and competing stakes and the potential for identification to sway one way or the other during change, they lobby one another for support of proposed actions and/or sympathies to specific viewpoints. Powerful combinations of stakeholders can result from this lobbying. Pfarrer, Decelles, Smith, and Taylor (2008) describe the role of "elite stakeholders" as facilitators of interaction between the organization and its other stakeholders and also as facilitators of discourse among stakeholder groups. They cite the example of Texaco's 1994 discrimination scandal where "elites such as print and TV media outlets disseminated information to the organization's other stakeholders, helping shape their opinions and perhaps galvanizing them into action" (p. 732).

Another great example of this can be found in the "muckraking" of early American socialist writers in the 1900s. The story of Upton Sinclair's book *The Jungle* about the meat-packing industry is a provocative example of how stakeholders can discover joint concerns (see Highlight Box 3.3). Neither Sinclair, the American socialists he was associated with, sympathetic congressmen, nor any single advocacy group could have accomplished the Food and Drug Administration Act alone. It was the powerful combination of Sinclair's call for attention, the public's outrage and lobbying of the President, and the reactions of Congress to the President's bid for reform that created the political climate to pass this law. The ways in which stakeholders interacted and came to bond around a common conclusion had a great deal of influence in creating change. Further, the combination of the public, the President, and Congress coming together as stakeholders was enough to overcome the lobbying efforts of industry stakeholders.

Roles Stakeholders Play in Change

Individuals, groups, and whole organizations can serve specific roles during change that may exert influence and impact the way implementation unfolds. I briefly describe four specific stakeholder roles here: opinion leaders, connectors, counselors, and journalists.

Opinion leaders have been discussed in the change literature for many years (cf. Kanter, 1983; Leonard-Barton and Kraus, 1985). Opinion leadership involves individuals or groups of stakeholders whose opinions tend to lead rather than follow other stakeholders. An innovation champion, a type of opinion leader, is said to be a leader, a sponsor, a diplomat, a salesperson, a risk-taker, and a problem-solver. In the opposite vein, the *innovation assassin* (Leonard-Barton and Kraus, 1985) (don't you love the metaphor!) advises people not to use the new change. Further, Zoller and Fairhurst (2007) describe resistance leaders as emergent and informal spokespersons who present dissent messages to those in power. In another example, Armenakis, Bernerth, Pitts, and Walker (2007), based on research in diffusion, argue that opinion leaders' adoption of new technologies and methodologies speeds up diffusion.

Scholars have studied social influence processes within organizational settings (Ibarra and Andrews, 1993; Zagenczky, Gibney, Murrell, and Boxx, 2008) and have examined cases of how innovations spread within networks due to social influence processes (Fulk, 1993; Kraut, Rice, Cool, and Fish, 1998; Timmerman, 2002). Additionally, they have studied the influence of change agents in the context of implementation of change. In a review of literature related to change agents (Lewis and Seibold, 1998), my colleague David Seibold and I make several observations about what is known about change agents in terms of their significance, common characteristics, and differences between internal change agents and external (e.g., consultants).

Just how opinion leadership plays a role in fostering attitudes about change, methods of implementation, or organizing resistance or advocacy of change is unclear. We do know that in organizations in general social influence is exerted through (a) overt statements made by others, (b) vicarious learning from observations of the experiences of others, and (c) normative group influence (Fulk, Schmitz, and Steinfield, 1990; Salancik and Pfeffer, 1978). It is likely that most social influence will travel through the pathways established in knowledge-sharing networks in organizations. We discussed in the last chapter how stakeholders tend to turn to sources of information considered knowledgeable, with whom they can exchange information and are in close proximity.

Malcolm Gladwell (2000) writes in his book *The Tipping Point* about opinion leaders he terms "salesmen" who have:

> a kind of indefinable trait, something powerful and contagious and irresistible that goes beyond what comes out of his mouth, that makes people who meet him want to agree with him. It's energy. It's enthusiasm. It's charm. It's likability. It's all those things and yet something more. (p. 73)

This sort of persuasive individual, if found within a given stakeholder's information knowledge network, might wield a good deal of influence on attitudes and action.

Connectors are another important role played by stakeholders during change. Connectors are those who help bridge gaps between different types of stakeholders. Gladwell's *Tipping Point* describes "connectors" as people who hold membership in many different social worlds, subcultures, and niches. Gladwell says of these people, "[their] ability to span many different worlds is a function of something intrinsic to their personality, some combination of curiosity, self-confidence, sociability, and energy" (p. 49). Because connectors have their "feet" in many different social worlds simultaneously, they are able to link those worlds together. They are fluent in many different value systems, languages, ideologies. The importance of connectors in change is then in (a) spreading knowledge and counter-knowledge about change initiatives, (b) bringing together diverse points of view on change from diverse stakeholder groups, and (c) brokering alliances among stakeholders that may create aligned goals for the change.

Several scholars discuss the importance of front-line or middle-level managers in connecting roles (cf. Coyle-Shapiro, 1999; Gallivan, 2001; Luscher and Lewis, 2008). Line supervisors have the potential to be effective translators of large-scale organizational change initiatives. They can provide the top manager perspectives to front-line employees and to outside stakeholders. They are uniquely suited to translate the vision of a change as well as important details of how implementation will take place. Further, front-line supervisors, and others in middle management roles, can translate front-line and other stakeholder concerns to decision-makers. Middle managers who interact with one another can also as serve as internal boundary-spanners across different functions and lines within an organization.

Christine Meyer (2006) has argued that middle managers are often derided as "foot-draggers" during change. However, her study of an international (Finnish, Swedish, Danish, and Norwegian) merger that resulted in the creation of Nordea – a large financial organization –illustrates how middle-level managers can play both destructive and constructive roles in change. The Nordea merger was described as an implementation "failure" due, in part, to the misalignment among middle-level managers and the absence of leadership and involvement from top managers. These critical connectors essentially pulled the organization in different directions simultaneously. Meyer proposed "whether middle management intervention is constructive or destructive in the process of operationalizing strategic intent [of change] depends on how the interests of the different groups of middle management are aligned" (p. 415).

Counselors are those in the organization who provide social support to other stakeholders during change. Several scholars have noted the importance of emotion and social support in the context of organizational change (Ashford, 1988; Miller and Monge, 1985; Zorn, 2002). Zorn provides several examples of the functions of emotion during organizational change, including "to signal engagement, disengagement, satisfaction or dissatisfaction with the change" (p. 161). Counselors are those in and around organizations who are best suited and most actively engaged in dealing with these emotions. Some emotions can be so raw and potentially destructive as to be "toxic." Peter Frost (2004) discusses the important role of "toxin handlers" in providing empathetic capacity to notice when and how painful situations turn toxic. Frost argues that toxin handlers "step into situations at work to dissipate or to buffer the toxins so that those who are in harm's way are rescued or protected and can get on with doing their organizational work" (p. 115).

Napier, Simmons, and Stratton (1989) describe how employees provided mutual social support during a merger of banks, "instead of just sitting in my corner and dealing with where *my* life was headed, we took more time [as a unit] to just talk about our feelings" (p. 115). One bank teller reported, "we got together on Friday after work for a bottle of wine and a good cry" (p. 116). One form of Social support can take the form of **emotional support** (providing a channel for venting emotions), **informational support** (providing answers to questions that are source of stress), and **instrumental support** (taking on some task for another person) (Miller, 1995). Ashford (1988) found that "sharing worries and concerns" was one of the most effective strategies to buffer against stress. Although a number of studies have been conducted suggesting the importance of social support during change and exploring the use of various coping strategies during change, we know very little about the sorts of individuals who are commonly cast in the "counselor" role.

Journalists serve the function of investigators and reporters during change. They may gather information from inside and outside the organization and are prone to share what they learn widely with other stakeholders. These stakeholders are not only high information seekers, they are high promoters of using data, sharing experiences, and opinion swapping. Most of the current change literature has focused only on information seeking as it relates to personal use. High information seekers, in that context, may use information to reduce uncertainty for themselves. In the context of the journalist role, information seeking is done as a service to the community of stakeholders. This is a role that has yet to show up in the change literature but nonetheless is a key one.

Journalists are not necessarily non-partisan. However, their function in this role is to gather and disseminate information, commentary, and opinion. They "report" on what is working; not working; what rumors are confirmed or debunked; how stakeholders of various types are reacting to change; and who is supportive or negative. They might also report on information gathered outside the organization or speculate on future plans for the change effort or reasons for why decision-makers selected it. The influence of opinion leaders may be heightened once a journalist reports on them. Journalists may spread information at the water-cooler, over drinks at the local watering hole, or do things akin to professional journalists like create or contribute to websites, blogs, wikis, and the like that describe the change process for others. They may also operate like roving reporters who pick up and then share the opinions of a wide array of stakeholders. Examples of journalists abound in the online world. "Sucks.com" sites (Gossett and Kilker, 2006) are one venue as are YouTube videos, and Facebook pages submitted by organizational stakeholders. "Sucks.com" catalogs a comprehensive list of corporate American "suck" sites (see Highlight Box 3.4) as well as more for government, universities, and even whole States and cities. These sites provide forums for stakeholders (e.g., consumers, employees, ex-employees) to complain about or discuss current operations in organizations, including change efforts.

Highlight Box 3.4: Sample of Sucks.com Sites

3M Sucks	Federal Express Sucks	Pepsi Sucks
Anheuser Busch Sucks	Hilton Sucks	Pfizer Sucks
AT&T Sucks	Kraft Food Sucks	RJR Nabisco Sucks
Boeing Sucks	Merck Sucks	Safeway Sucks
Cigna Sucks	Microsoft Sucks	Time Warner Sucks
Comcast Sucks	Nike Sucks	Xerox Sucks

In sum, the four stakeholder roles here, opinion leaders, connectors, counselors, and journalists can have tremendous impact on how change progresses in organizations. All of these are very social roles. In one way or another stakeholders who play out these roles help in interpretation, meaning-making, sense-making, and spread of information and opinion about change programs.

Stakeholder Model of Implementation of Change

A theoretical model (Lewis, 2007) I formulated helps to conceptualize the important factors that account for selections of communication strategies and the relationships that those strategies, once enacted, have with stakeholders' concerns, their interactions, and ultimately, their effects on outcomes for change. An updated version of the model is presented here (Figure 3.1) to help guide our discussion of the role of stakeholder interactions in the context of implementation of organizational change. This version of the model is somewhat different from the earlier version in the sense that it includes a variety of actors in the strategic communication portion of the model. In the earlier version, only implementers were treated as strategic communicators who design messages and communicative strategies to influence stakeholders. Consistent with Stakeholder Theory and the development in this book, I have altered the model to reflect the more accurate depiction of many possible communicators acting strategically during implementation of change. Not all stakeholder communication is reactionary.

Models are depictions of sets of important components of organizational (or other) life. In the most basic form they include components (usually in boxes or circles) and relationships (usually marked by arrows that illustrate direction of influence). Models are always oversimplifications of real life, but they are one tool to help us map out how important features of our social worlds impact one another. They also aid in the development of hypotheses that can be tested in research, which is one valuable pathway to furthering understanding.

We can start our tour of this model from the "back side" or the right side of the model – outcomes. Outcomes of implementation of change concern both what the model terms "observable system" and "results." These are topics that are discussed in detail in the next chapter. For now we can define the important differences between these two concepts. The **observable system** concerns what it is possible to notice through participation and observation. Observables in change implementation include the number of users of a new technology, the frequency of errors in use of a new procedure, the degree to which all expected users are all following a new policy, and the like. **Results**, on the other hand, concern whether the implementation effort achieves intended or unintended, desired or undesired consequences. Usually change programs are not initiated in order to alter processes, behaviors, and attitudes alone. Those outcomes are intended as precursors to some stated or unstated goal of the implementers or sponsors of change programs. Thus, change initiatives are intended to raise revenue, increase market share, increase productivity, reduce numbers of consumer complaints, etc. Although the outcomes of participation, implementation rate, appropriate user response may be achieved, results may not be always achieved. Typically, it is results that are ultimately used to judge the success or failure of change initiatives.

Unintended consequences of change programs are also part of results. If all the desired results are achieved but the company suffers some major embarrassment or injury as an additional result of a change, the ultimate judgment may be failure. Organizations sometimes pay dearly for unintended consequences of major change programs, including reputation damage; breakdowns in relationships with employees, customers, suppliers, or other important stakeholders; lost revenue during transition periods, among others.

The rest of the model is intended to account for major features of organizational and stakeholder activities during implementation that give rise to the observable system and results. The general perspective that frames this book, and is embraced by this model, concerns the critical contribution of stakeholder interactions as an important engine for the outcomes of change. Thus, in the next section of the model, moving left across the page, I have depicted stakeholders' concerns, assessments of each other, and interactions about change in and around the organization. We will discuss these critical components in detail in Chapter 8. You will notice that these various components of the change situation are depicted as having influence on one another in complex ways. Interactions among stakeholders and implementers may influence, and are influenced by, stakeholders' assessments of each other and stakeholders concerns about the change. As I have argued throughout this book, stakeholders make sense collectively in highly social ways. As Weick (1995) points out, "sensemaking is never solitary because what a person does internally is contingent on others" (p. 40). Stakeholders consider and may be influenced by the stakes others have in the organization and in the change, and the sensegiving attempts of others who attempt to frame the change in specific ways.

Sensemaking among stakeholders during change processes often leads to the construction of concerns about the impact of change. For example, even if the change may seem to support my values, it may threaten the values of a stakeholder group with which I identify. Such identifications as well as interactions with members of those stakeholder groups may lead to increased concerns about the change. In turn, as concerns rise or fall, my interactions regarding the change may lead to decreased support for the change and lack of enthusiastic participation in the change initiative. Of course positive reactions or conflicted reactions can be built through the same sort of process. I might start out negative but after interacting with other stakeholders come to hold a more positive outlook on the change or simply be more confused about what I think.

Working a layer back in the model to the communication strategies enacted by implementers and others, the model depicts how communication strategies (e.g., messages and styles of interactions) can serve as triggers for stakeholders' concerns and stakeholders' interactions with each other. As we discussed in Chapter 2, implementers, as well as other stakeholders, use different strategies to disseminate information and solicit input. For example, we noted that in some cases, implementers' attempts to involve stakeholders are widespread and in others they may be fairly limited. These and other dimensions of communication strategies, discussed in Chapter 5, prompt many stakeholder reactions to change programs.

The model predicts that both implementers' and stakeholders' communicative strategies, once enacted, will create opportunities for stakeholders to construct concerns about the change. For example, communication between stakeholders and implementers creates a frame that change is necessary, stakeholders may perceive even difficult changes (involving high demands on them, layoffs, painful or drawn-out transition periods) as ones they must endure. Where implementers' attempts to communicate the necessity of change do not result in stakeholders perceiving such a need, this may lead to an increase in stakeholders' uncertainty about going through painful change.

The model also depicts a link between stakeholders' interactions and communication strategy directions. This link is referencing, in part, that implementers monitor stakeholder interactions and make course corrections in their own communicative strategies to provoke the desired results. For example, implementers may observe the interactions of employees who are strongly opposed to a change effort and conclude that resistance is likely. One possible reaction to perceived employee resistance would be to reshape communication efforts to address the reasons employees are giving for their negative reactions to the change. This might involve soliciting further input from employees; providing extra incentives for enthusiastic participation; or threats for those who are noncompliant. Of course this is a process involving sensemaking and interpreting "what is going on" with stakeholders that may not accurately reflect stakeholders' view of things. Implementers may read things one way and stakeholders may read them in distinctly different ways. Communication among implementers and stakeholders may enable a construction of reaction to change that is common or may result in many disparate views that are only partially observed by the various communicators.

This link between stakeholders' interactions and communication strategy also suggests that stakeholders' interactions are, in part, triggered by their sensemaking of the strategic communication attempts by implementers. In a similar way as just described, stakeholders independently and socially make sense of the messages and communicative processes engaged in by implementers, and that sensemaking is part of the determination of their own further interactions with one another. If for example a stakeholder group perceives implementers focused more on another stakeholder group's input than their own, this may encourage them to engage with one another about ways to become more visible and important in the eyes of implementers. It might also suggest to them that their concerns aren't considered relevant and decrease their desire to provide input.

The model also predicts that communicator strategy choices are conditioned by important perceptions and strategic choices made at a more general level. Implementers and stakeholders alike base strategic communication choices on institutional factors that shape the organizational environment as well as their own perceptions of the change context.

As various individuals assess the situation of change in terms of important stakeholders; how the organization has typically changed in its history; the readiness or willingness of the organization to change; and the goals and needs of the organization in implementing the change, they select, create, and enact communication strategies. Institutional factors often act as constraints on communicators' strategy choices. Some practices of communication may be impossible to pull off given certain constraints and some may be promoted through the existence of strongly normative ways to do things.

For example, in the earlier example of the drive-thru pharmacy window, pharmacists might wish to end the practice. In order to speak out in an influential and strategic way against it, the pharmacists could have chosen any number of communicative strategies. They could have gone to the newspapers with a protest editorial; picketed in front of drive-thru pharmacies; asked all pharmacists to complain to their own companies through a letter-writing campaign. However, they decided to protest the practice through passing a resolution in their professional association. They may have made this choice because it is more professionally normative to do so. That is, it is a more usual way of lodging the opinions of their professional members.

The model provides a way to map out the strategic communication of implementers and stakeholders of change initiatives. It illustrates how antecedent factors encourage and constrain some strategic communication strategies; how those strategies once enacted lead to stakeholders' concerns, assessments, and interactions; and how those interactions, in turn, influence outcomes in the observable system and results of change. This process is fluid and complex and as discussed in Chapter 1, does not happen in isolation of events in the organization's larger environment. Stakeholders exist in all facets of an organization's world. Stakeholders' identifications, and various understandings of their own and others' stakes in the change and in the organization are constantly in flux. Multiple communicators in various stakeholder roles are operating simultaneously and as we have observed in an earlier discussion, multiple change efforts can be underway simultaneously. Further, the ways in which communication is enacted creates multiple forums for socially making sense of the change, messages, and the stories told about what is "really going on."

Conclusion

In summary, this chapter has provided an overview of Stakeholder Theory and how it applies to the implementation of organizational change. We have examined the important branches of Stakeholder Theory and noted that a complete understanding of any given organization's stakeholders can be a very complex matter. How individual stakeholders and stakeholder groups perceive themselves in relation to an organization can be complex, can change over time, and can sometimes lead to self-contradictory interests. The salience of identifications of individuals during change events can make mapping the stakeholder terrain very dynamic. Communication about change highlights different targets of identification, various perceptions of loyalties to different stakeholder groups, and the importance of change from different perspectives. This chapter has also provided an overview of four important roles performed by stakeholders during change and toured the model of implementation that frames this book. In subsequent chapters, the major areas of the model are further explored. We focus first, in Chapter 4, on the outcomes of change, understanding more about the importance of assessing outcomes as well as the difficulty of doing so. Chapter 5 describes five key strategy dimensions of implementer and stakeholder communication during change. Chapter 6 provides an important backdrop discussion of power and resistance in organizations, especially during change. In Chapter 7 we explore the important antecedents to implementers' and stakeholders' selection of strategies they enact. Chapter 8 focuses on interactions during change in highlighting how their storytelling, framing, and sensemaking are drivers of and result in communication and change outcomes. Chapter 9 completes our discussion of change in the context of stakeholder communication with a focus on practice.

References

Adams, J. S. (1980) Interorganizational processes and organization boundary activities. *Research in Organizational Behavior*, 2, 321–355.

Allen, M. W. and Callouet, R. H. (1994) Legitimation endeavors: Impression management strategies used by an organization in crises. *Communication Monographs*, 61, 44–62.

Armenakis, A. A., Bernerth, J. B., Pitts, J. P., and Walker, J. (2007) Organizational change recipients' beliefs scale: Development of an assessment instrument. *Journal of Applied Behavioral Science*, 43 (4), 481–505.

Ashford, S. J. (1988) Individual strategies for coping with stress during organizational transitions. *Journal of Applied Behavioral Science*, 24, 19–36.

Barron, D. (2001) Private politics, corporate social responsibility and integrated strategy. *Journal of Economics and Management Strategy*, 10, 7–45.

Burt, R. S. (1992) *Structural Holes: The Social Structure of Competition*. Cambridge, MA: Harvard University Press.

Coyle-Shapiro, J. A. M. (1999) Employee participation and assessment of an organizational change intervention: A three-wave study of Total Quality Management. *Journal of Applied Behavioral Science*, 35 (4), 439–456.

Deetz, S. (2001) Conceptual foundations. In F. M. Jablin and L. L. Putnam (eds.), *The New Handbook of Organizational Communication: Advances in Theory, Research, and Methods* (pp. 3–46). Thousand Oaks, CA: Sage.

Donaldson, T. and Preston, L. (1995) The stakeholder theory of the corporation: Concepts, evidence, and implications. *Academy of Management Review,* 20, 65–91.

Fireman, B. and Gamson, W. A. (1979) Utilitarian logic in resource mobilization perspective. In J. D. McCarthy and M. N. Zald (eds.), *The Dynamics of Social Movements: Resource Mobilization, Social Control and Tactics* (pp. 8–44). Cambridge, MA: Winthrop.

Freeman, E. (1984) *Strategic Management: A Stakeholder Approach.* Boston, MA: Pitman.

Frost, P. (2004) Handling toxic emotions: New challenges for leaders and their organizations. *Organizational Dynamics,* 33 (2), 111–127.

Fulk, J. (1993) Social construction of communication technology. *Academy of Management Journal,* 36 (5), 921–950.

Fulk, J., Schmitz, J., and Steinfield, C. W. (1990) A social influence model of technology use. In J. Fulk and C. W. Steinfield (eds.), *Organizations and Communication Technology* (pp. 117–140). Thousand Oaks, CA: Sage.

Gallivan, M. J. (2001) Meaning to change: How diverse stakeholders interpret organizational communication about change initiatives. *IEEE Transactions on Professional Communication,* 44 (4), 243–266.

Gladwell, M. (2000) *The Tipping Point: How Little Things Can Make a Big Difference.* New York: Little Brown and Co.

Gossett, L. and Kilker, J. (2006) My job sucks: Examining counterinstitutional web sites as locations for organizational member voice, dissent, and resistance. *Management Communication Quarterly,* 20 (1), 63–90.

Hendry, J. R. (2005) Stakeholder influence strategies: An empirical exploration. *Journal of Business Ethics,* 61, 79–99.

Ibarra, H. and Andrews, S. B. (1993) Power, social influence, and sense making: Effects of network centrality and proximity on employee perceptions. *Administrative Science Quarterly,* 38 (2), 277–303.

Jennings, P. and Zandbergen, P. (1995) Ecologically sustainable organizations: An institutional approach. *Academy of Management Review,* 20, 1015–1052.

Jones, T. M. and Wicks, A. C. (1999) Convergent stakeholder theory. *Academy of Management Review,* 24, 206–221.

Kanter, R. M. (1983) *The Change Masters.* New York: Simon and Schuster.

Kraut, R. E., Rice, R. E., Cool, C., and Fish, R. S. (1998) Varieties of social influence: The role of utility and norms in the success of a new communication medium. *Organization Science,* 9, 437–453.

Kuhn, T. (2008) A communicative theory of the firm: Developing an alternative perspective on intra-organizational power and stakeholder relationships. *Organization Studies,* 29, 1197–1224.

Kuhn, T. and Deetz, S. A. (2008) Critical theory and corporate social responsibility: Can/should we get beyond cynical reasoning? In A. Crane, A. McWilliams,

D. Matten, J. Moon, and D. Siegel (eds.), *The Oxford Handbook of Corporate Social Responsibility* (pp. 173–196). Oxford: Oxford University Press.

Leifer, R. and Delbecq, A. (1978) Organizational/environmental interchange: A model of boundary spanning activity. *The Academy of Management Review*, 3 (1), 40–50.

Leonard-Barton, D. and Kraus, W. A. (1985) Implementing new technology. *Harvard Business Review* (Nov–Dec), 102–110.

Lewis, L. K. (2007) An organizational stakeholder model of change implementation communication. *Communication Theory*, 17 (2), 176–204.

Lewis, L. K. and Seibold, D. R. (1998) Reconceptualizing organizational change implementation as a communication problem: A review of literature and research agenda. In M. E. Roloff (ed.), *Communication Yearbook 21* (pp. 93–151). Thousand Oaks, CA: Sage.

Lewis, L. K., Scott, C. R., and D'Urso, S. (unpublished) Development of collaborative communication: A case study of an interorganizational network.

Luscher, L. S. and Lewis, M. W. (2008) Organizational change and managerial sensemaking: Working through paradox. *Academy of Management Journal*, 51, 221–240.

McWilliams, A. and Siegel, D. (2001) Corporate social responsibility: A theory of the firm perspective. *Academy of Management Review*, 26 (1), 117–127.

Meyer, C. (2006) Destructive dynamics of middle management intervention in postmerger processes. *Journal of Applied Behavioral Science*, 42 (4), 397–419.

Miller, K. I. (1995) *Organizational Communication: Approaches and Processes*. Albany, NY: Wadsworth.

Miller, K. I. and Monge, P. R. (1985) Social information and employee anxiety about organizational change. *Human Communication Research*, 11, 365–386.

Mitchell, R., Agle, B., and Wood, D. (1997) Toward a theory of stakeholder identification and salience: Defining the principle of who and what really counts. *Academy of Management Review*, 22, 853–886.

Napier, N. K., Simmons, G., and Stratton, K. (1989) Communication during a merger: The experience of two banks. *Human Resource Planning*, 12 (2), 105–122.

Orlikowski, W. J. and Gash, D. C. (1994) Technological frames: Making sense of information technology in organizations. *ACM Trans. Inform. Syst.*, 12 (2), 174–196.

Pfarrer, M. D., Decelles, K. A., Smith, K. G., and Taylor, M. S. (2008) After the fall: reintegrating the corrupt organization. *Academy of Management Review*, 33 (3), 730–749.

Post, J. E., Preston, L. E., and Sachs, S. (2002) Managing the extended enterprise: The new stakeholder view. *California Management Review*, 45 (1), 6–28.

Rowley, T. J. (1997) Moving beyond dyadic ties: A network theory of stakeholder influences. *Academy of Management Review*, 22 (4), 887–910.

Rowley, T. J. and Moldoveaunu, M. (2003) When will stakeholder groups act? An interest- and identity-based model of stakeholder group mobilization. *Academy of Management Review*, 28 (2), 204–219.

Salancik, G. R. and Pfeffer, J. (1978) A social information processing approach to job attitudes and task design. *Administrative Science Quarterly*, 23, 224–256.

Scott, C. R. (1997) Identification with multiple targets in a geographically dispersed organization. *Management Communication Quarterly*, 10, 491–522.

Scott, C. R. (1999) The impact of physical and discursive anonymity on group members' multiple identifications during computer-supported decision making. *Western Journal of Communication*, 63, 456–487.

Scott, C. R., Lewis, L. K., and D'Urso, S. C. (2010) Getting on the "E" list: Email list use in a community of service provider organizations for people experiencing homelessness. In L. Shedletsky and J. E. Aitken (eds.), *Cases on Online Discussion and Interaction: Experiences and Outcomes* (pp. 334–350). Hershey, PA: IGI-Global.

Timmerman, C. E. (2002) The moderating effect of mindlessness/mindfulness upon media richness and social influence explanations of organizational media use. *Communication Monographs*, 69 (2), 111–131.

Weick, K. E. (1995) *Sensemaking in Organizations*. Thousand Oaks, CA: Sage.

Zagenczky, T. J., Gibney, R., Murrell, A. J., and Boxx, S. R. (2008) Friends don't make friends good citizens, but advisors do. *Group and Organization Management*, 33 (5), 760–780.

Zoller, H. M. and Fairhurst, G. T. (2007) Resistance leadership: The overlooked potential in critical organization and leadership studies. *Human Relations*, 60 (9), 1331–1360.

Zorn, T. E. (2002) The emotionality of information and communication technology implementation. *Journal of Communication Management*, 7 (2), 160–171.

Further Reading

Cheney, G. and Christensen, L. T. (2001) Identity at issue: Linkages between "internal" and "external" organizational communication. In F. M. Jablin and L. L. Putnam (eds.), *The New Handbook of Organizational Communication* (pp. 231–269). Thousand Oaks, CA: Sage.

Cheney, G. and Frenette, G. (1993) Persuasion and organization: Values, logics, and accounts in contemporary corporate public discourse. In C. Conrad (ed.), *The Ethical Nexus* (pp. 49–73). Norwood, NJ: Ablex.

De Bakker, F. G. A., Groenewegen, P., and den Hond, F. (2005) A bibliometric analysis of 30 years of research and theory on corporate social responsibility and corporate social performance. *Business and Society*, 44 (3), 283–317.

Dorewood, H. and Benschop, Y. (2003) HRM and organizational change: An emotional endeavor. *Journal of Organizational Change Management*, 16 (3), 272–287.

Garrety, K., Badham, R., Morrigan, V., Rifkin, W., and Zanko, M. (2003) The use of personality typing in organizational change: Discourse, emotions and the reflexive subject. *Human Relations*, 56 (2), 211–235.

Heath, R. L. (1994) *Management of Corporate Communication: From Interpersonal Contacts to External Affairs*. Hillsdale, NJ: Lawrence Erlbaum.

Kramer, M., Dougherty, D. S., and Pierce, T. A. (2004) Managing uncertainty during a corporate acquisition: A longitudinal study of communication during an airline acquisition. *Human Communication Research*, 30 (1), 71–101.

Lee, S. and Kim, B. (2009) Factors affecting the usage of intranet: A confirmatory study. *Computers in Human Behavior*, 24 (1), 191–201.

Levine, S. and White, P. E. (1961) Exchange as a conceptual framework for the study of interorganizational relationships. *Administrative Science Quarterly*, 22 (2), 235–247.

Lewis, L. K., Richardson, B. K., and Hamel, S. A. (2003) When the stakes are communicative: The lamb's and the lion's share during nonprofit planned change. *Human Communication Research*, 29 (3), 400–430.

Lines, R. (2007) Using power to install strategy: The relationships between expert power, position power, influence tactics, and implementation success. *Journal of Change Management*, 7 (2), 143–170.

Meyer, M. (2000) Innovation roles: From souls of fire to devil's advocates. *Journal of Business Communication*, 37 (4), 328–347.

Mumby, D. K. (1988) *Communication and Power in Organizations: Discourse, Ideology, and Domination*. Norwood, NJ: Ablex.

Noblet, A. J., McWilliams, H. H., and Rodwell, J. J. (2006) Abating the consequences of managerialism on the forgotten employee: The issues of support, control, coping, and pay. *International Journal of Public Administration*, 29, 911–930.

Putnam, L. L. (1989) Negotiation and organizing: Two levels within the Weickian model. *Communication Studies*, 40, 249–257.

Richardson, P. and Denton, D. K. (1996) Communicating change. *Human Resource Management*, 35 (2), 203–216.

Robinson, O. and Griffiths, A. (2005) Coping with the stress of transformational change in a government department. *Journal of Applied Behavioral Science*, 41 (2), 204–221.

Rogers, E. M. (1995) *Diffusion of Innovations*. New York: Free Press.

Scott, C. R. and Timmerman, C. E. (1999) Communication technology use and multiple workplace identifications among organizational teleworkers with varied degrees of virtuality. *IEEE Transactions of Professional Communication*, 42, 240–260.

Stevenson, W. B., Bartunek, J. M., and Borgatti, S. P. (2003) Front and backstage processes of an organizational restructuring effort. *Journal of Applied Behavioral Science*, 39 (3), 243–258.

Vaananen, A., Pahkin, K., Kalimo, R., and Buunk, B. P. (2004) Maintenance of subjective health during a merger: The role of experienced change and pre-merger social support at work in white- and blue-collar workers. *Social Science and Medicine*, 58, 1903–1951.

Yuan, Y., Fulk, J., Shumate, M., Monge, P. R., Bryant, J. A., and Matasanis, M. (2005) Individual participation in organizational information commons: The impact of team level social influence and technology-specific competence. *Human Communication Research*, 31 (2), 212–240.

4

Outcomes of Change Processes

There are only two tragedies in life: one is not getting what one wants, and the other is getting it

Oscar Wilde

Success is getting what you want; happiness is wanting what you get

Ingrid Bergman

We live immersed in narrative, recounting and reassessing the meaning of our past actions, anticipating the outcome of our future projects, situating ourselves at the intersection of several stories not yet completed

Peter Brooks

Organizational scholars have been trying to describe the outcomes of innovation and change processes for a very long time. Before we take

Organizational Change: Creating Change Through Strategic Communication,
First Edition. Laurie K. Lewis.
© 2011 Laurie K. Lewis. Published 2011 by Blackwell Publishing Ltd.

up discussion of how outcomes of change are assessed, let us first turn to the more general topic of how one makes assessments of organizational outcomes in general. Certainly it is important to attend to the goals and purpose of any organizational strategy in terms of what has been accomplished, what has not, and what is left to do. Further, assessment of the degree and quality of accomplishments as well as necessary and useful adjustments to goals as the initiative unfolds are important.

Goals are important for a few reasons. First, it is critical for communicators who propose and promote a change to make a case for it (we return to this issue in Chapter 7). Those whose cooperation in change is necessary must come to believe that its purpose makes sense. To gain cooperation, the change should be viewed as necessary (or at least advantageous) and appropriate to the purpose it is being put. One of the major pitfalls of change is the inability of leaders to "sell" a vision for the change to those who are responsible for pulling it off operationally. Since change always involves effort, that effort usually needs justification. For some audiences, minimal justification may be necessary; for other audiences or circumstances, this is a major undertaking. That is especially true when there is a good deal of pain involved in the change (e.g., lay-offs, ending something of long-held value). If implementers are not able to articulate goals for a change and provide a sense of purpose that other stakeholders can buy into, they are already starting on a path that is likely to run into resistance – and probably for good reason.

A second reason why goals are so important during change is that they provide an organization, and its stakeholders, with a metric for assessing distance traveled and direction of movement. Although goals can shift and be remade, they still provide us with markers as to where we started and where we were, at least at one time, headed. Like trail markers made by hikers in the woods, they provide data points marking a path. That direction might be altered, but the hikers are better off when they know where they've been and the trajectory they have been on. If nothing else, this prevents hikers, and organizations, from mistakenly traveling in circles.

A third reason why goals are important in organizations is that they provide a sense of legitimacy in portraying the organization as rational. Decision-making is supposed to be rational, based on an aim or direction; on information analysis; and on logical reasoning. External and internal stakeholders will often judge the soundness of an organization's decision-making in part upon its ability to chart a path targeting a pre-specified goal. Organizations that are unable or unwilling to specify such end points are likely to be considered as illegitimate, irrational, or even criminal /unethical. Externally powerful stakeholders such as boards of directors, contractual partners, investors, governmental oversight agencies, and the like often demand that organizations offer some sense of goals and purpose in order to achieve legal, financial, and institutional legitimacy. So, there are good reasons for organizations to create goals and to assess them. Although that may seem a rather easy and straightforward task, in fact it is quite complex.

Organizational research that attempts to assess outcomes of organizing processes will often measure **effectiveness** – the accomplishment of desired results – or **efficiency** – accomplishment of effectiveness with the fewest possible expended resources. For either type of outcome, there are numerous potential problems in pinning down useful assessments. I will highlight here five common problems with assessing organizational outcomes: knowing when to assess; from whose perspective to make assessments; how to assess some types of outcomes; correctly attributing causes and effects; and potential costs associated with doing genuine assessment.

Problems in Assessing Organizational Outcomes

Let us start with a simple question about assessment of outcomes of any organizational endeavor: When should assessment of outcomes take place? A concrete example in a more familiar context might aid this discussion. I live in New Jersey and it does snow here. Once in a while we get one of those snows that comes down all day. You wake up and find an inch or two on the ground. Then, you need to decide whether to shovel the driveway or wait and let a few more inches fall before you start shoveling. The longer you wait, the bigger the job, but the chances improve that you'll have to shovel fewer times. If you shovel at two in the afternoon and the snow stops, you have really good results – cleared driveway! If you wait another two hours and another two inches have fallen, your earlier results are completely erased and now you must reshovel. Of course, if you wait until six inches have fallen and some freezing rain falls on top of that, you may find you cannot shovel the snow at all – bad results. So, the question is at what point during the day do you assess your outcomes? If you assess your outcomes at 2:05 pm, you'd be very pleased. Later that afternoon, you might be very displeased, and even later that night after an inch of freezing rain, you may not only judge your shoveling a failure, but your future prospects may look dim as well!

One lesson from the snow-shoveling example is that timing of assessment of any outcome can play a major role in how we judge what we have accomplished. This is as true of organizational dynamics as it is of snow removal. Many of the examples and cases discussed in this book thus far provide further evidence of the principle that achieved results change over time. The Spellings Commission would likely have judged the impact of its Report as failure at the outset since the immediate negative reaction of so many stakeholders was so strong. However, over the months that stakeholders discussed, debated, and reconsidered actions relative to the Report, results became more favorable. The higher education community began to work towards accomplishing some of the goals highlighted by the Report. The Commission started to see fruits of its labor.

Not only is it hard to know when to assess outcomes, it is hard to know from what perspective to assess outcomes. To return to our snow example, my kids assess outcomes of snow in terms of (a) whether enough falls to get school canceled (good result) and (b) whether enough snow falls to afford good sledding (also a good result). My husband and I are more concerned with how fast we can have our driveway cleared and how many times we have to shovel. The local snow removal service likely judges outcomes in terms of how much revenue the snowfall produces. From their perspective, a few moderate days of snowfall is superior to one day accumulating to the same number of inches. If they can charge for two visits to clear driveways, they are better off and can probably do their job more efficiently on each day, so they don't have to pay workers for overtime.

In the case of organizational operations, many different stakeholder perspectives may be relevant and those different stakeholders may use very different metrics to assess organizations. As we discussed in Chapter 3, stakeholders not only identify with different roles and groups, they also occupy very different positions with regard to different organizational products and by-products. This can make stakeholders' assessments quite complex. If we consider the example of the Spellings Commission, we can predict that university and college faculty, higher education business officers, journalists, state governments, parents of college-age children, communities that support state-funded universities, employers of college graduates, and many other stakeholders will demand different things from higher education and thus view the outcomes in very different ways. As Pfarrer, Decelles, Smith, and Taylor (2008) argue, "an organization may be able to satisfy the demands of certain stakeholder groups only at the expense of others" (p. 732).

Further, as we discussed in the last chapter, even individual stakeholders might have more than one perspective on a specific organizational outcome. As a university professor, I may view some of the Spellings Commission recommendations as potentially insulting towards higher education. I might perceive a threat of a federalization that might restrict academic freedoms in higher educational institutions. However, as a parent of children who will be applying to universities one day, I may have a very different read on some of the recommendations of the Commission, and may see some merit in the indictments of higher education and the urgent need for reform. I might even recognize that higher education is not making enough progress on some of these issues. How I assess the attempts of higher education to address concerns raised in the Commission's Report will vary depending on what "hat" I have on.

One way for organizations to resolve the problem of multiple stakeholder perspectives in assessing organizational outcomes is to adopt a purely managerial viewpoint. In doing so, management and/or shareholder perspectives become paramount. In for-profit organizations a bottom-line consideration may become most important. For nonprofit organizations, the accomplishment of a central mission may be highlighted. For government agencies, accomplishing politically expedient goals that ensure the re-election of officials may be most sought. For any organization, survival can be an ultimate measure of success or outcome. However, due to **equifinality** – the principle that there are multiple paths to the same end – that can be a very ambiguous standard to use in assessment. Many different paths could permit an organization to survive. Some may be "better" paths by some other standard (e.g., the most ethical path to survival; the path that preserves the most stakeholders' demands; the path that highlights only shareholders' preferences) but all share the ultimate standard of survival. For example, in the current budgetary crisis many state governments and corporations are considering furloughs of employees. Under such plans, employees would take an unpaid day or two per month off work. The savings will enable organizations to save enough money that they need not lay off workers. Both layoffs and furloughs (two different paths to savings) can facilitate survival of the organizations, but have very different implications. Of course, critics of furloughs see other alternatives to budgetary savings – yet another stakeholder perspective implying other paths to survival.

A third problem in measuring organization outcomes concerns the difficulty in measuring some outcomes. Organizations are interested in many levels and types of outcomes. Some important activities of organizations concern things that are very hard to measure, such as how the public perceives the brand of the organization; whether employees/members have internalized important values of the organization; the degree to which an organizational philosophy is being lived out in practice; how customers and clients are benefited by an organization's operations. Although probably all organizations have some goals that are difficult to measure directly, nonprofit organizations often grapple with this problem (DiMaggio, 1988; Kanter and Summers, 1987). For many nonprofit organizations, bottom-line or easily quantifiable metrics often do not capture highly lofty missions. The mission of the Girl Scouts of America is a good example: "Girl Scouting builds girls of courage, confidence, and character, who make the world a better place." The Girl Scout organization has several more specific goals: discovering fun, friendship, and power of girls together; developing girls' full individual potential; relating to others with increasing understanding, skill, and respect; developing values to guide their actions and provide the foundation for sound decision-making; and contributing to the improvement of society. These are not easily measured, to say the least.

Our Homeless Net case provides another example of intractable mission (see Case Box 4.1). The homeless service providers have a shared mission to end homelessness. That is, that everyone in the United States will have an adequate, safe, affordable home. Although that may sound like a simple mission, the debate comes more in the manner in which the service providers operate. Some providers focus on what they do well and what they are rewarded for doing by funders – providing basic needs to persons who are homeless. Others argue that the focus ought to be eliminating the needs of these persons by resolving core causes of homelessness: lack of affordable housing; lack of medical care; and lack of a living wage. Similar debates are raised for other problematic situations. Should one put all donated monies towards finding a cure for cancer, or should a portion of money go to the care of those suffering from cancer? These issues are challenging not only in the sense that assessing such a large complex mission is difficult but also in the sense that not all stakeholders may agree what priorities ought to prevail along the path to the larger goal. Large complex missions often need to be addressed in small steps and small bites.

In order to encourage supporters of their organizations, nonprofits must demonstrate that they are able to accomplish their stated

Case Box 4.1: Homeless Net Struggles to Assess a Large Mission

Most homeless service providers actually make it easier to remain homeless. That is, they provide showers, food, temporary shelter against weather or criminal victimization, etc. and therefore do not work directly to end homelessness.

It is a complex problem to decide the amount of resources to devote to aiding people who are currently homeless and the amount that should be devoted to core causes of homelessness, namely (1) lack of available affordable housing for those who lose homes due to illness, death of provider, divorce, violence, discharge from military or prison; (2) lack of affordable health and mental health care; and (3) guarantee of a living wage that will let any full-time employee afford housing in the city or town in which they reside.

The leader of a nonprofit organization focused on the prevention of homelessness put it this way when asked why some service providers did not focus much on prevention. "We just find that the rest of the community does not participate around that [prevention]. We are not sure, we think that it could be linked to the fact that they are concerned about the way any possible attention might be drawn to them, that someone could perceive as negative. So they tend to only do things that they perceive the government to be pleased by them doing. ... We find that putting oneself in the position of taking money either from the local government or the federal government tends to stymie communication, and participation in what it really takes to end homelessness, and therefore you have a situation that tends to sustain it."

It is relatively easy for the providers in Homeless Net to demonstrate activity and levels of need (numbers of clients served, numbers of homeless persons of different categories, underserved homeless persons) but it is very difficult to determine progress on the ultimate goal to end homelessness. It is also hard for service providers to take the risk of focusing *only* on the ultimate goal as opposed to the side-goals that are necessitated by the condition of not achieving the main goal.

Source: Data segment related to CTOSH project.

goals. With missions that are very difficult to measure, this has become a major challenge for organizations (Ospina, Diaz, and O'Sullivan, 2002). Sawhill and Williamson (2001) use the example of a nature conservancy's struggle to develop metrics to assess its goal achievement. Although the conservancy had a clear philosophical mission "to preserve the diversity of plants and animals around the world by protecting habitats" they used very quantifiable measures to assess outcomes that didn't really get at the core mission. They measured the numbers of dollars collected towards their cause and the numbers of acres it owned. Doubtlessly these metrics had some appeal to specific stakeholders. However, they also did not really capture the mission of the organization. "The conservancy's goal, after all, isn't to buy land or raise money, it is to preserve the diversity of life on earth" (Sawhill and Williamson, 2001, p. 101). Since the extinction of species continued to spiral higher and higher every year since the organization's founding, from that perspective the organization was a failure. The Homeless Net organizations could come to a similar conclusion in that nationwide homelessness continues to increase despite their efforts. Overall, homeless service providers are losing the battle to prevent homelessness and can much more readily document "success" in terms of numbers of clients served. Ironically, that is not their true goal. In fact, the lower the need for their services, the closer they are to achieving their real stated goal!

Another potential problem in assessing organizational outcomes concerns errors in attributing causes and effects. An **attribution error** occurs when an observer attributes the cause of an observation incorrectly. When I hear a loud crash downstairs and assume that my children have broken something only to discover later that it is one of my cats that have caused the noise, I have made an attribution error. Cause and effect attributions are made all the time in organizations. Decision-makers who are striving to improve service, increase employee or customer loyalty, speed up production processes, decrease defects, perform what amount to experiments in cause and effect relationships. Managers will introduce an intervention of some sort, observe whether outcomes improve by some standard, and then draw conclusions about whether what they did "worked" or not. Although we all perform these sorts of experiments in our lives in many contexts all the time, they are fundamentally flawed as true experiments because they are not controlled. A true experiment where we can really assess cause and effect relationships requires important procedures such as random assignment to condition; controlled conditions (so nothing else varies except for the one thing we are studying); and strict objective measures over time. Usually, in the natural "experiments" that organizations conduct daily to figure out what is working and what is not, these conditions are not met and thus it is far easier to make errors in attributing cause and effect relationships.

For example, if an organization's production line introduces a new method of assembling part of the product at a particular workstation, the manager would likely want to know if the new method was (a) effective and (b) better than the previous method. The manager would have to first define "effective" and "better" and would likely already have a standard metrics to measure that, such as speed of production, number of quality defects, and/or number of times the line had to be stopped for adjustments to be made. The manager would have to assess the relative costs of this new method (e.g., if it involved more employees at that station, costs would be higher) and thus, what level of improvement would justify the additional costs. Once you have a target and metrics the experiment would commence. At some appointed time (and as noted earlier in this chapter, that can sometimes be hard to determine), a metric would be assessed. If the metric showed improvement over previous measures of the metric, the manager might conclude that the new method was indeed better. If the metric was equal to or less than previous measures, then the manager might conclude that the new method (a) was flawed, (b) was not worth additional cost, or (c) needs more time to show evidence of success. However, what if the week that the manager conducted her experiment her best three workers were all out with the flu? Or, what if the new method appeared to raise the production quality and speed on this line, but production and speed went up on all lines in that week? The manager would have a hard time discerning whether the rise in production on the experimental line was due to the new method or just a fluke of productivity in the whole plant that week.

Now, this line manager might eventually be able to gather enough data to eliminate other possible explanations of the new production method's success or failure; but things can get much more complicated in the larger contexts of organizations. It can be much more difficult to sort out cause and effect in cases where organizations are trying to influence the image of their brand; increase knowledge that potential customers have of their products; increase sales with a particular marketing campaign, or other large outcomes of organizational practice that are nearly impossible to study in a controlled way. Many factors could account for the effects of brand name awareness, product awareness, and sales. Whether one specific action taken by an organization is responsible for these outcomes, or some portion of them, can be very difficult to determine.

A final problem in assessing organizational outcomes concerns the costs of documenting failures and the perceived need to make accurate measurements. Given the political context of organizations that we discussed in Chapter 1, it may be that at times organizational leaders do not truly wish to accurately assess organizational outcomes. Often data, even assessment data, can serve symbolic functions in an organization. As Feldman and March (1981) argue, the mere fact that data is present during decision-making can provide legitimacy to the outcome. Data and information can often be used as a symbol of due diligence. This can be true even when the data does not properly support the decisions that are made. So, for example if the plant manager has a vested interest in the new line methodology in the earlier example, and has essentially already committed herself to the promotion of the new methodology across the organization, the data collected about its relative benefits over other methods may be moot. The collection of data may be for symbolic reasons only – to be able to claim that she "studied" the new method. In this case, assessment of outcomes of this new production method is made politically not in terms of objective metrics.

In some cases, documenting complete success might imply the end of the organization. Think of organizations whose mission is to eradicate disease. If that eradication is achieved, the purpose of the organization is fulfilled – complete success equals organizational death! The March of Dimes (see Highlight Box 4.1) actually faced such a crisis when Jonas Salk found the vaccine for polio. Following that discovery, the March of Dimes changed its focus to the prevention of birth defects since its primary mission had been accomplished and, ironically, they had a very difficult time finding financial support. It was only through quick adaptation that they were able to avoid financial crisis. Documenting success in this case was not beneficial.

In sum, assessment of organizational outcomes can be challenging. Assessments can be problematic in terms of when appropriate questions of results can be answered; inclusion of multiple perspectives in assessments; difficulty in measuring some outcomes; difficulty in determining cause and effect; and the political aspects of assessment of outcomes. We turn next to how change outcomes have been assessed by scholars and practitioners.

Highlight Box 4.1: March of Dimes Succeeds to the Brink of Organizational Death

The March of Dimes campaign to fight polio had been a remarkable victory. The organization had worked on all fronts, responding to the emergency of local outbreaks, funding and arranging long-term care for victims, mobilizing awareness, and paying for the research that led to the vaccine.

After 1955, the impetus that had led people to give money to the foundation ebbed away, and the March of Dimes was in something of a quandary. It still had debts owing to its massive spending on the vaccine, but people were not willing to be stopped in the middle of a movie for a disease that could now be easily prevented.

In 1958, the organization came up with a new mission. Its work on polio mostly behind it, the March of Dimes turned to another burning issue of infant health: birth defects. At the time, the term birth defects was not in use. Parents of a baby born with a debilitating condition were often not given any explanation for what affected their child. The numbers or percentages of babies born with these conditions were not known, and the diseases that affected children at birth were mostly mysteries.

The March of Dimes put its volunteer and fundraising organization to work in this new area. The foundation brought together scientists from diverse specialties to work together on birth defects, and as with polio, the March of Dimes had quick and concrete results. In 1961, research funded by the March of Dimes led to the development of the PKU test, which can identify and prevent some forms of mental retardation. In 1968, the organization funded the first successful bone marrow transplant used to correct a birth defect.

But birth defects had many causes, so this issue was not as focused as the fight against polio had been. Eventually, medical researchers identified approximately 3,000 distinct disorders causing birth defects. Some of these were genetic diseases, some were disorders caused by conditions *in utero*, and others were caused by problems with the birth itself, such as premature term. The March of Dimes continued to use many of the techniques it had deployed during its polio campaign to raise funds to combat birth defects.

Source: Adapted from http://www.answers.com/topic/march-of-dimes.

Assessing Change Outcomes

As discussed in Chapter 3, we can think of outcomes of change implementation in terms of the observable system – that we can notice through participation and observation – and results – that can be assessed in terms of what is achieved plus other consequences that arise. As noted in Chapter 1, Rogers (1983) proposed the concept of "routinization" – when the innovation/change has become incorporated into the regular activities of an organization and is no longer considered a separate new idea – as a descriptor for the "observable system." Others have used terms like "refreezing" (Lewin, 1951) and "institutionalization" (Goodman, Bazerman, and Conlon, 1980) to refer to the point where the change outcome is known and the process of change is complete.

Other scholarship has focused more on descriptors for the nature of outcomes of change. Scholarship as early as the 1970s acknowledged that implementation outcomes should not be assessed merely in binary terms (e.g., adopted/not adopted) as in diffusion research, but described in terms of some degree of use or partial adoption measure (Calsyn, Tornatzky, and Dittmar, 1977; Hall and Loucks, 1977). Also, terms like "reinvention" (Rice and Rogers, 1980; Rogers, 1988), "adaptation" (Leonard-Barton, 1988; Glaser and Backer, 1977), and "modification" (Lewis and Seibold, 1993) have been used to describe how the original idea of a change sometimes morphs during implementation. For some scholars this is viewed as a very positive outcome because it demonstrates that users alter the change to fit their own needs and goals. In earlier work with my colleague David Seibold, we introduced the terms of "fidelity" and "uniformity" to describe different dimensions of change outcomes. **Fidelity** describes the degree of departure from the intended design of the change. **Uniformity** describes the range of use of the change across adopting unit(s) or stakeholder groups. These two dimensions can be combined to describe how a change is "modified" in use in an organization. They can also be used to describe how and to what degree implementers intend for users to adapt change programs in use.

Implementation efforts that aim to produce a high degree of fidelity (match to a specific vision for use/participation) and a high degree of uniformity (all stakeholders using or participating in similar ways) suggest an implementation that is focused on producing a single model and enforcing or cajoling that specific model to be followed by all participants. The implementation of a sexual harassment policy might be a good example of this sort of effort. The desired observable system outcome is that everyone follows the same rules and guidelines for creating an environment that is non-discriminatory; non-threatening; and void of sexually charged language, displays or other inappropriate behaviors. It would not be a desirable outcome to have much, if any, variation in how stakeholders or various stakeholder groups applied such a new policy.

However, implementation of new software for data management might be a very different case. In such an effort, the implementers may encourage experimentation and different possible applications of the software across stakeholders. Perhaps accounting would use the data management system for keeping track of payments; the human resource department may use it to track applications; and the production unit would use it in some aspect of product quality control. In such a case, neither fidelity nor uniformity may be important in order to consider the implementation successful. Simple experimentation by different departments may be the only goal.

We can also consider cases where high fidelity and low uniformity could be important as well as where low fidelity with high uniformity would be useful. The case of high fidelity and low uniformity may occur where there is a specific vision by decision-makers and implementers for each different stakeholder group/unit for use or participation in the change. So, although differences across stakeholders are tolerated (in fact, desired), those differences are prescribed by the implementers in advance and not left to experimentation. The low fidelity and high uniformity situation might involve a context in which the organization has many possibilities for making use of a new innovation but needs to ensure that all stakeholders are ultimately participating in similar ways. This might involve a round of discussion and brainstorming in ways that the organization might make use of a new strategy, resource, or tool. Then, once the best use has been decided, it is implemented with the goal of uniform use/participation across all stakeholders. A new payroll system for keeping track of employee hours would be an example of this. There might be many ways to report work hours and keep track of vacation and sick leave; but it might be important that all units in an organization do it the same way so as not to create chaos in the payroll department. There could be some joint discussion about different alternatives (high fidelity to some designer's plan need not be mandated), but ultimately, everyone would need to do it the same way (high uniformity).

The fidelity and uniformity concepts provide us with language to describe both the intentions of implementers (e.g., how much fidelity and uniformity is desired at the outset) and the ways in which the observable system exists at any point after introduction of change. While I was still in graduate school I was part of a team that studied a large food manufacturing plant in the midwestern United States. "Kelco" (Lewis and Seibold, 1993) introduced a line technician program that involved new roles for a set of employees. Those who were placed in the line tech role had to learn either new technical or administrative skills since they had been recruited from either purely mechanic or production jobs. When our evaluation team came on the scene, we observed much variation in how the role of line technician was operating across shifts and across the plant. There had been an unclear definition of the role of line technician coupled with some poor support in training line technicians in new skills. This left the new line techs to invent their own roles based on their best guess as to what they should be doing or what they wanted to have as their own role.

Some line techs, who formerly had been production workers, focused their efforts on the administrative portion of the job and ignored the mechanical repair aspects of the job. Others, who formerly had been mechanics, focused efforts on the repair work and ignored many of the administrative parts of the job. As one interviewee put it, "they went with their strengths" – focusing efforts on those portions of the new job at which they already had competence. The result of these attempts to self-socialize into the new role was extreme low fidelity and low uniformity in the practice of the line technician program at Kelco. Because the implementers' intentions were to have high fidelity and high uniformity, this was a very undesired outcome for the organization.

An important note about goals needs to be considered here. Goals in organizations seem like very rational and fixed constructions that (a) are known at the outset of change, (b) are stable across the change process, and (c) can be assessed at any given point. After all that is the very definition of a goal – a guidepost by which we measure performance over time. However, it is likely that organizational goals are much more fluid than this rational depiction. First, goals are likely to be held differently by different stakeholders because they hold different stakes. Further, some goals may be hidden at times. Goals shift over time and through the process of enactment we discussed in Chapter 1. Individuals and collectives are able to rewrite history and convince themselves that the *real* goals (the ones now held) were present even at the start. Think of the classic example of the New Year's Resolution that many of us make each year. Or the goals we make about our grade performance that we make at the start of a term. We start out saying "I'll lose x amount of weight," "I'll get all As." But as the difficulty in reaching those goals (often ones we've set repeatedly) and various unpredicted barriers get in our way, we revise our goals ("I really meant to lose y amount of weight," or "stay on a healthy diet regardless of the weight I lose," or "I'm actually happy to get at least a B average this term"). We can sometimes convince ourselves, as well as others, that the previous goals never existed and measure performance against the revised goal.

In organizations it is perhaps even easier to experience shifting goals over time due to the complex nature of setting goals, assessing them, and reporting on them to stakeholders. How we frame a goal in terms of language like "improvement," "effectiveness," "more," "less," and "successful" to name only a few can become contested in organizations. It is a bad habit and perhaps a defensive strategy for organizations to be fairly poor at nailing down measurable goals and holding themselves publicly accountable for specific measurable results.

In my 2007 model (see Figure 3.1) I introduced a third way to describe the observable system – authenticity. **Authenticity** concerns the sincerity of stakeholders' compliance with implementers' expectations for their behavior. Inauthenticity arises when stakeholders suppress genuine emotions and "fake" their approval, liking, and/or enthusiasm for a change. Implementers may observe a desired level of uniformity and fidelity in stakeholder participation in change, but still not readily detect inauthenticity in stakeholders' responses. In cases where implementation involves mandated participation, where input by stakeholders is neither invited nor tolerated, some stakeholders' compliance may involve faking enthusiasm, support, and/or approval.

As already discussed, change often invokes the politics of organizational contexts, where display of genuine feelings and assessments of change may be risky. Feelings of disappointment, fear, frustration, anxiety, and even rage among stakeholders may need to be suppressed to avoid incurring some political cost. Such suppression can lead to increases in stress (Grandey, 2003), burnout (Schmisseur, unpublished; Tracy, 2000), emotional exhaustion (Schmisseur, 2005), and depressed mood (Erickson and Wharton, 1997) for individual stakeholders.

Also, the consequences of inauthenticity may be high for organizations and implementation efforts. The indirect costs of this outcome may include "**change burnout**" (exhaustion of an individual's capacity or willingness to continue to participate in change programs: Lewis, 2006); lack of vigilance in reporting and working to resolve problems in change implementation; and unit and organizational turnover. Harris and Ogbonna (2002) provide a good example of ritualistic cooperation (a form of inauthenticity) with a culture change in a UK hotel chain. The managers instilled an annual review of goals and progress as part of an effort to shift the culture. The front-line interpretation of this practice illustrates inauthenticity and the undesirable organizational outcomes of this review:

> Every three months or so we get a pack – yeah. Yeah – "this is how we're suppose to act this month." Yeah, yeah – this is now your philosophy for life! Oh, when we say "for life" we actually mean until we change our minds next year! It's like a ceremonial event – we troop into the room, get lectured on what the company wants and troop back out again. It's just one of those things we do. After a few years you don't even question it anymore! (p. 38)

Clearly, these front-line workers were not internalizing the cultural shift that implementers desired. They approached the goal setting meeting as a mere symbolic event that was to be endured but not truly embraced as an important activity. In another example, the same authors describe how organizational members fake their transformation of attitudes and values in pure performance for their supervisors:

> Oh God! We've got rules for everything – how to greet, how to act, how to smile, when to smile, what to say – it's all bollocks! I mean you just do what you want but obey the rules when the boss has got his beady little eye on you! (p. 44)

These examples illustrate how inauthenticity can potentially harm the organization's efforts at accomplishing results. If the outcomes achieved are merely "for show" and not true change, the likelihood of achieving the desired results that are expected to arise from the change effort is low. Further, as you can hear in the comments of these front-line workers, cynicism, annoyance, and misrepresentation become commonplace.

Scholars have examined individual stakeholder outcomes related to change in terms of attitudes like "willingness" (Miller, Johnson, and Grau, 1994) and "liking of change" (Lewis and Seibold, 1996), and individuals' abilities to cope and their general well-being (Rafferty and Griffin, 2006; Noblet, McWilliams, and Rodwell, 2006; Robinson and Griffiths, 2005). This approach has generally focused on the degree to which stakeholders' (generally employees) reactions to change become precursors to managerial goals being met or to resistance. Examination of outcomes related to stakeholders' alteration of roles, status, skills, job security, hours worked, internalization of the change philosophy, etc. are far more rare in the literature. Further, it is extremely rare in the literature to see examination of outcomes for stakeholders other than employees.

Assessing Results of Change

In the 2007 model I discussed the idea of "results" as a separable concept from observable system outcomes. *Results* concern not just what the change program looks like in practice but whether it accomplishes implementers' preconceived goals. Results also concern the material conditions created by the change as well as unintended consequences.

In terms of goals, research on change outcomes tends to use concepts of "success" and "failure." As we observed earlier in this chapter, those are highly debatable terms depending on how, when, and by whose standard outcomes are assessed. Results are similarly subject to these effects. On an organizational level it is not only a problem that assessment of results is difficult to do, it is also something that may not be done often. Doyle, Claydon, and Buchanan's (2000) survey of a group of UK managers suggests that systematic, formal evaluation of change outcomes is rare. In fact, in their study 67% agreed that the "change process cannot be evaluated effectively because there are too many overlapping initiatives running at one time" –an indicator of the problem noted earlier in making accurate attributions of cause and effect relationships. Additionally, this study found that the learning process as a result of organizational development activity was neither systematic nor effective. Fifty-four percent of respondents agreed "we don't have the luxury of time to pause and reflect on what we've done in change" and 53% agreed "we tend to repeat mistakes in implementing change because there was no time to learn from what happened in the past" (p. S64). I found a similar result in a study (Lewis, 1999), with an international sample of implementers, in that very few respondents reported use of formal evaluation as a means to assess change programs.

For the most part, researchers have asked organizational leaders, implementers, and decision-makers to assess results of change initiatives. When other stakeholders are asked for an evaluation of success, it is usually in terms of the organization's original goals. Very little exploration of individuals' goals or perspectives of results has been done in change scholarship. Further, little is done to effectively measure whether "original goals" are widely shared, understood, and recalled.

One excellent place to begin examining the results that change has for different stakeholders would be to focus on the **material conditions** that are produced or altered through organizational change. Material conditions would focus on things like employee pay and benefits; community members' experienced levels of noise and air pollution; speed or efficiency of service to an organization's clients, etc. These sorts of results change the day-to-day reality for stakeholders. They are very separable issues from organizational results that usually have to do with the survival, economic well-being, or competitive advantage and the like.

Unintended consequences are yet another way to describe results for both organizations and for individual stakeholders. Harris and Ogbonna (2002) define this concept as "used to imply unforeseen or unpredicted results to an action (often negative in nature)" (p. 34). Jian (2007) defines this as "consequences that would not have taken place if a social actor had acted differently but that are not what the actor had intended to happen" (p. 6). Examples of unintended consequences include negative results for employees such as lowered job or organizational satisfaction; lowered trust in the organization; organizational turnover; and stress.

Some researchers have studied cynicism as an unintended consequence of organizational change. Reichers, Wanous, and Austin (1997) suggest that failed change programs and inadequate sharing of information about intended change can lead to cynicism which in turn can lead to lowered commitment, satisfaction, and motivation. Further, Doyle *et al.* (2000) found that "constant change ... seems to have fostered self-interest, fatigue, burnout and cynicism, to have damaged relationships and to have reduced organizational commitment and loyalty" (p. S65).

Our case study of Ingredients Inc. (see Case Box 4.2) provides an excellent example of how change burnout can be problematic. As we learned in Chapter 1, Ingredients Inc. experienced at least 9 large to moderate changes over a 12-month period. The employees were reeling from a series of new announcements of, in some cases, unexpected changes. There were many different messages received about how extensive changes would be. Laster (2008) found in this case that employees who had more foreknowledge of changes to come fared better. In another study of multiple change by Grunberg and colleagues (2008), multiple changes created anxiety and uncertainty and produced deterioration in many attitudes of employees concerning their work and the organization. However, these authors did find that most employees rebounded in attitudes over time.

Case Box 4.2: Ingredients Inc. – Foreknowledge and Change Burnout

Amy, an employee of Ingredients Inc., said of the ongoing change, "I think that whoever planned a merger, an acquisition, a relocation, and in my group, a reorganization of personnel ... whoever planned to do all that within a four-month period must have been smoking something."

Employees recalled the communication about the changes differently. Some reported more forewarning about the complexity and number of changes to come, while others reported that they were only told about one change (the merger). The result was that different sets of employees experienced the ongoing change in different degrees of expectation.

Laster found that the more employees perceived that the change messages forewarned of numerous changes to come, the more likely they were to be satisfied with the changes, be able to cope with them, and trust the implementers. It appears that even though cynicism and burnout are real potential problems during periods of frequent change, communication can mitigate these negative outcomes.

Source: Adapted from Laster (2008).

Jian's study (2007) of a financial company in the midwestern United States reveals several examples of unintended consequences, including the loss of trust between employees and senior management. Jian describes how rumors became a sore rub for senior management:

> the senior management accused employees of rumor mongering and undermining the change. ... The CEO commented in a management meeting, "There are a whole bunch of people that don't get it yet ... There are kind of, two different categories of people that don't get it. There are those that truly don't understand ... And there are those who don't want to understand ... (p. 23)

Unintended consequences can be understood from the perspective of managers' intentions or the intentions of other actors and stakeholders involved in a change effort. A union strike that results in the unintended shut down of a plant would count here just as much as the stress caused by managers' decisions to increase production requirements. The more stakeholders acting in a situation, the more likely unintended consequences are to occur.

Causes for Implementation Failures and Successes

Change scholars have investigated many reasons for the failure or success of change programs in organizations. In a survey of consultants, researchers, and managers, Covin and Kilmann (1990) found that eight themes emerged as having the most impact on results (see Table 4.1 for summary of their study and also of themes in studies by Ellis, 1992; Fairhurst, Green, and Courtright, 1995; Miller *et al.*, 1994; and Bikson and Gutek, 1994). They include issues related to managers' behaviors and communication; general communication; participation practices; vision; and expectations. Other research has called attention to these and other themes such as willingness or readiness for change; impacts of uncertainty and stress caused by change; and politics. Less attention has been paid to factors that tend to encourage success aside from a good deal of research on effects of involvement and participation. What does exist about achievement of successful results has been dominated by a focus on a few specific types of change. In our review of literature (Lewis and Seibold, 1998) David Seibold and I found that of the 18 works examining practice advice for success in change, 11 addressed the implementation of new technologies and 7 addressed manufacturing technologies. It will be hard to determine general theories of success and failure of change until more studies are conducted using broader samples.

In a study (Lewis, 2000) with an international sample of 76 implementers in for-profit, nonprofit, and governmental sectors implementing a broad sample of different types of changes (e.g., management programs, reorganization, technologies, customer programs, merger, quality programs, recruitment programs, and reward programs), I found that implementers tended to identify potential problems that might cause failure in terms of fear or anxiety of staff; negative attitudes; politics; limited resources; and lack of enthusiastic support. Problems that implementers identified as having the largest impact on perceived success of change programs were those concerning the functioning of the implementation team and overall cooperation of stakeholders. However, they also considered these kinds of problems to be least anticipated and the least encountered.

Table 4.1 Factors predicting failure and success of change programs

Factors Predicting Failure	Factors Predicting Success
Top Managers	Presence of Change Champion
Forcing change	
Behaving inconsistently	*Top Managers*
Having unrealistic expectations	Demonstrated support for change
Lack of enthusiastic support	
	Willingness and Readiness for Change
Responsibilities	High value congruence
Misplaced or unclear	
Lack of Openness to Change	*Good Communication*
Fear or anxiety about change	Establishing a clear vision/purpose
	Establishing legitimacy of program
High Unresolved Uncertainty and Stress	Use of widespread participation
About job security, pay, rewards, job	Active solicitation of input
evaluation, personal competency, social	Active dissemination of information
and work-related priorities	
	Effectiveness of Implementation Team
Lack of Good Communication	Availability of resources
Poor communication	
Purpose/vision of program unclear	
Lack of Meaningful Participation	
Threats to Power	
Political tactics	
Organizational Structure /Resources	
Role conflict and role ambiguity	
Status differences	
Reward structures	
Limited resources	
Resistance Encountered	
Active discouragement of change	
Nonuse of change	
Ignorance of change	
Social influence against change	
Negative attitudes about change	

A large body of work on important contingencies that impact failure or success of planned change concerns resistance to change. We will return to this topic in Chapter 6, but for now will note some of the general trends in research on resistance. Whether resistance is a predictor of success or failure is debated in the literature. While that may sound counterintuitive, Markus (1983) points out a reasonable explanation, "[resistance can be functional] by preventing the installation of systems whose use might have on-going negative consequences" (p. 433). Essentially, resistance can be the manifestation of a correct judgment that the change is a bad idea for the organization. Piderit (2000) and Dent and Goldberg (1999) have also suggested that the notion of "resistance to change" as a vilified concept – the ultimate archenemy of implementers – be retired. Piderit's complaints about how the concept has been used in the literature includes: (a) that the largely positive intentions of "resistors" are generally ignored in the research, (b) dichotomizing responses to change as "for" or "against" oversimplifies the potential attitudinal responses that are possible, and (c) the term has lost a clear, core meaning in the multiple ways it has been used in the literature. Piderit points out through her review that resistance has typically been viewed as something less powerful stakeholders do to slow down or sabotage a change effort. She argues that the language of resistance tends to favor implementers viewing those who oppose change as obstacles to success.

Two major concerns arise from this standard treatment of resistance. First, thinking of resistance as an obstacle to "right thinking" blinds the implementer to potentially useful observations of flaws in the change initiative. That is, if implementers are not open to the possibility that the change program might be flawed, and they treat any negative commentary as mere resistance, it is easy to dismiss it without consideration. Efforts are directed at fixing the resistors rather than reconsidering or altering the change initiative itself. Piderit quotes Krantz (1999, p. 42) on the use of the concept of resistance in organizations as "a not-so-disguised way of blaming the less powerful for unsatisfactory results of change efforts." Piderit refers to this tendency as the fundamental attribution error (discussed above as the wrongful attribution of cause and effect). Evidence that practitioners are guided towards such an error abounds in the practice-oriented literature. Popular press books on change implementation often have sections or chapters devoted to resistance to change. Many present their advice about strategies and specific tactics in terms of their ability to reduce or forestall resistance (Lewis, Schmisseur, Stephens, and Weir, 2006).

A second concern about resistance as it is typically used concerns cueing behavior. Implementers who assume resistance in stakeholders may actually promote that response. Think of the last time someone close to you started their sentence with "I know you are going to hate this, but ..." It usually sets up an automatic thinking process for you to search for the worst interpretation of what you hear next. A similar reaction may be triggered when implementers introduce change efforts with warnings of how "none of us will like this but" or "this will be a challenge for some of you." Zorn, Page, and Cheney (2000) provide an example of this in their study of the cultural transformation by Ken, the manager, who introduced change by telling his subordinates they should be "scared, frightened, and excited of the changes that are about to happen" (p. 530).

We can be certain in considering resistance in change initiatives that a good deal of noncompliant behavior is considered problematic by implementers and that from their perspectives much of it is believed to be born of ignorance, fear, stubbornness or some political motive. For some more enlightened implementers, signs of resistance may be signals that the change has flaws or needs adjustment so that it can be used in a successful way. Such implementers might treat those who raise objections or concerns about the change as loyal, committed, and/or ethical stakeholders who have the organization and its stakeholders uppermost in mind. In either case, the resistance and the reactions to that resistance by implementers and other stakeholders certainly have large impacts on change initiatives.

Another research area pointing to important sources of explanation for success and failure concerns managers' expectations and influence. King (1974) conducted a field study in which managers' expectations for success or failure of an organizational change effort were manipulated (some being led to believe success was more likely; some being led to believe success was less likely). Findings revealed that the results were related more to the managers' expectations than to qualities of the change program itself. Other research has pointed to the importance of managers' cues and encouragement in the behavioral and attitudinal responses of stakeholders (Isabella, 1990; Leonard-Barton and Deschamps, 1988).

Conclusion

This chapter has focused our attention on various ways in which organizations perceive, enact, and assess outcomes and results. We have seen that assessment of outcomes is a very important strategic activity that aids in planning, hindsight learning, and course-correction. However, we have also noted that assessment can be a very difficult task. Assessment of outcomes in organizations in general can be fraught with challenges in understanding the moving target of goals; the politicization of goal assessment; the attribution of error; and the problems associated with timing and means of assessing outcomes. In the context of organizational change different stakeholders can come to widely different assessments of outcomes. Also, the material conditions of stakeholders of change can vary widely.

Change outcomes have been treated in different ways in the literature including focus on "original goals" as baseline for comparison (e.g., fidelity); focus on degree of implementation or outcome achievement; measurement of the similarity of adoption of change across users (e.g., uniformity); and in terms of the genuine "buy-in" of key stakeholders (e.g., authenticity). Further, scholars have measured unintended consequences of change programs that can sometimes create additional challenges and burdens for both organizations and individual stakeholders even when overall intended outcomes and results are achieved.

A number of factors have been identified in the change literature as having predictive value in explaining and accounting for failure and success. Most of the research has explored predictors of failure, with a special focus on "resistance." In Chapter 6 we return to the topic of resistance in some detail.

This review and discussion of outcomes of change processes has called attention to the importance of multiple perspectives in defining and assessing "what has happened" as a result of initiating change. Stakeholders and implementers have various perspectives on those outcomes; may certainly differ on how and when to assess them; and may even be self-conflicted as to assessing them at any given point. Understanding that "calling" a success or failure in a change process is a highly social activity is an important first step in grappling with the challenges of measuring outcomes – a topic we return to in Chapter 8.

In the 2007 model (Figure 3.1) stakeholder concerns, assessments of each other, and stakeholder interactions are driven by the strategic communication strategies enacted by implementers and stakeholders. As discussed in Chapter 2, implementers and stakeholders make use of different strategies to disseminate information and solicit input. In Chapter 5 we will discuss a more nuanced view of these general strategic approaches among others.

References

Bikson, T. K. and Gutek, B. A. (1994) Implementation of office automation. *MIS Quarterly*, 18, 59–79.

Calsyn, R. J., Tornatzky, L. G., and Dittmar, S. (1977) Incomplete adoption of an innovation: The case of goal attainment scaling. *Evaluation*, 4, 127–130.

Covin, T. J. and Kilmann, R. H. (1990) Participant perceptions of positive and negative influences on large-scale change. *Group and Organization Studies*, 15, 233–248.

Dent, E. B. and Goldberg, S. G. (1999) Challenging "resistance to change." *Journal of Applied Behavioral Science*, 35 (1), 25–41.

DiMaggio, P. J. (1988) Nonprofit managers in different fields of service: Managerial tasks and management training. In M. O'Neill and D. R. Young (eds.), *Educating Managers of Nonprofit Organizations* (pp. 51–69). New York: Praeger.

Doyle, M., Claydon, T., and Buchanan, D. (2000) Mixed results, lousy process: The management experience of organizational change. *British Journal of Management*, 11, S59–S80.

Ellis, B. H. (1992) The effects of uncertainty and source credibility on attitudes about organizational change. *Management Communication Quarterly*, 6 (1), 34–57.

Erickson, R. J. and Wharton, A. S. (1997) Inauthenticity and depression: Assessing the consequences of interactive service work. *Work and Occupations*, 24, 188–213.

Fairhurst, G. T., Green, S., and Courtright (1995) Inertial forces and the implementation of a socio-technical systems approach: A communication study. *Organization Science*, 6 (2), 168–185.

Feldman, M. S. and March, J. G. (1981) Information in organizations as signal and symbol. *Administrative Science Quarterly*, 26 (2), 171–186.

Glaser, E. M. and Backer, T. E. (1977) Innovation redefined: Durability and local adaptation. *Evaluation*, 4, 131–135.

Goodman, P. S., Bazerman, M., and Conlon, E. (1980) Institutionalization of planned organizational change. In B. M. Staw and L. L. Cummings (eds.), *Research in Organizational Behavior* (Vol. 2, pp. 215–246). Greenwich, CT: JAI Press.

Grandey, A. A. (2003) When "the show must go on": Surface acting and deep acting as determinants of emotional exhaustion and peer-rated service delivery. *Academy of Management Journal*, 46 (1), 86–96.

Grunberg, L., Moore, S., Greenberg, E. S., and Sikora, P. (2008) The changing workplace and its effects: A longitudinal examination of employee responses at a large company. *Journal of Applied Behavioral Science*, 44 (2), 215–236.

Hall, G. E. and Loucks, S. F. (1977) A developmental model for determining whether the treatment is actually implemented. *American Educational Research Journal*, 14, 263–276.

Harris, L. C. and Ogbonna, E. (2002) The unintended consequences of culture interventions: A study of unexpected outcomes. *British Journal of Management*, 13, 31–49.

Isabella, L. A. (1990) Evolving interpretations as a change unfolds: How managers construe key organizational events. *Academy of Management Journal*, 33, 7–41.

Jian, G. (2007) Unpacking unintended consequences in planned organizational change. *Management Communication Quarterly*, 21 (1), 5–28.

Kanter, R. M. and Summers, D. V. (1987) Doing well while doing good: Dilemmas of performance measurement in nonprofit organizations and the need for a multiple-constituency approach. In W. W. Powell (ed.), *The Nonprofit Sector: A Research Handbook* (pp. 154–166). New Haven, CT: Yale University Press.

King, A. S. (1974) Expectation effects in organizational change. *Administrative Science Quarterly*, 19 (2), 221–230.

Krantz, J. (1999) Comment on "challenging 'resistance to change.'" *Journal of Applied Behavioral Science*, 35 (1), 42–44.

Laster, N. M. (2008) Communicating multiple change: Understanding the impact of change messages on stakeholder perceptions. Dissertation Abstracts International (UMI No. AAT 3342339).

Leonard-Barton, D. (1988) Implementation as mutual adaptation of technology and organization. *Research Policy*, 17, 251–267.

Leonard-Barton, D. and Deschamps, I. (1988) Managerial influence in the implementation of new technology, *Management Science*, 34, 1252–1265.

Lewin, K. (1951) *Field Theory in Social Science*. New York: Harper and Row.

Lewis, L. K. (1999) Disseminating information and soliciting input during planned organizational change: Implementers' targets, sources and channels for communicating. *Management Communication Quarterly*, 13, 43–75.

Lewis, L. K. (2000) "Blindsided by that one" and "I saw that one coming":The relative anticipation and occurrence of communication problems and other problems in implementers' hindsight. *Journal of Applied Communication Research*, 28, 44–67.

Lewis, L. K. (2006) Employee perspectives on implementation communication as predictors of perceptions of success and resistance. *Western Journal of Communication*, 70 (1), 23–46.

Lewis, L. K. and Seibold, D. R. (1993) Innovation modification during intraorganizational adoption. *Academy of Management Review*, 2, 322–354.

Lewis, L. K. and Seibold, D. R. (1996) Communication during intraorganizational innovation adoption: Predicting users' behavioral coping responses to innovations in organizations. *Communication Monographs*, 63, 131–157.

Lewis, L. K. and Seibold, D. R. (1998) Reconceptualizing organizational change implementation as a communication problem: A review of literature and research agenda. In M. E. Roloff (ed.), *Communication Yearbook 21* (pp. 93–151). Thousand Oaks, CA: Sage.

Lewis, L. K., Schmisseur, A., Stephens, K., and Weir, K. (2006) Advice on communicating during organizational change: The content of popular press books. *Journal of Business Communication*, 43 (2), 113–137.

Markus, M. L. (1983) Power, politics, and MIS implementation. *Communications of the ACM*, 26, 430–444.

Miller, V. D., Johnson, J. R., and Grau, J. (1994) Antecedents to willingness to participate in a planned organizational change. *Journal of Applied Communication Research*, 22, 59–80.

Noblet, A. J., McWilliams, H. H., and Rodwell, J. J. (2006) Abating the consequences of managerialism on the forgotten employee: The issues of support, control, coping, and pay. *International Journal of Public Administration*, 29, 911–930.

Ospina, S., Diaz, W., and O'Sullivan, J. F. (2002) Negotiating accountability: Managerial lessons from identity-based nonprofit organizations. *Nonprofit and Voluntary Sector Quarterly*, 31, 5–31.

Pfarrer, M. D., Decelles, K. A., Smith, K. G., and Taylor, M. S. (2008) After the fall: reintegrating the corrupt organization. *Academy of Management Review*, 33 (3), 730–749.

Piderit, S. K. (2000) Rethinking resistance and recognizing ambivalence: A multidimensional view of attitudes toward an organizational change. *Academy of Management Review*, 24 (4), 783–794.

Rafferty, A. E. and Griffin, M. A. (2006) Perceptions of organizational change: A stress and coping perspective. *Journal of Applied Psychology*, 91 (5), 1154–1162.

Reichers, A. E., Wanous, J. P., and Austin, J. T. (1997) Understanding and managing cynicism about organizational change. *Academy of Management Executive*, 11 (1), 48–58.

Rice, R. E. and Rogers, E. M. (1980) Re-invention in the innovation process. *Knowledge*, 1, 499–514.

Robinson, O. and Griffiths, A. (2005) Coping with the stress of transformational change in a government department. *Journal of Applied Behavioral Science*, 41 (2), 204–221.

Rogers, E. M. (1983) *Diffusion of Innovations* (3rd edn.). New York: Free Press.

Rogers, E. M. (1988) Information technologies: How organizations are changing. In G. M. Goldhaber and G. A. Barnett (eds.), *Handbook of Organizational Communication* (pp. 437–452). Norwood, NJ: Ablex.

Sawhill, J. and Williamson, D. (2001) Measuring what matters in nonprofits. *The McKinsey Quarterly*, 2, 96–107.

Schmisseur, A. M. (unpublished) The art of well-being: Managing emotional dissonance in the workplace.

Schmisseur, A. M. (2005) Beyond the client service interaction: An examination of the emotional labor of change implementers. Unpublished doctoral dissertation, University of Texas at Austin, Texas.

Tracy, S. J. (2000) Becoming a character for commerce: Emotion labor, self-subordination, and discursive construction of identity in a total institution. *Management Communication Quarterly*, 14 (1), 90–128.

Zorn, T. E., Page, D., and Cheney, G. (2000) Nuts about change: Multiple perspectives on change-oriented communication in a public sector organization. *Management Communication Quarterly*, 13 (4), 515–566.

Further Reading

Ashford, S. J. (1988) Individual strategies for coping with stress during organizational transitions. *Journal of Applied Behavioral Science*, 24, 19–36.

Harvey, A. (1970) Factors making for implementation success and failure. *TMS Management Science*, 16, B312–B321.

Larsen, J. K. and Agarwalla-Rogers, R. (1977) Re-invention of innovative ideas: Modified? Adopted? None of the above? *Evaluation*, 4, 136–140.

Vaananen, A., Pahkin, K., Kalimo, R., and Buunk, B. P. (2004) Maintenance of subjective health during a merger: The role of experienced change and pre-merger social support at work in white- and blue-collar workers. *Social Science and Medicine*, 58, 1903–1915.

5

Communication Approaches and Strategies

Never tell people how to do things. Tell them what to do and they will surprise you with their ingenuity

George S. Patton

It is a bad plan that admits of no modification

Publilius Syrus, 1st century BC

Make it so

Jean-Luc Picard, Captain of the Starship *Enterprise*

As implementers make decisions about how to introduce change to stakeholders, they make basic and sometimes sophisticated choices of communication strategies. **Structured implementation activities** (SIAs) are defined as a set of actions purposefully designed and carried out to introduce users to the innovation and to encourage intended usage

Organizational Change: Creating Change Through Strategic Communication,
First Edition. Laurie K. Lewis.
© 2011 Laurie K. Lewis. Published 2011 by Blackwell Publishing Ltd.

(Lewis and Seibold, 1993). Implementers are responsible for SIAs that will announce change; explain the process of change; create necessary skill-building and information dissemination activities; alter reward and evaluation systems; and socialize stakeholders into their necessary roles in the change program. There are numerous models and methods for accomplishing these implementation communication tasks and the various approaches have different implications for the roles of stake-holders; the nature, timing, and frequency of communication; and most importantly the design of messages about change. This chapter will examine strategic models for the implementation of change; explore five specific dimensions of communication strategies; and discuss the use of different channels for communication by both implementers and stakeholders involved in change processes.

An Overview of Strategic Implementation Models

From at least the late 1970s, scholars have been conceptualizing and investigating general strategies for the introduction of change in organizations. Two very general approaches have been described as the "adaptive" and "programmatic." Roberts-Gray and Gray (1983) and Roberts-Gray (1985) suggest that **adaptive approaches** fit the change/innovation to the organization (and its stakeholders) and that **programmed approaches** alter the organization (and its stakeholders) to accommodate the change. In another distinction, between the "**rule-bound**" and "**autonomous**" approaches, some authors suggest that implementation strategies can be either centrally controlled and designed (rule-bound) or be flexible and open to redefinition or reinvention even at the lowest levels of the organization (autonomous). The combination of these four general strategic types yields an interesting set of combinations (see Table 5.1).

Paul Nutt (1986, 1987) developed four models of change implementation (intervention, participation, persuasion, and edict) that somewhat mirror these combination strategies. Edict is the "my way or the highway" model much like the Rule-bound/Programmatic model in which the implementer or decision-maker is firmly in control and draws very little on other stakeholders' input. The participation model is much like the Autonomous/Adaptive model where implementers merely set some initial conditions and then empower lower level stakeholders and users to be involved heavily in decision-making and reinventing the change. Nutt's persuasion model focuses on turning over the implementation

Table 5.1   General strategic approaches – combination models

Autonomous/Adaptive	**Autonomous/Programmed**
Implementer team empowers lower-level employees/other stakeholders in designing best use and form of change. Reinvention of the change to suit organizational and/or stakeholder needs is focus.	Implementer team empowers lower-level employees/other stakeholders to develop best use and form of change. However, some joint form of change plan is then agreed as an ideal model for organization.
Rule-bound/Adaptive	**Rule-bound/Programmed**
Implementer team is in control, but a pre-set initial vision of the change is not necessarily goal. Users/ stakeholders encouraged to adapt the change to fit needs; potential uses; future creative use.	Implementer team is in control and high fidelity is primary goal. Organization and stakeholders are forced or encouraged to bend to accommodate the change.

effort to experts and so might fit into the Autonomous/Programmed box in Table 5.1. In Nutt's intervention model an adaptive approach is taken but the implementer team takes an active role in selling the change, so it may fit well into the Rule-bound/Adaptive category.

In keeping with the model presented in Chapter 3, I argue here that implementers' desires for different combinations of uniformity and fidelity in outcomes of change have implications for which of these strategies they might select. For example, if it is essential to gain high uniformity and fidelity, a more adaptive approach may be undesirable. On the other hand, where creativity and multiple and various applications of a change (e.g., new technology or tool) are goals, an autonomous/ adaptive approach might provide the best general approach. In fact, we might diagnose problematic implementation efforts by examining if there was a match of the intended outcome, in terms of fidelity and uniformity, and the alignment of an overall implementation strategy that would seem well geared to achieve those ends.

These overarching models of implementation strategy guide how implementers make communication choices as they introduce, monitor, and adjust change along its process of integration into an organization. We next examine specific dimensions of the communication strategy choices of implementers and other stakeholders during change. Implementers' strategic communication is highly influenced by the strategic implementation model they adopt whereas stakeholders are most influenced by their perceptions of the change context.

Communication Strategy Dimensions

In much of the literature on implementation of change in organizations, implementers are assumed to employ strategic communication in order to improve the likelihood of successful outcomes/results and reduce stakeholder resistance. It is much less common for scholars to address the strategic communication of other stakeholders. Stakeholders, particularly employees, are usually treated as receivers of implementers' communication and as reactionary in their communication surrounding change efforts. Resistance is typically portrayed as an emotionally triggered activity engaged in to slow down or stop a change that is perceived as threatening to stakeholders' self-interests. At times it is presented as a side effect of change processes caused by a knee-jerk distaste for change coupled with misunderstanding of implementers' information about the change. We will take a distinctively different perspective on stakeholders' strategic communication here.

The model described in Chapter 3 presents five dimensions of strategic communication that can be applied to either implementers or stakeholders. In this chapter we will further explore these dimensions of communication and highlight how implementers are often focused in different ways than stakeholders (see Table 5.2).

Table 5.2 Communication strategy dimensions: Implementers' and stakeholders' foci

	Implementers' Foci	Stakeholders' Foci
Disseminating Information/ Soliciting Feedback	• Official view of plan/purpose • Answering questions • Correcting misinformation • Listening for rumors • Soliciting insights • Inviting active participation	• Alternative views of change plan/purpose • Asking questions • Seeking outside expertise • Providing additional expertise and insight • Knowledge production

Table 5.2 (*Continued*)

	Implementers' Foci	*Stakeholders' Foci*
One-sided or Two-sided Message	• Positive selling • Acknowledging and refuting others' arguments • Forewarning of some negatives to provide realistic preview for positive stakeholders	• Raising new arguments • Engaging over refutation provided by implementers • Inoculating fellow stakeholders to implementer arguments
Gain or Loss Frame	• Focus on how cooperation with change provides advantage or how lack of cooperation will run risk of loss • Gains/losses will be in terms of organization well-being; central mission of organization; individual stakeholders' gains and losses	• Identifying new gains and losses not noted by the implementers • Refutation of some predictions of gain/losses as unlikely or more likely
Blanket/ Targeted Messages	• Blanket message or marketing to specific stakeholders • Determining high-value interests and information needs of key stakeholders	• Tailoring messages for each stakeholder group or using blanket strategy • Sharing targeted messages with other stakeholders for comparison/ consistency
Discrepancy/ Efficacy	• Communicating need and/or urgency for change • Communicating "we can do it" message to stakeholders	• Supporting, refuting, and/or questioning need, urgency, and efficacy of messages • Advocating alternative "need" messages

Dissemination/Soliciting Input

Strategic communicators in the context of change processes disseminate information and solicit input. They mix these activity foci in different ways and with different motivations. Table 5.2 suggests the key foci of implementers' and stakeholders' communication along this dimension. Along the dissemination/soliciting dimension we can use the participatory styles from Chapter 2 as a general way to describe the communication. We expect that this style choice will be rooted in implementers' general strategic approach to implementation (see Table 5.1). For example, in the Rule-bound/Programmatic approach to implementation we should expect that implementers are most interested in presenting a preformulated idea of what the change entails and why it is being introduced. They are likely most interested in communication that promotes a compliance with implementers' vision; limits discussion of alternatives; and focuses on instruction and correction not reconsideration or adaptation. Implementers' input solicitation will likely focus on discovering the level of accuracy of stakeholders' interpretations of the change effort. Thus, this approach to implementation is likely to involve a more symbolic style of participation (either Bankrupt Participation or Ritualistic Participation).

The communication style of the rollout of Gap Inc.'s cultural change (see Highlight Box 5.1) serves as a good example of this approach. In 2002 Gap managers rolled out a cultural transformation to encourage its 150,000 employees to work together across functions, borders, and brands. The campaign involved encouraging employees to share purpose, values, and behaviors that leaders hoped would dominate the culture and guide the company. The communication strategy involved multiple phases beginning with indoctrination of 2,000 senior leaders who then passed along training and messages about the change to their employees. From the description provided in *Communication World*, this campaign provides a clear example of ritualistic participation in that stakeholders were informed about the change and extensively socialized into the new ways of thinking at Gap but their input and participation were used as a means to inculcate the new cultural meanings and as a check on their learning and understanding – not as input that might alter the overall cultural change. For implementers who are utilizing a general strategic approach to implementation that falls into the autonomous/adaptive approach, we'd expect to see a participatory style more like privileged or widespread empowerment. In such an implementation effort, soliciting input is resource-focused – where

Highlight Box 5.1: Gap's Campaign for Cultural Transformation

The internal communication team had an unprecedented opportunity to develop and execute a comprehensive communication and rollout strategy that would at once educate, empower, and re-recruit employees to get behind the company and the PVBs (Gap's Purpose, Values, and Behaviors) ...

... the communication team focused first on ... the leaders, garnering their support for and understanding of the PVBs ... Full-day immersion meetings called Leadership Summits were developed to accomplish this goal. The meetings were highly interactive and engaging, requiring active participation. Once the senior leadership had been fully immersed in the PVBs and given time to process the information ... they were able to effectively share the cultural shift with their teams.

In order to communicate the guidelines to Gap's remaining employees, customized and culturally relevant communications were required. Executive and senior leaders held 60-minute presentations during regular business update meetings to introduce the PVBs. These presentations were scripted to inspire teams, generate enthusiasm, and set the stage for the full rollout.

The communication team designed interactive workshops about the PVBs for headquarters employees ... These workshops defined and applied the guidelines in terms of employees' real work needs through exercises and role-playing.

Throughout the rollout effort the communication team surveyed the mind-set and levels of interest of leadership through focus groups and surveys in order to continually refine content and methods. The team also established a "Your Voice" channel on the company intranet, GapWeb, for employees to ask questions, voice concerns, and receive direct responses about the guidelines.

Source: Nash (2005), pp. 42–43.

stakeholders' views and ideas are considered critical in design and implementation decision-making. We'd expect to see more emphasis on inviting active participation and soliciting insights along with the traditional activities of providing details of the change, describing the purpose, and answering questions.

We have already discussed much of the research that suggests positive benefits of more participative approaches to change implementation. As stakeholders become more engaged around designing, modifying, and even clarifying the change effort, they tend to feel more satisfied with it and more likely to be supportive. Another example of a corporation completely transformed with a widespread empowerment model is told in the story of CEO Jorgen Vig Knudstorp leading the 76-year-old Danish toy-maker Lego through change (see Highlight Box 5.2). Knudstorp employed the resource approach towards stakeholders, using their input in critical design and business decisions to improve the product and its delivery. In Knudstorp's communication, listening was not merely to confirm whether stakeholders were "getting his vision." Listening was a means to gather intelligence and put decisions into the hands of those who were best equipped to make them.

Stakeholders' strategic communication will also vary in terms of the focus on dissemination and/or solicitation activities. The model predicts that their choices of strategic communication will be based on their perceptions of the change context (we will return to this topic in the next chapter). Initially, stakeholder groups will be receivers of change announcements. Then, they will be involved in clarification and sense-making activity that involves asking questions and offering opinions to one another and to implementers. They may propose, especially to one another, alternative views of the change plan and purpose (reinterpreting it according to their best understandings or in terms of some version that suits political interests). This is the sense of "authoring" that we talked about in Chapter 1. Stakeholders may explore the change through seeking expert (as they define it) advice and information from non-official channels/persons. In organizational systems where participation is invited and/or channels for upward feedback are open, they may also participate in providing their own expertise, insights, and suggestions. And, as we discussed in Chapter 2, they will be party to the production of knowledge through participation in networks surrounding stakeholders of the change.

We should not assume that stakeholders necessarily want to encourage widespread participatory practices any more than will some implementers. In fact, some stakeholder groups may perceive that their stakes are best met by having a more dominant role in the change initiative and be less willing even than implementers to consider an adaptive approach to implementation. Such stakeholders may question why some stakeholder groups or individuals even have a "seat at the table." They may be interested in forestalling lengthy discussions or creative

Highlight Box 5.2: CEO of Lego Transforms Company Through Widespread Empowerment Strategy

To survive, the company needed to halt a sales decline, reduce debt, and focus on cash flow. At the same time, I had to build credibility. You can make a lot of things happen if you are viewed without suspicion, so I made sure I was approachable.

... Implementing a strategy of niche differentiation and excellence required a looser structure and a relaxation of the top-down management style we had imposed during the turnaround because the company needed empowered managers. For example, I stopped participating in weekly sales-management and capacity-allocation choices and pushed decisions as far down the hierarchy as possible.

... I realized the power of customer contributions in 2005, when the company started involving a couple of enthusiastic fans in product development and I started systematically meeting with adult fans of Lego. Since then, we've actively encouraged our fans to interact with us and suggest product ideas. An amazing number of grown-ups like to play with Legos. While we have 120 staff designers, we potentially have probably 120,000 volunteer designers we can access outside the company to help us invent.

... Managing user contributors requires corporate transparency and a respect for customers' ideas. We never take customers' enthusiasm for granted. We reward them by showing that we listen to and care about their feedback. When I attend fan events, I tell customers that while I can't implement every idea they propose, ... the more we hear an idea, the more thought we give to it. I also tell customers that they fulfill another vital role: They are an avenue to the truth. And in today's world, a CEO needs every avenue to the truth that he or she can find.

Source: O'Connell (2009), p. 25.

sessions that generate alternative versions of how the change might be installed. Part of a stakeholder's hesitancy to engage in more empowered participation by multiple stakeholders might concern the delay that such practices often bring to decision-making. Also, by involving more voices and engaging in more information assessment and knowledge

---

Case Box 5.1: Spellings Stakeholders Solicit Input and Disseminate Information

Some stakeholder groups were more on the sidelines of the initial controversy: "I think most faculty don't know what in the world was going on. And that's not a criticism of them, but as I travel and I make speeches and all this ... not very many faculty [are] clued into this. They ... [see] it as something that was going on in Washington, and a lot of things go on in Washington, and so what?"

Reactions were perhaps more largely influenced by the reactions of higher education leaders; business officers; media and other stakeholders who were following the Commission's whole process.

Many administrators helped in translating the meaning and importance of the report to other important stakeholders. As one business officer commented, "Well, I've had discussions about this with our provost. We are at very different ends of the scale [in our reactions]."

Further, several administrators described using the Report to open up dialogue with their boards. Alumni were another group of stakeholders with little initial awareness of the Report or the work of the Commission. As one association leader said, "To the extent that alumni were aware ... it [is] largely because they were made aware of it by their presidents."

Source: Adapted from Lewis, Ruben, Sandmeyer, Russ, and Smulowitz (unpublished).

---

creation, the odds of a favored existing alternative winning out diminishes. A stakeholder who has an early strong preference may argue against a widespread empowerment strategy if that preference has already been embraced by implementers.

It is also important to remember that stakeholders' communication is not merely aimed at influencing the decisions and opinions of implementers. Much of their interaction and persuasive attempts will be aimed at potential allies among other stakeholders including those who are undecided or opposed. Stakeholders who do not have the "definitive" status (recall in Chapter 3 Mitchell *et al.*'s designation of stakeholders who are seen as urgent, legitimate, and powerful) likely to garner implementers' attention, will often need partners to be able to influence the direction of change efforts. And, even where influence attempts directed at implementers fail, lobbying key stakeholders could alter the on-the-ground reality of the change process regardless of the official stance of implementers.

Employees can drag feet; advocacy groups can protest and call attention to organizational practices; customers and clients can ignore new policies; and professional associations can denounce new practices. All of which can ultimately forestall a change initiative or alter outcomes. Thus, stakeholders will aim dissemination of information about the change, its costs and consequences, likely success or failure, and implications for individual groups of stakeholders, at many potential audiences. They will also likely invite the input of outside experts and experienced individuals, and may convene formal or informal sessions among interested stakeholders to discuss and formulate opinions about the change. The Spellings case (see Case Box 5.1) is a good example of how stakeholders mobilized to find many different ways to engage one another as well as target some communication toward the would-be implementers of change (the Spellings Commissioners).

Sidedness

A second dimension of communication strategy (see Table 5.2) concerns the degree to which communicators' messages focus on their own viewpoint or discuss a balanced perspective on the change. Persuasion researchers refer to this as "sidedness" (Allen, 1991). A **one-sided message** "simply presents arguments supporting the advocated position; a **two-sided message** in addition to presenting supporting arguments, also discusses opposing arguments" (O'Keefe, 1993, p. 87, italics added). A further distinction involves whether the two-sided messages are "refutational" or "non-refutational." **Refutational** messages not only refer to the opposing arguments, they also make a case against them. **Non-refutational** messages merely mention the opposing arguments.

The relative effectiveness of one- and two-sided messages in altering a receiver's attitudes has been studied in health campaigns (e.g., persuading public to get breast cancer screening or quit smoking) and political and marketing contexts. The general conclusion of this research is that two-sided refutational messages are most persuasive (Chebat, Filiatrault, Laroche, and Watson, 2001; Crowley and Hoyer, 1994).

Research suggests that two-sided messages are likely to increase the perceived credibility and trustworthiness of the communicator. Other research has shown that these sorts of messages work most effectively when the audience is highly involved with regard to the object of persuasion (the topic is one they find salient and relevant) (Chebat and Picard, 1985) and for audiences who are initially negatively inclined (Pratt, 2004).

Persuasion research also suggests that two-sided refutational messages can be used to "inoculate" a receiver to future counter-arguments. Inoculation is used here in a metaphorical sense:

> ... just as a biological vaccination confers resistance to viruses by injecting a weakened version of the viral agent into the body, triggering the production of antibodies that later protect against stronger viral attacks, an attitudinal inoculation treatment subjects people to a counterattitudinal message (i.e., a weakened attack) with refutations, motivating attitude bolstering prior to a stronger persuasive attack, thereby conferring resistance. (Compton and Pfau, 2009, p. 11)

To make inoculation work the message must contain threat, counter-arguments, and refutations. The "threat" concerns calling attention to vulnerability in an existing attitude (e.g., your current position has a potential weakness). The threat component motivates people to process the inoculation message content (i.e., the counter-arguments and refutations). As we hear both the communicator's arguments, counter-arguments against those claims, and refutations to the counter-arguments, we are better prepared to face criticism of our adopted position in social contexts. Compton and Pfau (2005, 2009) suggest that inoculation treatments are consistent and effective in bolstering resistance to subsequent persuasive attempts in political, marketing, public relations, and health contexts.

These authors also report a number of side benefits of inoculation messages including that they tend to enhance perceived issue involvement and intent to talk to others about the target issue. Some research suggests that by equipping listeners with the arguments to fend off critics of a position, they make it more likely that such persons will be willing to engage those with a different point of view. In a study by Lin and Pfau (2007) on a hotly contested issue in Taiwan politics (the future relationship with the People's Republic of China), they found that inoculated participants increased in confidence in their initial attitudes, were more likely to speak out on behalf of those attitudes, even with those who disagreed, and were more likely to resist the counterattitudinal persuasion of others.

Compton and Pfau (2009) also discuss how inoculation can be spread through social networks. They argue that inoculation messages will promote involvement and word-of-mouth-communication in audience members. Some have speculated that the "pass-along" messages that these audience members share with others may be even more persuasive than the originals. Compton and Pfau argue that "talk as reassurance" (finding support for views through conversations within one's social network) and "talk as advocacy" (proselytizing specific campaign information) can result in increased exposure of more people to the messages and influence subsequent behaviors. Essentially, this approach to persuasion suggests that fostering rumor mills, seeded with inoculations against counter-arguments, is a potentially powerful persuasive communication strategy. That is very counter to usual advice given to implementers to squelch or control venting and rumor communication. The water-cooler moments of venting don't always occur face-to-face. In the Spellings case stakeholders exchanged opinions and persuasive appeals in articles and response statements published in higher education outlets including *Inside Higher Education* and *Chronicle of Higher Education*. In the content analysis of the over 1,300 core articles and individual responses published over a two-year period following the publication of the Spellings Report, 56% were coded as primarily supporting or primarily refuting or questioning the Report. Only 6.2% were coded as "balanced" (e.g., pointing to positive points on various "sides" of the issue). Although the study of these data did not explicitly code for "sidedness" it does provide an indication of the tendency of these stakeholders to focus on presenting one side of the issue (even if some of the refutational messages may have been two-sided).

Examples of the responses to the articles published about the Spellings case (see Case Box 5.2) illustrate what one-sided and two-sided messages sound like. In the first two one-sided messages, the stakeholders simply present their point of view on the idea of federally mandated standards of accountability in higher education. The third message acknowledges the difficulties in assessing outcomes (in his/her comparison to assessing pornography and note that implementation of standards will be difficult), but proceeds to support an argument that measurement is needed. Further, this two-sided message provides a refutation of a counter-argument in the second paragraph concerning the complexity of measuring learning outcomes.

Case Box 5.2: One- and Two-sided Messages from Spellings Stakeholders

One-Sided Messages

Posted by Assistant Professor on February 15, 2006 at 1:35 pm EST

The idea of the federal government dictating learning outcomes through assessment frightens me. This development threatens to align curriculum with tests, which provides politicians and their funding agents with inroads into the classroom. High stakes testing in the academy will redefine collegiate learning from a complex mesh of leadership, spiritual, intellectual, social, moral, and identity development. ...

Posted by Smith on June 22, 2006 at 12:05 pm EDT

With testing and accountability comes federally mandated standards, which is tantamount to a federally mandated curriculum. Are you ready for a National Curriculum? Remember the "Bill of Rights" for higher ed. is a thinly disguised attempt to squelch academic freedom. I really think that it's another way for neo-cons to influence and control ... well, everything.

Two-sided Message

Posted by VP of Strategy at Private Nonprofit Institution on February 21, 2006 at 11:50 am EST

Measuring a high quality education is a bit like recognizing pornography: it is hard to define, but you probably know it when you see it. Do we give up the fight against pornography because it is so difficult to define? I certainly hope not. The key to any successful policy implementation lies in the details, but you do not give up simply because it is difficult to implement, as is the case with assessing outcomes in higher education.

Some of the misguided paternalistic comments here suggest that only academia can save students from the perils of consumerism in higher education, but then argue that the complexity of measuring learning puts it beyond the effective reach of regulation. It is a personal challenge to stave off cynicism and simply assume that academia simply refuses to change even as students behave more and more like consumers (i.e., they exercise their ability to inform themselves and then choose) and already hold institutions accountable for outcomes based on their personal experience.

It is my experience in higher education that outliers garner a disproportionate share of attention. Believe it or not, most students do not seek a "cheap" solution or an easy degree. Students know a valuable education when they receive one, and are quick to tell their family, friends, and colleagues when they were well served, and when they were poorly served in higher education. Accountability and assessment is alive and well in higher education, but perhaps most faculty are just too afraid to admit it.

Source: *Inside Higher Education*, online responses to articles.

We have very little evidence of persuasive effects of sidedness or inoculation in organizational contexts. However, a study by Griffith and Northcraft (1996) found that "balanced" (two-sided messages) about a new technology significantly affected performance of new users in a positive direction. The persuasion evidence appears to support the strategy of two-sided messages that have the benefits of boosting credibility and, if refutational arguments are included, of inoculating the audience to counter-arguments of others. This logic would, of course, apply equally well to stakeholders as to implementers. For example, a stakeholder opposed to a change might inoculate her audience of other stakeholders against the refutations that implementers might make against her position.

Although acknowledging and directly addressing the downsides to change may be advisable according to the research on sidedness, we know that organizational spokespersons are sometimes loath to admit to negative information about important initiatives. Evidence suggests that communicators often have distaste for delivering bad news or even previewing that a message contains bad news. This has been referred to as the **"mum effect."** McGlone and Batchelor (2003) argue that reference to a negative object can be a threat to face for the recipient and the communicator. That is, as a communicator delivering bad news I might look bad and by avoiding delivery of bad news (or putting it softly) I might improve my self-presentation by appearing more humane. They argue that substitution of a euphemism is a common strategy of indirect communication to avoid or mitigate face threats. So, one might say "I have to use the restroom" instead of a more vulgar description of the actual need one has. In a change context, a manager might avoid the term "lay-offs" and replace it with "reduction of headcount," "off-boarding," or "reengineering" (see Highlight Box 5.3 for more examples). In fact, Smeltzer's study (1991) of change announcements found that euphemisms like "rightsizing," and "enhanced voluntary severance" were often used when discussing layoffs and that employees reacted negatively to euphemisms and to overly positive announcements. They also found that managers' euphemistic terms were frequently the target of employee jokes.

Highlight Box 5.3: Companies Use Euphemisms to Avoid Saying "Layoffs"

Last week, when American Express (AXP, Fortune 500) CEO Kenneth Chenault said the company would slash 7,000 jobs, or 10% of its workforce, he called it part of a "re-engineering plan."

Days later, Fidelity Investment president Rodger Lawson described 1,300 layoffs in a memo to staff as "cost improvement plans."

Experts say executives use opaque jargon to minimize the public relations damage of mass firings …

Silicon Valley companies seem particularly fond of inventing over-the-top management-speak. In a blog post last month, Tesla Motors CEO Elon Musk referred to a 10% staff cut at the electric car startup as part of a "Special Forces Philosophy."

At eBay (EBAY, Fortune 500) 1,500 job losses in October were a result of an employee "simplification."

Last month Yahoo (YHOO, Fortune 500) CEO Jerry Yang explained in an e-mail to employees that a 10% staff cut was a way for the company "to become more fit."

Source: Yi-Wyn (2008).

McGlone and Batchelor's study found that when subjects' identities were concealed from recipients of messages, they were more likely to deliver more polite euphemistic language when they were told they would later meet receivers of the messages than when they were led to believe no such face-to-face meeting would take place. This result suggests communicators' concern for their own face was the motivator for using euphemism. This is ironic when considered in light of Smeltzer's study that suggests that negative reaction and ridicule are sometimes the result of use of euphemism.

Implementers' concerns with their own self-presentation (face) may result in the delivery of euphemistic or ambiguous change messages that disguise unpleasant news or ignore discussion of potential risks or downsides of change programs. **Equivocal communication**, commonly referred to as "double-speak," uses language strategically to give an appearance of responsiveness that if truly delivered in a clear, direct manner would create negative repercussions (Bavelas, Black, Chovil, and Mullet, 1990). Thus a manager might find a way to deflect or ignore questions raised about a potential negative of a change program (e.g., "the situation is evolving and we are gathering more information," "overall, our organization is very healthy," "of course we are keeping everyone's best interests in the forefront of our planning").

In an interesting study by Susan Kline and colleagues, communication professionals were asked to rate a number of messages that were given by hypothetical organizational spokespersons during a crisis. Kline and colleagues expected that equivocal messages would be deemed more appropriate for use in crises with **avoidance-avoidance goal conflicts**. "Avoidance-avoidance goal conflicts arise when the message options available to respond to a question have multiple negative outcomes in relation to one's aims, yet a reply must be made" (Kline, Simunich, and Weber, 2009, p. 44). The professionals in the study found the equivocal messages delivered in these circumstances to be appropriate and linked to higher levels of corporate reputation. They also found that judgments of the appropriateness of equivocal messages were related to assessments that goals of multiple stakeholders were being addressed in the messages.

We have reason to believe that perceived deception or incompleteness in provided information can be detrimental to the credibility of implementers and also can endanger the success of the change program (Schweiger and DeNisi, 1991). If equivocal messages are used, they must be delivered with skill to avoid these negative outcomes. And, even if such messages can be successful from the perspective of the sender, ethical considerations should be made that might militate against their use.

Gain or Loss Frame

The third strategic communication dimension (see Table 5.2) concerns whether the persuasive message is framed in terms of gains or losses. A **gain frame** emphasizes the advantages of compliance with the persuader's message and a **loss frame** emphasizes the disadvantages of noncompliance. For example, an implementer can stress that if stakeholders are cooperative and able to make a change program successful, they will help position the company to earn greater market share and the possibility of significant raises for employees will be greater. On the other hand, a loss-framed message might suggest that *unless* employees cooperate with the change initiative, the possibility of a significant loss of market share might mean layoffs or even the closing of the organization. It is possible that a message might contain one or both types of appeals.

Bartunek, Rousseau, Rudolph, and DePalma (2006) argue that recipients of change programs often "gauge organizational change in terms of their own perceived or anticipated gains or losses from it, the extent to which change makes the quality of some aspect of their work or work life better or not" (p. 188). This would suggest that communicators who wish to persuade would want to consider the appropriate emphasis of potential gains and losses associated with a change effort and with rejection or failure of the change effort.

In general, research has suggested that people are more willing to take a risk to avoid (or minimize) losses than to obtain gains (O'Keefe and Jensen, 2006). Further, evidence suggests that negative information is particularly powerful compared with parallel positive information (Kellerman, 1984). However, O'Keefe and Jensen's analysis of the research on gain- and loss-framed appeals concludes that loss-framed appeals are not generally more persuasive than gain-framed appeals. Researchers also have explored characteristics both of situations and of message receivers to see if these act as moderators of the effectiveness of gain- and loss- framed messages. Broemer (2002) found that for individuals who were highly ambivalent (neither for nor against) at the outset, negatively framed messages (loss-framed) were more persuasive. Level of perceived risk might also be a potentially important moderator of these effects. Some researchers have argued that in high-risk situations (e.g., detection of a possible disease) people respond better to loss-framed messages (e.g., if you don't get tested, you could become seriously ill) (Rothman, Bartels, Wlaschin, and Salovey, 2006).

It is unknown how stakeholders might perceive the concept of risk in organizational change situations. An organizational change might be presented as survival-oriented. That is, if implementers' warn convincingly that the change is necessary to keep the organization going, this may trigger a high-risk scenario for many stakeholders. Other situations may trigger a high-risk perception on part of some stakeholders who think their personal stakes are threatened by the change (e.g., employees who fear layoffs; customers who fear service quality will decline; community members who are concerned about increases in pollution or congestion).

Clearly, determining the relative appropriateness and effectiveness of these different message frames is complex in that it is likely contingent on source, context, message, and receiver characteristics. What is interesting for our present purposes is to consider, in the context of organizational change, both how different communicators may use these frames, and with what side effects, in addition to any persuasive advantage they may hold. Even if neither frame is generally more persuasive, there may be other consequences for the communicator who employs one or the other, particularly if a certain frame is used repeatedly.

Consider, for example, the "chicken little" scenario where an implementer forwards a case for each of a subsequent set of changes in an organization based on the potential for great catastrophe if the change is not implemented successfully. If a "sky is falling" loss-frame is adopted repeatedly by the same communicator, credibility of that communicator may wane over time. A similarly deleterious effect may arise from a "rose-colored glasses" gain-frame pattern where a communicator is always touting some new change as the next best thing since sliced bread.

Generally, the message-framing literature does not consider implications of the ongoing relationship between the persuader and audience since the context of the research to date has been in many-to-one campaigns were the persuader was unknown or nonparticular (e.g., health campaigns, political advertisements). These message frames tend to be studied in experimental contexts where there is no existing prior relationship history between the communicator and his/her audience or anticipation of future relationship. In organizational contexts, especially where change is frequent and overlapping, we would expect to see numerous messages about change, often from the same people who are engaged in ongoing relationships. Further, the same individuals will be engaged with one another on a number of topics unrelated to change. How those messages form patterns and shed light on the credibility of the communicators may have larger explanatory power than the original form of the appeal (gain- or loss-framed). For example, in the current US battle for control over the political landscape, Republican lawmakers oppose much that the President and Democrats in Congress wish to enact. The Republican arguments against the President's proposals frequently are stated in terms of "unless we defeat the President's initiatives, bad things will happen" – a loss frame. In response, the Democratic Party continues to portray the Republican Party as the "party of no." This pattern, identified by the Democrats, of Republicans always being doomsayers of any Presidential proposal or action, may have negative side effects on the credibility of members of the Republican Party. If on the other hand the Republicans were to adopt a gain frame, where they forwarded arguments that defeating the President's proposals would advantage the country in some specific ways, it might present them in a different light. It would lead them to more discussion of what could be accomplished, and what positive vision might then be possible. For example, instead of arguments about what will happen if future generations are saddled with debt, Republicans might envision alternative uses of the money not spent including increases in personal wealth.

In the Ingredients Inc. case (see Case Box 5.3) we see evidence of a gain frame in the presentation of the expectations for the merger. In the opening and final paragraphs of the memo, the organization's leader suggests that the merger will "result in a more focused and competitive company" and that the result "is a focused organization with the ability to grow and prosper in a very competitive marketplace." Clearly, the communicators designed the message to emphasize how success of this change would enable gains to be made. They did not emphasize potential losses from failure of the merger – despite rising statistics that suggest merger failure rates are quite high.

In contrast, some of the official communication forwarding the Spellings Commission's arguments calling for change in higher education in the United States came much closer to adoption of a loss frame (see Case Box 5.4). Although the wording did not go so far as to speculate about the dim future for Americans based on the problems in higher education, it did go so far as to hint that a trend of poor performance existed, leaving the reader to imagine the scenario playing out in full.

Case Box 5.3: Memo to Ingredients Inc.

Ingredients Inc. has decided to merge Eastern Company and Midwest Company into a single operating company. Both companies are very successful and the combination of the two will result in a more focused and competitive company.

Eastern and Midwest will be led by (Midwest CEO) **as Chief Executive Officer**. He will be responsible for leading the overall integration of the two companies, managing ongoing business activities through his executive management team and the continued development of innovative new products.

To maximize the marketplace potential of Eastern and Midwest, Ingredients Inc. is naming (Eastern CEO) **as President.** He will be responsible for leading the combined sales organizations, sales support and the activities of the combined bakery RandD and product development (applications) as well as all marketing functions for the combined entity.

The new company will be headquartered in Midwest City, where all back office support activities will reside. The combined Supply Chain organization will be led by Brian Smith, VP Operations, Midwest; Finance/IT by Michael Crossman, VP Finance, Midwest; and Research and Development by Simon Davis, VP Technology, Midwest. Chris Coleman, VP Finance, Eastern, will assume new division-wide responsibilities as the VP Procurement.

The current Eastern and Midwest Sales organizations will not be affected by the merger, as well as the Eastern Plant manufacturing support services and Caravan Product Development Group, who will remain in Eastern City to provide the same level of customer support and service as experienced in the past.

As the transformation process unfolds, certain positions and individuals will be affected by the relocation of responsibilities. Although the exact timing has yet to be determined, appropriate arrangements and separation packages will be provided on an individual basis.

Company consolidation is a difficult process, especially since it impacts people who are loyal, hard-working and contribute to its success. However, by integrating Eastern's high-touch sales and service focus, with Midwest's excellence in manufacturing and RandD, Ingredients Inc. can offer products and services that are more closely aligned to the customers' needs. The result is a focused organization with the ability to grow and prosper in a very competitive marketplace.

Source: Laster (2008), p. 174.

Case Box 5.4: Official Statement by the Department of Education on Spellings Commission Report

The Commission's Final Report determined that while America's colleges and universities have much to be proud of, they are not well-prepared for the challenges of an increasingly diverse student population and a competitive global economy. Our system of higher education has become dangerously complacent despite the fact that, in the Commission's words, "Other countries are passing us by at a time when education is more important to our collective prosperity than ever."

... Too many Americans just aren't getting the education that they need. There are disturbing signs that many students who do earn degrees have not actually mastered the reading, writing, and thinking skills we expect of college students.

Source: US Department of Education (2006).

Targeted or Blanket Messages

In a fourth dimension of strategic communication choices (Table 5.2), communicators must decide whether their messages should be tailored (targeted) or more general (blanket). In a study (Lewis, Hamel, and Richardson, 2001) my colleagues and I examined the different communication strategies employed by nonprofit change implementers. We found that two of the models (**Equal Dissemination** and **Equal Participation**) involved blanket strategies wherein the same message or communication style was adopted across all stakeholders. In the Equal Participation model attempts are made to give all stakeholders a chance to provide input to the change process. Implementers we interviewed often described this as a burdensome process. Inviting opinion and input also meant that the implementer had to deal with all advice, suggestions, complaints, and disappointments when some had not been incorporated into final decisions. However, many implementers thought that this was a necessary step to ensure that the change would ultimately receive the support it needed. It was also possible through the use of this model for change programs to be dropped as a result:

One curator described a long effort to promote a change in the landscape of the museum grounds that would have required a tremendous public relations effort and fund-raising campaign to carry out successfully. After encountering resistance from the museum's friends group and getting a no confidence vote from her immediate superior (who had previously shown support for the change), she decided to quietly "let the project die." (Lewis *et al.*, 2001, p. 21)

In the **Marketing**, **Need to Know**, and **Quid Pro Quo** models distinctions among stakeholders were made either with regard to what messages were communicated or with regard to time and/or attention afforded. A senior vice president of a nonprofit provided an apt description of what we eventually labeled the Quid Pro Quo model, "There's a pecking order with our communication. Whoever pays the most dues gets listened to the most. Just like in any business, your biggest vendor or supplier is going to have the most clout" (Lewis *et al.*, 2001, p. 21). Essentially, implementers based decisions on what to talk about, how much to talk, and how early to communicate with stakeholders, on what they needed that stakeholder to provide to the change effort.

The Marketing and Need to Know models were extensions of this idea in the sense that implementers attempt to provide stakeholders with information that they need or desire (Need to Know) and/ or information in an explicitly tailored way (Marketing) to make it more likely to ignite the flow of resources and cooperation for the change. At times these models were invoked to prevent giving some stakeholders too much information. For example, one CEO suggested that he did not want board members to know enough detail that they might be tempted to micro-manage the change effort, so their information was kept broad. One interviewee expressed the general philosophy of the marketing models this way: "All [stakeholders] take a different communication strategy. You couldn't throw one message out and [have] it work for all the people you work with. They're too diverse and come from too many different places" (Lewis *et al.*, 2001, p. 25).

Some scholars (Leonard-Barton, 1987; Leonard-Barton and Kraus, 1985) have suggested that change implementation is an "internal marketing campaign" and that change messages should be tailored. However, Smeltzer's 1991 study of change announcements found that in only a few rare cases in their sample did management attempt to adapt the message to multiple audiences. They cite the example that an organization's announcement that a 1% merit pool was available was not differentiated for those making $15,000 annually from those earning

$100,000 annually. In a study in 1992, Smeltzer and Zener found that organizations did not differentiate between internal and external audiences in the announcement of layoffs. Contrastingly, Allen and Callouet (1994) explored the use of influence strategies targeted to different types of stakeholders in the context of organizational crisis management. Their findings suggest that organizations do adapt their communication strategies differently for different stakeholders and that they sometimes combine messages intended for one stakeholder group (e.g., regulators) with those meant for other audiences (e.g., media or community).

Although it is potentially useful to tailor messages to certain stakeholder groups, it is somewhat silly to suggest that communicators in an organizational context can completely segment their audience. As we observed in Chapter 3, stakeholders have relationships with one another and so they likely share messages, information, evidence, and arguments with one another. Therefore, the strategy to target specific persuasive messages for specific stakeholders may not be well accomplished without acknowledgment of that reality. At a minimum, communicators must be aware that any potentially conflicting arguments or information they provide to different stakeholders could ultimately be discovered.

Discrepancy and Efficacy

In a fifth strategic communication dimension (Table 5.2), communicators weigh the degree to which they emphasize messages focused on suggesting the urgency to initiate change (**discrepancy messages**) and /or messages promoting the sense that the change goals can and will be accomplished (**efficacy messages**). Armenakis and colleagues (cf. Armenakis, Harris, and Field, 1999; Armenakis and Harris, 2002; Armenakis, Harris, and Mossholder, 1993) discuss the importance of discrepancy and self-efficacy messages in examination of creating readiness for change. These authors argue that stakeholders need to believe that (1) change is needed and (2) the organization has the capability for successful change.[1] Numerous researchers have documented the importance of stakeholders' beliefs that change is needed (see Armenakis, Bernerth, Pitts, and Walker, 2007, for review). According to this perspective messages targeting this goal need to result in a realistic rather than exaggerated case in order to lead to stakeholders' acceptance of change. The Spellings case provides an excellent example of a discrepancy message (see Case Box 5.4) wherein the Department of Education and the Spellings Commission warn of other nations "passing us by."

The danger of overdoing a discrepancy message is that it may be constructed by stakeholders in such a way that they end up feeling hopeless in recognition of a huge performance gap or competitive disadvantage. If the gap between where the organization is operating and where it needs to be operating is perceived as too huge, stakeholders may be demotivated to attempt to change things. Efficacy messages are used to help overcome the sense of hopelessness that discrepancy messages sometimes produce. These messages project a "can do" attitude and announce to stakeholders that obstacles can be overcome and even seemingly insurmountable odds can be conquered. Witness Barack Obama's "Yes, we can!" message in light of a litany of social, military, economic, and environmental challenges that he devoted a great amount of time to in campaign speeches.

Reger, Gustafson, Demarie, and Mullane's (1994) work on reframing of organizational change argues that stakeholders tend to hold fairly rigid schemas about their organizations. A **schema** is a cognitive structure that represents what is known about some object including its attributes. We also may develop, or have introduced, an "ideal schema" – an image of what we want this organization to be. These authors call the difference between the actual organizational schema and the ideal organizational schema an "**identity gap**." This is a very similar idea to the "performance gap" notion mentioned earlier. A narrow identity gap may be demotivating because stakeholders may perceive change as unnecessary or not worth the effort. A wide identity gap can be a source of organizational stress if the stakeholders perceive change as unattainable and that consequences of failure to change are severe. These authors suggest that there is a "**change acceptance zone**" wherein the motivation to change (perceived need) is high enough to create some stress; but the perception of potential success is also high enough to provide the impetus to try.

With regards to efficacy messages in general, O'Keefe (2007) points out that in some circumstances such messages can have a deleterious effect on the audience in that they put the responsibility for results squarely on the shoulders of the message recipient. This can have the impact of creating negative side effects (e.g., in the health context it may lead to stigmatizing those with unhealthy conditions as being personally responsible for their circumstance) where guilt for lack of success or for the existence of the performance gap may result. Change communicators might be wise to consider both the ethical dilemmas associated with communication strategies that may give rise to stress and/or guilt and the potential side effects of invoking such emotion. For example, stakeholders who come to feel too negative in their role in an organization may decide that disassociation may be a better course than complying with the change effort. If you have been part of a failing organization for a number of years and a change agent is now trying to motivate new policies and practices based on that record of failure, you may feel enough guilt, embarrassment, or resentment that even in light of a compelling efficacy message may lead you to drop out rather than forge on to the new, better future.

In other approaches to this dimension of communication strategy some scholars have explored the role of expectations in change outcomes. For example, King's study (1974) of managers' expectations for the success or failure of change initiatives, revealed that higher expectations were related to higher productivity. Fairhurst's study (1993) of vision of organizational change also demonstrated that daily interactions of stakeholders around vision and its meaning can be a very powerful determinant of change outcomes.

Channels for Communicating

Rogers (1995) defines a communication **channel** as "the means by which messages get from one individual to another" (p. 18). We may distinguish broadly between interpersonal and mediated channels. **Interpersonal channels** primarily involve face-to-face communication, and **mediated channels** make use of some form of mass media or technology. Although scant research has focused on the effectiveness of different channels for communicating during change, some theoretical and descriptive scholarship exists in the literature.

Erik Timmerman (2003) has proposed a model of media choice over the lifetime of a change effort. As we noted in Chapter 2, Timmerman proposes that a set of source, organizational, media, message/task, receiver, and strategic factors will influence the choices of media that implementers use to disseminate information. Specifically, Timmerman argues that during the "action phase" of implementation – where the decision to change is enacted – implementers are likely to communicate through one-to-many announcement methods that include meetings and are relatively efficient means to contact multiple recipients. During the integration phase – wherein the change becomes stabilized into day-to-day routines – he proposes that "users" (stakeholders) will provide evaluation messages via informal media, including informal face-to-face discussions and group meetings. He further suggests that a preplanned, top-down programmatic approach to implementation is likely to be associated with "official" media that emphasize one-way communication. An adaptive approach that is more emergent and responsive to stakeholders as conditions and reactions are altered during the course of an implementation effort will involve use of both formal and informal media, as well as channels that are more interactive and that will accommodate feedback about the implementation effort.

In my own work (Lewis, 1999) evidence, from a study of 76 leaders of implementation efforts from a wide variety of organizations, suggests that popular channels for dissemination of information during change are small informal discussions, general informational meetings, and word of mouth (staff member to staff member). The most popular channels for soliciting input are also small informal discussions followed by "checking in with line supervisors," and "unsolicited complaints or praise." In my analyses of these data I found implementers' associated use of general informational meetings and their assessments of the success of the change. In a later study (Lewis, 2006) of *employees'* perceptions of use of channels and their assessments of success, I found that the most commonly used channels to receive information were "word of mouth (employee to employee)" followed by "small informal discussion." The most frequently used channels for providing input were "talking with my supervisor," and "participation in small informal discussions." I also found that frequency of use of all the tested channels for both receiving information and providing input was unrelated to perceptions of success of change efforts. The study showed that value of employee input and clarity of vision for the change *are* predictive of success perceptions. Taken together these results suggest that what is communicated is far more predictive than the channel or frequency of communication by channel.

By and large we know very little about the prevalence or effectiveness of different channels used during communication about change, although some authors advocate heavily for some channels as more effective. Larkin and Larkin (1994), for example, argue, "above everything else communication should be about changing employees. And senior executive communication doesn't do that – only communication between a supervisor and employees has the power to change the way employees act" (p. 87). Young and Post, in their review of "exemplary companies" (identified by peer organizations), strongly endorse face-to-face communication. Fidler and Johnson (1984) set forth several propositions about the use of interpersonal and mediated channels for communication during planned change implementation. They propose that interpersonal channels are more suited to meet specific needs of organizational members in overcoming risk and complexity associated with a change. However, when neither risk nor complexity is a major factor, mediated channels are proposed as more effective in providing general information.

Conclusion

In summary, this chapter has provided a description of important communicative approaches to implementation; dimensions of communicative strategies; and use of channels for communication. Much of this terrain is new in the change literature, and to some extent new to organizational communication in general. We have seen very little empirical or theoretical exploration of how change messaging or strategic approach to communication on the part of any stakeholder (including implementers) is more or less likely; more or less common; or more or less likely to be connected to other attempts on the parts of other communicators, among many questions.

Although there is a rich tradition of study of persuasive messages within the communication and socio-psychological disciplines, we really know little of how these message strategies work within the unique contexts of organizations, and even more specifically, change processes. We know little of the impact of specific conditions of organizations wherein those who would be persuasive and those who are considered "audiences" know one another; have history; have anticipated future interaction; are bound by roles arranged within hierarchical structures; and have numerous material and spatial associations with one another (e.g., exchange labor for pay, share office space). Clearly this is an area ripe for future research.

However, there is considerable evidence to suggest that the ways in which messages are designed and delivered are capable of influencing the sensemaking of stakeholders who participate in change communication. The ways in which stakeholders interpret messages and communication strategies of implementers and other stakeholders have a critical role in how they form beliefs, cognitions, emotions, and behavioral intentions regarding change initiatives. In Chapter 7 we will examine the organizational and institutional antecedents to these strategic communication choices on the part of both implementers and stakeholders. In Chapter 8 we will return to the effects of these strategic efforts on the interactions among stakeholders.

Note

1. Armenakis and colleagues also contend that (3) convincing organization members that it is in their best interest to change (valence), (4) showing that those most affected by the change are supportive (principal support), and (5) establishing that the desired change is right for the focal organization (appropriateness) are also critical to change messages.

References

Allen, M. (1991) Meta-analysis comparing the persuasiveness of one-sided and two-sided messages. *Western Journal of Speech Communication*, 55, 390–404.

Allen, M. W. and Callouet, R. H. (1994) Legitimation endeavors: Impression management strategies used by an organization in crises. *Communication Monographs*, 61, 44–62.

Armenakis, A. A. and Harris, S. G. (2002) Crafting a change message to create transformational readiness. *Journal of Organizational Management*, 15, 169–183.

Armenakis, A. A., Harris, S. G., and Field, H. S. (1999) Making change permanent: A model for institutionalizing change. In W. Pasmore and R. Woodman (eds.), *Research in Organizational Change and Development* (Vol. 12, pp. 97–128). Greenwich, CT: JAI Press.

Armenakis, A. A., Harris, S. G., and Mossholder, K. W. (1993) Creating readiness for organizational change. *Human Relations*, 46, 681–703.

Armenakis, A., Bernerth, J., Pitts, J., and Walker, H. (2007) Organizational change recipients' beliefs scale: Development of an assessment instrument. *Journal of Applied Behavioral Science*, 43, 481–505.

Bartunek, J. M., Rousseau, D. M., Rudolph, J. W., and DePalma, J. A. (2006) On the receiving end: Sensemaking, emotion, and assessments of an organizational change initiated by others. *Journal of Applied Behavioral Science*, 42 (2), 182–206.

Bavelas, J. B., Black, A., Chovil, N., and Mullet, J. (1990) *Equivocal Communication*. Newbury Park, CA: Sage.

Broemer, P. (2002) Relative effectiveness of differently framed health messages: The influence of ambivalence. *European Journal of Social Psychology*, 32, 685–703.

Chebat, J. C. and Picard, J. (1985) The effects of price and message sidedness on confidence in product and advertisement with personal involvement as a mediator variable. *International Journal of Research in Marketing*, 2 (4), 129–141.

Chebat, J. C., Filiatrault, P., Laroche, M., and Watson, C. (2001) Compensatory effects of cognitive characteristics of the source, the message, and the receiver upon attitude change. *Journal of Psychology*, 122 (6), 609–621.

Compton, J. and Pfau, M. (2005) Inoculation theory of resistance to influence at maturity: Recent progress in theory development and application and suggestions for future research. In *Communication Yearbook 29* (pp. 97–145). New York: Lawrence Erlbaum.

Compton, J. and Pfau, M. (2009) Spreading inoculation: Inoculation, resistance to influence, and word-of-mouth communication. *Communication Theory*, 19 (1), 9–28.

Crowley, A. E. and Hoyer, W. D. (1994) An integrative framework for understanding two-sided persuasion. *Journal of Consumer Research*, 20, 561–574.

Fairhurst, G. T. (1993) Echoes of the vision: When the rest of the organization talks total quality. *Management Communication Quarterly*, 6, 331–371.

Fidler, L. A. and Johnson, J. D. (1984) Communication and innovation implementation. *Academy of Management Review*, 9, 704–711.

Griffith, T. L. and Northcraft, G. B. (1996) Cognitive elements in the implementation of new technology: Can less information provide more benefits? *MIS Quarterly*, 20, 99–109.

Kellermann, K. (1984) The negativity effect and its implication for initial interaction. *Communication Monographs*, 51, 37–55.

King, A. S. (1974) Expectation effects in organizational change. *Administrative Science Quarterly*, 19 (2), 221–230.

Kline, S. L., Simunich, B., and Weber, H. (2009) The use of equivocal messages in responding to corporate challenges. *Journal of Applied Communication Research*, 37 (1), 40–58.

Larkin, T. J. and Larkin, S. (1994) *Communicating Change: How to Win Support for New Business Directions*. New York: McGraw-Hill.

Laster, N. M. (2008) Communicating multiple change: Understanding the impact of change messages on stakeholder perceptions. Dissertation Abstracts International (UMI No. AAT 3342339).

Leonard-Barton, D. (1987) Implementing structured software methodologies: A case of innovation in process technology. *Interfaces*, 17, 6–17.

Leonard-Barton, D. and Kraus, W. A. (1985) Implementing new technology. *Harvard Business Review*, 63 (6), 102–110.

Lewis, L. K. (1999) Disseminating information and soliciting input during planned organizational change: Implementers' targets, sources and channels for communicating. *Management Communication Quarterly*, 13, 43–75.

Lewis, L. K. (2006) Employee perspectives on implementation communication as predictors of perceptions of success and resistance. *Western Journal of Communication*, 70 (1).

Lewis, L. K. and Seibold, D. R. (1993) Innovation modification during intraorganizational adoption. *Academy of Management Review*, 18 (2), 322–354.

Lewis, L. K., Hamel, S. A., and Richardson, B. K. (2001) Communicating change to nonprofit stakeholders: Models and predictors of implementers' approaches. *Management Communication Quarterly*, 15, 5–41.

Lewis, L. K., Ruben, B., Sandmeyer, L., Russ, T., and Smulowitz, S. (unpublished) Sensemaking interaction during change: A longitudinal analysis of stakeholders' communication about Spellings Commission's efforts to change US higher education.

Lin, W. K. and Pfau, M. (2007) Can inoculation work against the spiral of silence: A study of public opinion on the future of Taiwan. *International Journal of Public Opinion Research*, 19, 155–172.

McGlone, M. S. and Batchelor, J. A. (2003) Looking out for number one: Euphemism and face. *Journal of Communication*, 53 (2), 251–264.

Nash, J. (2005) A comprehensive campaign helps Gap employees embrace cultural change. *Communication World* (Nov–Dec), 42–43.

Nutt, P. C. (1986) Tactics of implementation. *Academy of Management Journal*, 29, 230–261.

Nutt, P. C. (1987) Identifying and appraising how managers install strategy. *Strategic Management Journal*, 8, 1–14.

O'Connell, A. (2009) Conversation. Lego CEO Jorgen Vig Knudstorp on leading through survival and growth. *Harvard Business Review* (Jan), 25.

O'Keefe, D. J. (1993) The persuasive effects of message sidedness variations: A cautionary note concerning Allen's (1991) meta-analysis. *Western Journal of Communication*, 57, 87–97.

O'Keefe, D. J. (2007) Potential conflicts between normatively-responsible advocacy and successful social influence: Evidence from persuasion effects research. *Argumentation*, 21, 151–163.

O'Keefe, D. J. and Jensen, J. D. (2006) The advantages of compliance or the disadvantages of noncompliance? A meta-analytic review of the relative persuasive effectiveness of gain-framed and loss-framed messages. In C. Beck (ed.), *Communication Yearbook 30* (pp. 1–44). Mahwah, NJ: Lawrence Erlbaum.

Pratt, C. B. (2004) Crafting key messages and talking points – or grounding them in what research tells us. *Public Relations Quarterly*, 49 (3), 15–20.

Reger, R. K., Gustafson, L. T., Demarie, S. M., and Mullane, J. V. (1994) Reframing the organization: Why implementing total quality is easier said than done. *Academy of Management Review*, 19 (3), 565–584.

Roberts-Gray, C. (1985) Managing the implementation of innovations. *Evaluation and Program Planning*, 8, 261–269.

Roberts-Gray, C. and Gray, T. (1983) Implementing innovations: A model to bridge the gap between diffusion and utilization. *Knowledge: Creation, Diffusion, Utilization*, 4, 213–232.

Rogers, E. M. (1995) *Diffusion of Innovations* (4th edn.). New York: Free Press.

Rothman, A. J., Bartels, R. D., Wlaschin, J., and Salovey, P. (2006) The strategic use of gain- and loss-framed messages to promote healthy behavior: How theory can inform practice. *Journal of Communication*, 56, 5202–5220.

Schweiger, D. M. and DeNisi, A. S. (1991) Communication with employees following a merger: A longitudinal field experiment. *Academy of Management Journal*, 34 (1), 110–135.

Smeltzer, L. R. (1991) An analysis of strategies for announcing organization-wide change. *Group and Organization Studies*, 16 (1), 5–24.

Smeltzer, L. R. and Zener, M. F. (1992) Development of a model for announcing major layoffs. *Group and Organization Management*, 17 (4), 445–472.

Timmerman, C. E. (2003) Media selection during the implementation of planned organizational change. *Management Communication Quarterly*, 15 (3), 301–340.

US Department of Education (2006) Highlights of the Final Report. September 19.

Yi-Wyn, Y. (2008) Laid off? No you've been "simplified": When it is time to announce layoffs, executives embrace euphemism to soften the blow – to their companies. *Fortune*, November 11.

Young, M. and Post, J. E. (1993) Managing to communicate, communicating to manage: How leading companies communicate with employees. *Western Journal of Communication*, 22, 31–43.

Further Reading

Allen, M. (1993) Determining persuasiveness of message sidedness: A prudent note about utilizing research summaries. *Western Journal of Communication*, 57, 98–103.

Armenakis, A. A., Harris, S. G., Cole, M. S., Fillmer, J. L., and Self, D. R. (2007) A top management team's reactions to organizational transformation: the diagnostic benefits of five key change sentiments. *Journal of Change Management*, 7 (3–4), 273–290.

Baronas, A. M. K. and Louis, M. R. (1988) Restoring a sense of control during implementation: How user involvement leads to system acceptance. *Management Information Systems Quarterly*, 12, 111–124.

Berman, P. (1980) Thinking about programmed and adaptive implementation: Matching strategies to situations. In H. M. Ingram and D. E. Mann (eds.), *Why Policies Succeed or Fail* (pp. 205–227). Beverly Hills, CA: Sage.

Chebat, J. C., Filiatrault, P., Laroche, M., and Watson, C. (2001) Compensatory effects of cognitive characteristics of the source, the message, and the receiver upon attitude change. *Journal of Psychology*, 122 (6), 609–621.

Hale, J. L., Mongeau, P. A., and Thomas, R. M. (1991) Cognitive processing of one- and two-sided persuasive messages. *Western Journal of Speech Communication*, 55, 380–389.

Holt, D. T., Armenakis, A. A., Field, H. S., and Harris, S. G. (2007) Readiness for organizational change: The systematic development of a scale. *Journal of Applied Behavioral Science*, 43 (2), 232–255.

Marcus, A. A. (1988) Implementing externally induced innovations: A comparison of rule-bound and autonomous approaches. *Academy of Management Journal*, 31, 235–256.

O'Neal, E. C., Levine, D. W., and Frank, J. F. (1979) Reluctance to transmit bad news when the recipient is unknown: Experiments in five nations. *Social Behavior and Personality*, 7 (1), 39–47.

Smith, H. J. and Keil, M. (2003) The reluctance to report bad news on troubled software projects: A theoretical model. *Information Systems Journal*, 13, 69–95.

Tesser, A. and Rosen, S. (1975) The reluctance to transmit bad news. In L. Berkowitz (ed.), *Advances in Experimental Social Psychology* (Vol. 8, pp. 193–232). New York: Academic Press.

Zaltman, G. and Duncan, R. (1977) *Strategies for Planned Change*. New York: John Wiley & Sons, Inc.

6

Power and Resistance

Power abdicates only under stress of counter-power
Martin Buber

People don't resist change. They resist being changed!
Peter Senge

Our resistance to overtime was seen as a rejection of the company's philosophy of forced cooperation by team members
Laurie Graham, *On the Line at Subaru-Isuzu: The Japanese and the American Worker*

Resistance is a perennial concept in the organizational change literature. It would be hard to find a popular press book about organizational change that did not include a section or even a chapter on resistance and how to prevent or forestall its effects. The notion of resistance brings to mind images of domineering implementers forcing

Organizational Change: Creating Change Through Strategic Communication,
First Edition. Laurie K. Lewis.
© 2011 Laurie K. Lewis. Published 2011 by Blackwell Publishing Ltd.

unwanted change on stakeholders who are fearful and reticent to alter familiar practices (just because change is uncomfortable and/or "everyone hates change") and thus rebel. Stan Deetz (2008) puts it really well: "The very word evokes the sense of reclaimed autonomy of the oppressed working against domination. And its positive connotations are easy when the good guys are the weak guys and the bad guys powerful" (p. 387).

However, this leaves us with a romanticized depiction of resistance. It is actually far more complex to understand the various motivations for proposing and counter-proposing; for weighing in for or against; for acting in self-interests, organizational interest, and/or stakeholder group interest; for aligning with power or powerlessness; for forcing, threatening, coercing, and punishing; for raising expectations and raising doubts; for challenging, questioning, refuting, ridiculing, and ignoring; and a variety of other actions that have been described at one point or another as "resistance" or as "power" in the context of organizational change. This chapter will consider both the issues of power and resistance as they set a backdrop to understand implementers' and stakeholders' roles, as there is push and push back regarding change in organizations. We start with consideration of power.

Power During Organizational Change

Critical perspectives on organizations highlight practices of power, coercion, and domination that preserve a managerially approved status quo (Deetz, 2005; Fleming and Spicer, 2008). These tactics on the part of the powerful are sometimes met, say critical scholars, with opposition, subversion, and resistance. A managerial reading of the same set of dynamics might suggest that managers' decisions are often rejected and refused due to misguidedness, misinformed beliefs, and knee-jerk emotional reactions against discomfort, unfamiliarity, and/or the idea of change itself. Stakeholders might see power as something they themselves possess in the context of change: that they might cause change in the change initiative; that they might shape change through resistance efforts. They might see resistance as beneficial, as necessary even.

Power has been defined in many ways. Power can generally be used to refer to one's ability to influence a target (Yukl, 1994) or to the capacity to effect (or affect) organizational outcomes (Mintzberg, 1983). Mumby (2001) notes that another view of power focuses on the "potential or dispositional quality of actors" (p. 588). In this conceptualization, issues of autonomy and dependence that are part of the structural features of organizations become important. He further points to Lukes's (1974) argument that power may be exercised through the shaping or determination of an individual's wants. Thus, power may be exercised through causing another to act in accordance with one's wishes; through the threat of control; and through the manipulation of an individual's view of his own stakes and desires. Scott (1987) cites Emerson's (1962, p. 32) definition of power:

> It would appear that the power to control or influence the other resides in control over the things he values, which may range all the way from oil resources to ego-support, depending on the relation in question. In short, power resides implicitly in the other's dependency.

Thus, my secretary might have power over me in the sense that I depend on her to do tasks in order for me to accomplish my goals. I'm dependent on her and thus she derives a source of power over me due to that. One of the appealing things about Emerson's definition is that it acknowledges the possibility of mutual dependency.

> Power relations can be reciprocal: one individual may hold resources of importance to another in one area but be dependent on the same person because of resources held by the latter in a different area. And just as the degree of individual dependence may vary by situation, so may the degree of mutual dependence or interdependence. (Scott, 1987, p. 283)

I have graduate students who work for me in a program assistant role. As a supervisor, I have power over their continued employment. I also rely on their execution of tasks in order to manage the programs for which I'm responsible – thus *they* have some power over me in a sense. However, I also am part of the graduate faculty that rules over these students in terms of policy; I sit on committees that impact their requirements and progress toward degree. Thus, there are many levels and realms of interdependence.

In Boonstra and Gravenhorst's (1998) review of power approaches to change implementation, they define power as "dynamical social process affecting opinions, emotions, and behavior of interest groups in which inequalities are involved with respect to the realization of wishes and interests" (p. 99). This definition calls attention to the fact that power relations are not merely about material outcomes and status. They are also about people's personal values, self-esteem, and relationships.

Seeking approval, craving praise, face needs, etc. also are at play in power relationships. That a person in power over me has the ability to embarrass me in a public "dressing down" or build up my self-esteem, is also part of our understanding of power.

All of these definitions of power in the context of organizations emphasize shared qualities: influence; inequalities; outcomes relative to individual and organizational goals. Less noticed in many definitions of power is that power may be exercised unconsciously and invisibly (Boonstra and Gravenhorst, 1998; Lukes, 1974). For example, the mere existence of available power – **latent power** – may be enough to trigger compliance regardless if any power is overtly exercised. Latent power can serve as the threat of the exercise of power.

In the Spellings case (see Case Box 6.1) we see the clearest example of this among the cases in this book. Department of Education Secretary

---

Case Box 6.1: Spellings Commission's Latent Power Recognized

In a statement that followed the release of the Spellings Commission Report, it was noted that the Secretary of Education would be considering the six recommendations and other proposals. The outcome of that process would include an action plan for the future of higher education.

Many stakeholders who read the report and the statement came to believe that the Commission recommendations implied a takeover of higher education at a federal level through quantitative and standardized testing and other forms of increased government intervention.

One stakeholder, Senator and former Secretary of Education Lamar Alexander, who clearly recognized the latent power of the Department of Education to force change on the higher education community, suggested that he might offer an amendment to the Higher Education Act to prohibit the Department from issuing final regulations on these issues until Congress could convene and make decisions. He advocated convening leaders in the higher education community first to encourage self-monitoring and self-correction. The result of inaction was that the federal government would have to act.

Source: Adapted from Ruben et al. (2008).

Margaret Spellings and the Spellings Commission held a good deal of latent power. The specter of the Department of Education moving to impose new regulations, policy, and/or accreditation standards on higher education hovered over this change effort. Through their report the Commissioners supported higher education attempts to self-correct. However, it was certainly understood by those in the higher education community that latent power could be activated to force some of the change they were suggesting. As Ruben, Lewis, and Sandmeyer (2008) describe the culture of higher education, "recommendations that are perceived to threaten the autonomy of higher education strike at the heart and soul of the academy particularly if a perceived threat to that principle comes from outside the academy, and if it appears that the outsiders may have the power to enforce change, vigorous resistance is a predictable response" (p. 11).

We can also observe in the case description that the actions of Senator Alexander represented another example of latent power. The latent power of a senator to introduce (and perhaps secure) legislation that would limit the ability of the Department of Education to make rules pertaining to higher education would doubtlessly be perceived as a threat to Secretary Spellings. In fact, actions of Congress regarding Spellings' later rule-making efforts prompted a form of resistance (or counter-resistance to the resistance she perceived) from Secretary Spellings. She issued a personal statement in *The Politico*, "Congress digs a moat around its Ivory Tower": "While business leaders embrace the future, Congress is vigorously defending old structured and outdated practices in higher education at the behest of entrenched stakeholders who advocate the status quo" (Ruben *et al.*, 2008, p. 99).

A variety of scholars (French and Raven, 1959; Pfeffer, 1981; Pfeffer and Salancik, 1978) have theorized different bases of power including **position power** and **expertise power**. Mintzberg (1983) also discusses several external and internal means of influence including social norms (e.g., ethics, standards of conduct, professional expectations), formal constraints (e.g., laws, rules, regulations), pressure campaigns, and direct controls. For example, in use of position power, change agents and other stakeholders might rely upon formal authority and tactics such as demands, threats, and control that are well facilitated by having control over resources (e.g., pay, benefits, promotions, ability to grant "exceptions").

An expertise model of power would be based upon perceptions of a communicator's competence, professional capability, and effectiveness

Case Box 6.2: Homeless Net Recognizes Expertise Power of Implementers

Monica, Trevor, and Derek were considered experts by the homeless service providers in areas of communication and communication technologies, including assessment of communication, training on how to use the communication technologies, and issues with the listserv.

Despite that status of "expertise," there was no guaranteed success with implementation. Although the professors devoted considerable energy into state-of-the-art equipment, sophisticated software, and collaboration tools, it was the simple listserv that served this community best. The members of the community relied on their own sense of needs over the expert advice of the consultants.

Source: Adapted from Scott, Lewis, Davis, and D'Urso (2009).

on the job (Boonstra and Gravenhorst, 1998). The Homeless Net case (see Case Box 6.2) provides a good example of "expertise power." My colleagues Craig Scott, Scott D'Urso, and I (aka Derek, Trevor, and Monica) were considered content experts with regard to the communication technologies we were trying to implement. We were also considered experts in terms of general issues around communication. What we came to realize however was that while we were experts on the technologies we were trying to implement, our expertise on the circumstances of work for the homeless service providers was more limited.

Strong cultural preferences for face-to-face communication dominated this network. The context of the work, clients, culture, and backgrounds of the service providers militated against adoption of some of these tools – perhaps for good reasons. So, having expertise, even if recognized by the stakeholders of a change effort, may not be enough to guarantee success in terms of what the implementers set out to do. However, the resistance experienced in this case – ignoring some tools – may have proven to be adaptive in a positive way. The service providers were able to embrace the tools that worked for them, and did not expend resources learning and incorporating tools into work that were not viewed as useful. They may have made wise choices. As Derek (Scott *et al.*, 2009) notes: "I initially thought our project was about training people to use technology and then expecting them to comply. It turned out to be about providing opportunities for people, seeing what worked for them in their situation, and then learning from that" (p. 88).

Other important resources of power for individuals in organizations include information (especially unique information), and coalition power and group support. Boonstra and Gravenhorst (1998) argue that building networks and strong cohesive groups can advantage individuals who wish to wield power in organizations.

Lines (2007) investigated how change agents' power base makes a difference in implementing change. In a study of a large European telecommunications company struggling with consequences of deregulation, rapid technological change, and globalization, Lines found that different change agents, with different bases of power, selected different tactics to aid the implementation of change in their organizational units. Change agents with high expertise power tended to use participatory methods of introducing change and had more success with implementation of change when they were perceived as content experts. However, they also found that those change agents with high position power had more success than those with low position power and it appeared to make no difference whether they used participatory approaches to change. Of course we must qualify the researcher's measurement of "success" in this study. Lines assessed success in terms of observations of managers within the organization in which she collected her data. Other stakeholders may have judged the success of these change efforts in different ways.

In meaning-centered approaches to power in organizations, scholars (Cooney and Sewell, 2008; Kunda, 1992; Putnam, Grant, Michelson, and Cutcher, 2005) have demonstrated the important roles of interpretation and symbols in the exercise of power. Management of meaning can create legitimacy for decisions, plans, processes, goals, etc. In an often unnoticed manipulation, stakeholders' ideas about what is good and useful about a change effort can be altered in ways they identify with and result in acceptance of new structures and systems even if those changes are not in alignment with self-interests. Foucault (1984) argues in fact that power is most effective when it is masked to those who are controlled.

In these approaches, control over meanings in organizations is key to power. Dominant and taken-for-granted meanings in organizations lend themselves to bases of power. Those who are able to successfully maintain or shift meanings in ways that benefit themselves (or groups to which they belong) are able to define reality for other stakeholders. For example, Robert Gephart's study (Gephart 1984, 1988, 1992; Gephart, Steier, and Lawrence, 1990) of industrial accidents and disasters illustrates how different stakeholder groups (e.g., company, government investigators, families of employees) compete to shape interpretations of such events.

According to Boonstra and Gravenhorst (1998), in this genre of power literature, power is defined as "capacity to shape reality and to perform somebody in such a way that he or she does what one wants without any need of explicit power" (p. 108). In the "**management of meaning**" symbols are constructed to define reality for others. That new reality then implies certain actions and understanding over others. For example, defining an event as a "crisis" may be used to legitimate drastic action. Once stakeholders accept the definition of their reality as crisis then many other things may be implied – need to act quickly; need for someone to take charge; lack of time for questioning leaders; short-term focus; need for sacrifices; high stakes; and acknowledgment of external threats. The creation of new, shared meanings is an important part of the management of meaning. One part of this process can involve creating and recreating the history of an organization or an organizational decision. Once communicators can convince enough people to "read" the history the same way, a logical (i.e., taken for granted) conclusion can define the current reality and imply actions that are desired.

We say more about reframing in Chapter 8, but for now will note that many stakeholders participate in management of meaning. For example, Cooney and Sewell (2008) describe how shop stewards in an Australian automotive manufacturing plant developed a strategy of resistance that was based on reframing the managerial account of change. The employee representatives were able to "redefine the rationale given by the management based on improved competitiveness for the firm, as something that was worthy in principle but that could not be achieved in practice because of flawed decision-making based on short-term self interest" (p. 698).

Power is likely to underscore much organizational behavior and structure. Implications of granting too much power or yielding power during change can be far-reaching and those in power are likely not to want to give up their own power or see potential competitors or adversarial stakeholders increase theirs. Cooney and Sewell's study further illustrates this point. They found evidence that the management team appropriated the expertise of employees born of their own day-to-day knowledge of operations and incorporated it into the change effort in a way that did not give up power nor elevate the status of the employees in terms of their power. This is illustrated by the authors' description of how the union representatives were consulted regarding changes in the work process:

> Rather than embedding the union representatives within the design and implementation teams, the project manager held separate meetings with the design engineers, project engineers, and the union representatives. The project manager shuttled design and implementation ideas backward and forward between the groups so that management, rather than the groups themselves, retained control of the discussion and, ultimately, ownership of the design concepts and implementation strategies. (Cooney and Sewell, 2008, p. 702)

In this way, the management group was able to take up the ideas of the employees without granting them any power. The managers were also able to appropriate the ideas of employees and alter the change in ways that made it more palatable to employees and thus increase compliance. However, as the authors point out, the employees were not able to participate as recognized or equal partners.

Zorn, Page, and Cheney's (2000) depiction of the NUTS! case (introduced in Chapter 2) serves as another illustration of power and control strategies during change. These authors discuss the "hidden means by which control and power are controlled and maintained" (p. 546). They discuss the **concertive control** strategies that are used in the case. Concertively controlled organizations rely on the strong loyalty and identification of stakeholders (usually employees) to foster a frame of decision-making that puts the organization's interests first, above any individual interests. The stakeholders in such an organization accept the decision-making premises of the organization. Employees in such an organization essentially police one another and themselves by reminding one another of the values, mission, goals, and best practices of the organization. One of the features of concertive control is that it is unobtrusive (that is, employees don't feel they are being controlled at all). Examples of what Zorn *et al.* refer to as concertive control in the NUTS! case include the employees choosing to spend unpaid weekend days on experience days or training days; volunteering to make presentations on the NUTS! book to the group; and giving in to Ken's suggestions that they support the change. "The women generally acted in accord with Ken's position, but they also engaged in persuading themselves of the correctness of this position … Two or three of the less outgoing women

Highlight Box 6.1: JAR Technologies Experiences Concertive Control

JAR's environment that bred that past success has changed significantly. During the 1990s, NASA and US government defense budgets shrank significantly at the same time that a large commercial space market was growing rapidly. Commercial customers usually are not looking for the best solution, but rather one that is "good enough," produced quickly and at cost that will turn a profit.

In the late 1990s, JAR managers began an aggressive campaign to change the company value system to focus on cost/schedule rather than technical excellence. As a result, managers at JAR espoused the "discourse of enterprise" to justify the changes that needed to be made at JAR. This included espoused beliefs in customer-oriented thinking; continuous improvement, and a turbulent environment to which the organization must adapt. As one manager expressed, "We need to be careful to give rather than the Cadillac, give the Chevrolet if that's the case."

A second discourse also emerged in addition to the discourse of enterprise. This discourse was one related to JAR's successful past. "Most of the managers at JAR had come up through the engineering ranks and still strongly identified with the company's long-time commitment to technical excellence."

The result of the two competing discourses created a confused set of messages where both the espoused values of enterprise and the reward of "excellence" were mixed. Both employees and managers noticed the contradictions.

The authors of this study conclude that the managers may themselves come to be controlled by the concertive control system they implement for their employees. That is, the managers had become so strongly identified with the original set of values, they had a hard time pulling off the change themselves. This led to contradiction in their rhetoric.

Source: Adapted from Larson and Tompkins (2005).

told the participant observer that even though they feel uncomfortable or self-conscious making a presentation from NUTS!, they believed it was the right thing to do" (Zorn *et al.*, 2000, p. 552).

One important way in which concertive control and other powerful forms of controlling meaning are fostered in organizations is described in the work of Michel Foucault (1995) as he discusses the idea of

Discourse. Gail Fairhurst (2011) describes Foucault's Discourse as "a system of thought with its own linguistic tool bag, or collection of terms and metaphors for key concepts and ideas; categories for understanding; themes for stories; and familiar arguments for us to draw upon to describe, explain or justify" (p. 32). The use of familiar Discourses (e.g., Continuous Improvement, Innovation, Excellence) can be used as a guidepost for stakeholders to interpret "correct" thinking and action. Organizational leaders can reinforce such Discourses through repetition of the familiar language of these sets of concepts, ideas, and related stories.

An aerospace company's experience with change provides an example of how powerful Discourse in an organization can create challenges in transitions to new ways of managing meaning. Larson and Tompkins (2005) illustrate how concertive control – created in large part through a Discourse of Excellence – during change in an aerospace company constrained managers as well as workers (see Highlight Box 6.1). The power of highly identified organizations is that concertive control may lead to inertia. It is hard for even those who create concertive control systems to avoid the logic and values that become taken for granted – the familiar Discourses. Even when there seems a sensible reason for changing the value system, managers themselves may have a hard time making the switch.

Each of the approaches reviewed in this brief section on power in the context of organizational change presents a slightly different view on how issues of control, manipulation, and the blending or submission of different interests in organizations can be accomplished. Although this is by no means a thorough review of the vast literature on power in organizations, it provides a backdrop for the discussion of resistance in the context of organizational change that we turn to next.

Resistance During Change

As noted in Chapter 4, resistance is often vilified by popular press books and feared by managers as the root cause of change failure. Employee or other stakeholders' unwillingness to enthusiastically embrace a change and execute new procedures and tasks; adopt new philosophy or attitudes; discard old practices and the like is often blamed for change failure and labeled as resistance. Resistance is often characterized as a negatively valenced activity driven by fear, ignorance, stubbornness, or some nefarious political motive. Rarely are resistors considered to be focused on the improvement and protection of their organization or of change efforts. Rarely are they regarded as partners in the change process. Thus, the response to resistors on the part of implementers is usually to detect them, alter or discredit their views, and then persuade or pressure them into silence and/or at least a minimally acceptable level of cooperation.

Before considering resistance in detail we should consider for a moment why implementers, and other people in powerful positions in organizations, treat resistors in the ways that they do. I would argue that managers are not inherently closed to input because of some Machiavellian view of their leadership roles. In fact, I've known managers who espouse a very respectful, democratic, and participatory view of management who are completely closed to negative feedback, questions of the soundness of their plans, and who routinely disregard critique. They see themselves as leaders who truly have an open door and who are interested in the views of all stakeholders and they embrace values of open dialogue and mutual respect for difference and yet they sometimes behave in ways completely opposite to those values. I must admit, I have found this to be true of myself at times – usually when I'm convinced of the soundness of my own ideas.

One explanation of this contradiction can be found in an understanding of the difference between our espoused theories and our theories-in-use. Our **"espoused theories"** – those we claim as the premises of our choices of action – do not always match our **"theories-in-use"** –those we actually act out in real life. Chris Argyris (2000) writes that managers' "theories-in-use" often follow what he calls "Model I", which values being in control; winning and not losing; suppressing negative feelings; and acting as rationally as possible. Argyris describes how managers, shaped by these values, tend to advocate for their own position, make evaluations of our own and others' performance, and offer attributions about others' intentions in ways to remain in control, maximize wins, and suppress negative feelings.

> This means that we act in ways that encourage neither inquiry into our views nor the robust testing of the claims that we make. Indeed, the only test possible under these conditions is one that uses self-referential logic: "Trust me, I know what I am doing." (p. 5)

Argyris argues that Model I thinking and actions create defensiveness, self-fulfilling prophecies (e.g., cueing resistance), self-sealing processes, and escalating error. He further argues that people in organizations, programmed by such values, develop "defensive routines" that are designed to prevent embarrassment or threat. These defensive routines prevent learning.

Argyris describes a nice example of the use of defensive routines as he reports what happened in a learning experiment with some managers (see Highlight Box 6.2). After having been taught about the concept of

Highlight Box 6.2: Defensive Routines in Implementing Strategy

The executive [made it] clear that he was asking for a major change. The general manager became very upset ...

The facilitator intervened to ask the executive what he was feeling and thinking as he heard the general manager's reaction. The executive said that the response confirmed his fears; the general manager wanted individuals to be candid – up to a point. "I think that I may have made an error in raising the question," the executive said.

The general manager apologized, saying he realized that he was violating what he espoused in the plenary session and in his first response to the executive's question. "But you know," he said, "it is not easy to hear this."

"Yes," responded the executive, "and it is not easy to say it."

The general manager then encouraged others to speak. Several agreed with the executive. The facilitator asked, "What normally goes on at these meetings that leads people to hold back on such data?" The responses were candid. Participants described several organizational defensive routines involving "going along" with a higher-level executive when they believed that the supervisor was wrong but was also emotionally committed to his or her position. For example, one said, "I saw you [the general manager] as wanting this strategy. This is your baby: The strategy makes good sense and thus is not easy to refute. I figured given your strong commitment to it and the lack of support that I would get from others, it made sense to go along. I must say I did not realize until now that others had similar doubts."

... The general manager's initial reaction of dismay and bewilderment was an example of an individual defensive routine. His reaction was inconsistent with what he had been espousing, and was automatic and skillful.

Source: Argyris (2000), pp. 178–179.

defensive routines, a general manager engaged in discussion with his own managerial subordinates about implementation of his proposed strategy. Just prior to this discussion, the general manager had espoused a strong value for and commitment to the principles of a Model II thinking wherein defensive routines are avoided and principles of information sharing, discussing "undiscussables," subjecting point of view to public testing, and commitments to valid data are embraced. However, when a subordinate actually questioned his ideas, he reacted with a strong negative response that quickly communicated to the "resisting" subordinate that the espoused theory was not actually in use. The dysfunction of both the subsequent self-editing behavior of the resistant subordinate and the controlling behavior of the general manager were then recognized and processed by the facilitator. This example shows how difficult it can be for people to alter their theories-in-use even when they are highly committed to doing so.

It would not be an overstatement to say that mountains of literature have been written about resistance (see special issue of *Management Communication Quarterly*, 2008, for a timely set of articles related to the topic). It is challenging to sort out what exactly is meant by the term and how it is distinct from similar terms and actions. Terms that are related in some ways to resistance include: voice, dissent, complaining, foot-dragging, cynicism, and sabotage. Issues that are raised in discussions of the differences of these terms include what counts as resistance; the likelihood to have impact on the object of resistance; and individual versus collective resistance. Piderit (2000) notes that the term itself is truly a metaphor borrowed from physics that is meant to describe a "restraining force moving in the direction of maintaining the status quo" (p. 784). A traditional construction of resistance suggests that this is an act of disobedience, defiance, and/or is a reactive process by which employees (or others) oppose initiatives by change agents.

Resistance is often blamed for failure of change efforts. However, this description privileges a managerial or implementer perspective. One could just as easily say that installation of a change is indicative of a failed resistance campaign or that implementation of a change in its original proposed form is a sign that improvement efforts (i.e., resistance) failed. Thus as Piderit (2000) and Dent and Goldberg (1989) have cautioned us, we should be careful to consider resistance as a range of actions with many different possible rationales and consequences. Starting with the assumption that it is a dysfunctional problem of change is not advisable.

Piderit's review of the resistance literature concludes that there are three manifestations of resistance: cognitive, emotional, and behavioral. The cognitive view relates to an individual's beliefs about the change. An emotional dimension refers to an individual's feelings associated with the change. Protest, dissent, and sabotage would be included in the behavioral dimension. Consideration of the full range of complex reactions that stakeholders may have to change programs opens up a more nuanced conversation.

First, we should observe that a given stakeholder's response might not necessarily be consistent across these dimensions (feelings can contradict logic); consistent over time; or driven by a single source. Response to change is far more fluid than some of the practice literature would have us believe. It is easier to think of individuals as "for us" or "against us," or to think of stakeholders in groups of "good guys" or "bad guys." It is also easy for some of us to champion the cause of the weak and less powerful as somehow more inherently correct and wise. None of this sort of stereotyping is likely to help us to understand change processes very well.

As we discuss forms and function of resistance in this chapter, I will be presenting a view that resistance can serve many masters; can both increase and decrease effectiveness of change as judged from different stakeholder perspectives; and should be regarded as potential energy in any change effort. As Maurer (1996) observes, "the energy of resistance can be a powerful and frightening force" (p. 25). Energy in a change effort is absolutely necessary. It is an affirmative action to make change. Doing nothing cannot usually bring about change – except perhaps in the case of aging. However, even survival (of a human being or an organization) requires affirmative action. Ford, Ford, and D'Amelio (2008) argue in a similar vein that resistance can keep a change "in play" and in the conversation. "If people want a change to die … they would be better off not talking about it than engaging in existence-giving 'resistance' communications that provide energy and further its translation and diffusion" (p. 368).

Forms of Resistance

We can array the ideas related to resistance in many different ways, but for simplicity's sake we discuss them here in terms of subtle and more forceful versions of resistance. This should not be considered as

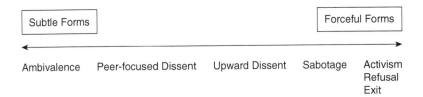

Figure 6.1   Forms of resistance

a stand-in for degrees of effectiveness, but rather a convenient description of intensity from an observer's point of view.

At the subtle end of the continuum (see Figure 6.1) are those reactions that some managers describe as resistant but that others have referred to as "ambivalence" (Larson and Tompkins, 2005; Piderit, 2000) or "reluctance" (Watson, 1982). A masters student, Jessica Castles (unpublished), in my organizational change seminar developed the following definition of resistance with this idea in mind, "a state of hesitation in which stakeholders are reluctant to fully embrace a change effort due to legitimate concerns about the potential consequences of its application" (p. 5). Castles points to the arguments of Dent and Goldberg (1989) in explaining that people do not resist change per se, rather they resist the negative consequences that could potentially accompany that change such as uncertainty, fear, loss of status or power, and/or personal harm. The phase of contemplation of those possible consequences is no doubt marked by ambivalence for many stakeholders.

It is also possible that ambivalence stems from a struggle between two or more desirable, yet contradictory alternatives. In the JAR case introduced earlier in the chapter, the JAR managers attempted to introduce a change from one philosophy of organizing (based on excellence) to another (based on expedience).

> Many managers still identified strongly with the old value system at the same time they were convincing themselves and others of the need to change that value system. As they struggled to reconcile these two discursive identities, they communicated in ways that reflected this ambivalence. (Larson and Tompkins, 2005, p. 11)

Piderit (2000) also reminds us that the three dimensions of our reactions to change (cognitive, emotional, behavioral) need not be complementary at any given point in time. For example, our feelings and beliefs may contradict one another. We may have very negative feelings about a layoff but believe it is necessary for the organization's survival. Piderit also argues that even contradiction within one of these three dimensions is possible. Contradictions such as those that Piderit points out can result in ambivalent responses along the dimensions of beliefs ("this is partly a good idea, but I'm not sure I believe it will work"), emotion ("I think this is exciting, but I'm fearful of the risk we are taking"), and behavioral intentions ("I'm planning to cooperate, but I'm not sure I'm going to be enthusiastic about it at first"). Piderit argues that most employees (and one might argue the same is true about other stakeholders) will experience some ambivalence during any change.

I have a hard time considering these reactions as "resistant" in the sense that most managers mean it. Lack of enthusiastic support seems different to me than pushing back. Suggesting that absence of immediate support is somehow indicative of a problem implies that stakeholders should not individually think about change or should not attempt to anticipate possible threats, downsides or concerns. As much is suggested in the classic management advice book *Who Moved My Cheese?* (Johnson, 1998) where the mice are praised for not "overanalyzing" as the Littlepeople are prone to do (see Highlight Box 6.3).[1] This attitude that stakeholders (usually seen in this context as employees) should not think about change initiatives seems to me to be incredibly odd. I have no idea how an organization could think it might benefit from discouraging critical thinking among its stakeholders – especially its own employees!

The lesson of *Who Moved My Cheese?* seems to be spelled out in part in the book's foreword by Kenneth Blanchard, "while in the past we may have wanted loyal employees, today we need flexible people who are not possessive about 'the way things are done around here.'" As he praises the exceptional book as being transformative for those who read it and embrace its principles, he argues that men would be better off to do "simple things that work" when it comes to change. He adds that even if some change is not good or is unnecessary it is "to our advantage to learn how to adapt and enjoy something better" (p. 18). Read: Leave the thinking to someone else!

In a discussion by readers of the book in the last section of *Who Moved My Cheese?* working professionals discuss some attempts to resist change in their own organizations. Jessica reports that what she got from the story is that change is so commonplace that she'd be better off to just adjust to it quickly. She recalls a story of a time that her fellow workers and she resisted a change (to reduce sales force by

Highlight Box 6.3: Mice Don't Overanalyze Change

Sometimes they [the Littlepeople] did well, but at other times their powerful human beliefs and emotions took over and clouded the way they looked at things ...

One morning [the mice] arrived at Cheese Station C and discovered there was no cheese.

They weren't surprised. Since Sniff and Scurry had noticed the supply of cheese had been getting smaller every day, they were prepared for the inevitable and knew instinctively what to do ... the mice did not overanalyze things ... The situation and Cheese Station C had changed. So Sniff and Surry decided to change.

Later that same day, Hem and Haw [Littlepeople] arrived ... They had not been paying attention to the small changes that had been taking place each day, so they took it for granted their cheese would be there ... "What! No Cheese?" Hem yelled. He continued yelling, "No cheese? No Cheese?" as though if he shouted loud enough someone would put it back.

"Who moved my Cheese?" he hollered.

Finally, he put his hands on his hips, his face turned red, and he screamed at the top of his voice, "It's not fair!"

Haw [Littleperson] just shook his head in disbelief. He, too, had counted on finding cheese at Cheese Station C. He stood there for a long time, frozen with shock. He was just not ready for this.

... While Sniff and Scurry had quickly moved on, Hem and Haw continued to hem and haw.

They ranted and raved at the injustice of it all. Haw started to get depressed.

Source: Johnson (1998), pp. 27–35.

selling digitally), "because we believed then that the backbone of our business was our large sales force, who called on people door-to-door. Keeping our sales force depended on the big commissions they earned from the high price of our product. We had been doing this successfully for a long time and thought it would go on forever" (p. 82). Laura chimed in with "maybe that's what it meant in the story about Hem and Haw's arrogance of success. They didn't notice they needed to change what had once been working" (p. 82).

Thus, the reader is left with the impression that those who resist new ideas based on successful experience with longstanding practice are "arrogant" and that they should be quick to move on when cued to do so (presumably by management). They should do this despite anticipated costs (in this case the apparent layoffs of a large sales force). The discussion goes on to characterize the "Hems" in their own organizations as "too comfortable or too afraid to change" (p. 86). Further, those who didn't change were "let go." Others offered that, "The good news is that while our Haws were initially hesitant, they were open-minded enough to learn something new, act differently and adapt in time to help us succeed" (p. 86). None of the stories shared in this final discussion in the book point to examples where the change was discovered to be wrong-headed or that a reluctant Hem or Haw turned out to be right in resisting the change effort.

There is a scary, "drink the Kool-Aid" sort of message in this book's discussion. As Angela describes identifying with Hem, "I'm a little bit like Hem, so for me, the most powerful part of the story was when Haw laughed at his fear and went on to paint a picture in his mind where he saw himself enjoying 'New Cheese.' It made going into the Maze less fearful and more enjoyable. And he eventually got a better deal. That's what I want to do more often" (p. 87).

The book provides us with a lens by which anything short of immediate and absolute enthusiasm and compliance can be viewed as dysfunctional "resistant" behavior by many in management. Further, the book, promoted as a tool to get your employees in the right mindset for change (by asking them all to read it and emulate the mice), sends a message that stopping to consider the wisdom of a proposed or introduced change is tantamount to resistance. And, that, the author implies, is bad.

Aside from initial or long-term ambivalence or reluctance – depicted by Hem and Haw in the cheese book – other "resistant" reactions to change can be characterized as complaining, cynicism, and pointed humor. Contu (2008) describes these types of reactions as decaf resistance. "**Decaf resistance** just as decaf coffee, makes it possible for us to enjoy without the costs and risks involved. We can have the thing (coffee) without actually having it" (p. 374). So, in these forms of resistance the individuals involved do not really challenge the power structure or practices head on. They don't run the risks associated with a frontal attack. Contu and others (Fleming, 2005; Fleming and Spicer, 2008; Mumby, 2005) argue that "decaf" resistance strategies permit the resistor to express they are not "buying into the dominant ideology" through these disobedient and irreverent behaviors, but also underscore the power of those ideologies because the resistors do ultimately submit to them. That is, they make noise without really changing anything.

My children sometimes use sarcasm in response to an order from mom or dad. They sometimes roll their eyes. I'm sure they'll get to an age where they will find witty ways to parody their parents (okay, they already do a fairly good impression of both of us!). All of these reactions to our parental control are a form of "decaf resistance." They offer the kids a way to vent, to provide a voice that questions our rules or rulings on certain issues. However, they avoid a form of resistance (e.g., running away from home, absolute refusal to comply) that might completely alter family relationships or the power structure between parent and child. In focusing on the "decaf" strategies my kids embrace a form of voice without running the risks of the "real" resistance – fundamentally changing our family structure. A similar process can be seen in stakeholders of organizational change. Further, scholars are paying more attention to these forms of resistance in observing that they can lead to important consequences.

Another way to refer to this kind of resistance is **peer-focused dissent**. Such efforts are directed at co-workers, family, and other stakeholders in informal and sometimes anonymous settings such as underground publications including websites, cartoons, newsletters, and zines. Gossett and Kilker (2006) claim that dissent scholars have largely dismissed peer-focused dissent because they deem it to be unproductive in terms of reaching audiences (supervisors, management, owners) who can activate real change in the organization. Gossett and Kilker argue that individuals may turn to peer-focused dissent when they are concerned about negative repercussions of dissent focused on decision-makers. Such risks might include damage to important relationships, being labeled a trouble-maker, or suffering retaliation, not to mention the possibility of being ignored or failing to successfully alter the change effort.

In their study, these authors examined the resistance messages posted on the RadioShackSucks.com website. This website was created as a place where disgruntled Radio Shack customers, employees, and ex-employees could vent, complain, and eventually organize against Radio Shack. Despite attempts by the corporation to silence the website (including legal action arguing that the site constituted "corporate sabotage"), it has continued with only short-term interruption for several years. The content analysis provided by Gossett and Kilker found that

34% of the coded data were "job-related information and rumors" and 27% were "work-related gripes and complaints." Most relevant to the topic of change, the study found that one type of "complaint" concerned criticism of the ethics or logic of specific company policies. In a post about the company's staffing policy:

> With the current turnover rate of both new and veteran managers (at least in my old district), they no longer have to pay their "higher" wages and salaries. They just bring in some newbie who will do the same work for lower pay ... AND they convince these rookie managers to work anywhere from 60–80 hours a week, and when they burn themselves out, district just brings in a new rookie. (Gossett and Kilker, 2006, p. 74)

These authors draw the conclusion that the posts on this website are not just misdirected complaints that should be addressed towards management directly. Rather, they argue that "the lack of member dissent within official organizational channels may not be indicative of a disengaged workforce but rather evidence of a system that denies its members safe, easy, and effective ways to make their voices heard" (p. 75).

A substantial portion (25%) of the postings on this site concerned strategizing more overt individual and collective acts of resistance. Part of this discourse concerned discussions of the pros and cons of leaving the organization; fantasy discussions of how to sabotage the organization; and interaction about a class action suit alleging that the company intentionally misclassified salespeople as managers to avoid paying overtime. Seemingly as a result of the promotion of the suit on this website, a high percentage (50% compared to 10–20% of other similar suits) of eligible employees signed on to it.

The result of the peer-focused dissent, at least in the Radio Shack case, certainly is suggestive of the potential of social networking to increase the power of sets of stakeholders. As we noted earlier in this chapter, building networks and strong cohesive groups can advantage individuals who wish to wield power in organizations. As Gossett and Kilker note, "without the social network formed by RadioShackSucks. com, it seems doubtful that more than 3,200 geographically dispersed employees would have come together quickly enough to take advantage of this $100 million dollar class action suit" (p. 79). Thus, peer-focused dissent can sometimes result in a more forceful form of resistance. The lack of productive upward channels to harness, address, and perhaps even embrace the feedback of stakeholders appears to run the risk of prompting a more forceful form of resistance.

Upward dissent can be represented on Figure 6.1 further down the scale toward forceful resistance. In these actions, stakeholders attempt to influence those who can make a difference in the organization. The scholarship of Jeffrey Kassing (Kassing, 2002, 2005, 2006, 2009) and Johny Garner (Garner 2009a, 2009b; Garner and Wargo, 2009) and others have investigated triggering events, types of strategies, frequency of use, and characteristics of dissenters and contexts of dissent. Garner (2009a) has found that employees self-report higher frequency use of direct factual appeals (providing information, expertise, appeals to logic), coalitions (getting assistance from the audience, recruitment attempts, asking if others feel the same), inspiration (appeal to values or morals), and solution presentation (providing a realistic solution). In a study of multiple attempts at upward dissent, Kassing's (2009) subjects self-reported higher frequency of direct factual appeals and solution presentation. They also reported that as dissent was repeated over time, there was increased likelihood to use more face-threatening appeals of circumvention (i.e., going around supervisor to speak to someone higher in the chain of command) and threatening resignation.

The dissent literature has found a number of triggers and goals for dissenting. Kassing (2009) notes that triggers of employee expressions of dissent include climate (e.g., workplace freedom of speech), individual characteristics (personality, argumentativeness, verbal aggressiveness), relational issues (e.g., quality of superior–subordinate relationship, management treatment of co-workers), and organizational factors (organizational role, tenure).

Also, in an interesting study by Garner (2009b) seven primary goals (providing guidance, getting advice, obtaining information, changing the audience's opinion, changing the audience's behavior, gaining assistance, and seeking emotional support) were tested to determine the frequency and corresponding strategies employed. Using a self-report methodology, Garner learned that the most frequently reported primary goals of dissent communication were obtaining information and getting advice on how to deal with a dissatisfying circumstance. Although these data may reflect selective memory (in that subjects were asked to recall a time when you "complained about a dissatisfying circumstance at work involving a policy or supervisor") or socially desirable responses (e.g., subjects may have been hesitant to report attempts to seek audience opinion change or presuming to give guidance), they suggest that dissent may be considered, in part, a sensemaking and/or social support mechanism as much as an effort to change the course of an organization's actions/policies/plans.

Less of the dissent literature has attended to non-employee stakeholders. An exception is the study by Garner and Wargo (2009) that examined the comparative perceptions of church leaders and parishioners in terms of how dissent was communicated. They found that leaders reported that church members were informal and indirect in expressing dissent. An example is the use of **"lateral dissent"** – wherein a member would express dissent to someone other than the leader in hopes it would get relayed to the leader. However, members reported expressing dissent directly to their leaders. The different perceptions may suggest that leaders misperceive some feedback if it is too subtle as dissent – such as the tactic of complimenting a practice as a way of indicating it has been unacceptably absent other times (e.g., "I liked how many hymns we sang today").

For another example of non-employee dissent, Coca-Cola's introduction of thermometer-loaded vending machines (Fast Company, 2009) serves us here. In 1999, Coca-Cola executives decided to introduce vending machines that charged more on hot days (and less on cold ones). Customers, predictably, were outraged by the innovation. After expression of dissent by consumers and negative press coverage by newspapers, Coca-Cola pulled the machines.

In perhaps the most forceful version of resistance, stakeholders move to actions that deliberately forestall or sabotage change efforts. Sabotage can take the form of "clandestine activities" (Real and Putnam, 2005) such as petty thefts, horseplay, and carelessness; acts designed to slow down or slowly kill off a change initiative by neglect (e.g., absenteeism at training or work, feigning ignorance about new procedures, restricting output to produce evidence of change failure); to more overt acts such as walkouts, strikes, lawsuit, or even workplace violence.

Harris and Ogbonna (2006) note that sabotage costs US firms up to $200 billion annually. Further, they suggest that service sabotage – organizational members' behaviors that are intentionally designed negatively to affect service – is likely to be especially problematic. Their research found that employee characteristics (e.g., risk-taking proclivity, need for social approval by work colleagues) are associated with sabotage behavior. Given their finding that sabotage is related to the personalities of employees, these authors draw the conclusion that HR professionals and supervisors should screen for such characteristics when recruiting and hiring employees. To my mind, this is a troubling conclusion in that if we start screening out certain personalities from our organizations – especially those with more critical and /or analytical tendencies – I worry about both the ethical and practical results. The following discussion of dispositional resistance assessment further develops this point.

Dispositional Resistance

A pocket of research has focused on identifying personality character-istics of change resistors. The work of Shaul Oreg (2003, 2006) has focused on isolating **dispositional resistance** – "an individual's ten-dency to resist or avoid making changes, to devalue change generally, and to find change aversive across diverse contexts and types of change" (Oreg, 2003, p. 680). Oreg's (2003) development of a measure of a "Resistance to Change Scale" that assesses the dispositional tendency to be change-averse, is based on a characterization of "resistance" as rooted in several ideas from the resistance literature: reluctance to lose control; cognitive rigidity; lack of psychological resilience; intolerance to the adjustment period involved in change; preference for low levels of stimulation and novelty; and reluctance to give up old habits.

Although I can certainly imagine a person with this profile being more likely to resist (or at least not prefer) change, I could also imagine a very different profile for someone who demonstrates resistance as dis-cussed so far in this chapter. For example, a person who is cautious; analytical; has high value for consistency, stability, and routine; who is inclined towards discernment; has high standards of evidence-based decision-making; has high self-esteem (and thereby trusts his/her own judgment) and independence; and strong commitments to organiza-tional, moral or professional ethics might not score high on Oreg's scale but might also be inclined to be a "resistor" in the sense we have been discussing here.

It seems Oreg's resistor would be of the type typically regarded by management as a menace to change efforts (reluctant, fearful, unneces-sarily worried, unhappy with the concept of change), whereas my por-trait might describe a resistor who could be engaged in careful, thoughtful, principled consideration of the pros and cons of a change effort, desiring to be convinced and unwilling to merely go along just because someone suggested change was necessary or beneficial.

Oreg's scale has shown validity and has been predictive in the case of imposed change (that the stakeholder had no choice about) of some measures of affective reactions to change (e.g., "I'm worried about what things the change will be like after the move," "This whole move makes me kind of angry") and functioning at work during change (e.g., "Due to the move I tend to be very distracted these days," "I find that I'm not as efficient or productive as usual these days"). Oreg (2003) has not measured behavioral resistance in terms of cynicism, dissent, or sabotage as an outcome of dispositional resistance so we do not yet know if this scale is useful in predicting the sort of resistance responses that we have been discussing in this chapter. However, even if it is predictive of those responses, I think it tells only one part of the picture of those who are inclined to be more negatively oriented towards any given change. By focusing too much on isolating a personality type that is generally disdainful of change, we run the risk of dismissing valid concerns, useful input, and thoughtful assessment of change efforts that may come from some of our most valuable stakeholders – those who put their energies towards critically analyzing organizational decision-making and actions. Also, if we quickly move from identifying resistors as types, to dismissing all complaints as rooted in fundamental personality flaws, we disallow for responsibility to be appropriately placed on the way that implementation efforts proceed and for the quality of change initiatives to be key factors in explaining resistance and/or failure.

Value of Resistance

The term **Principled Dissent** (Graham, 1986) – expression of dissatisfaction for reasons of justice, honesty, or organizational benefit – is used to describe the sort of ethically based dissent that few ascribe to resistors of change efforts. This sort of dissent brings with it potential benefit to organizations and to change efforts that are driven by a sincere interest in those outcomes. However, we also need to recognize that any form of resistance, even that which is motivated by self or group interests, may lead to a beneficial conclusion of a change effort from one or more perspectives.

Resistance in its varied forms in the context of organizational change serves a variety of functions. First, as Maurer (1996) argues, it brings energy to the change initiative. Minds are on the change; flaws are more likely to be discovered; faulty assumptions more likely exposed; and implications spelled out. It serves as "necessary safeguard" (Garner and Wargo, 2009) against self-delusion and groupthink. Other positive consequences of the nurturing of upward dissent and participation in general include increased commitment, trust, perceptions of fairness, and willingness to be cooperative in change efforts. Many of these

Highlight Box 6.4: Moving Cheese Might Require Thoughtful Consideration

"Leaders CAN make the wrong decisions, and sometimes only vigilance by 'everyday' workers can prevent increased costs to the organization by stopping ill-considered change before it occurs."

"The message I got: Be a nice little lemming and jump off the cliff with the rest of the wonderful little rodents who follow our leaders blindly until they take mercy on you and let you drown."

"But, in the context of someone making profit or gaining power by change, this book is dangerous. Unquestioning acceptance of change encourages unethical behavior on the part of those who orchestrate change. It could even be argued that it is unethical to encourage blind acceptance of such changes. One only needs to look at history or read the news to see this pattern emerge. Enron comes to mind. So do most political dictatorships."

"Any company that subjects their employees to this dribble [sic] (plus the dreaded group activities that go with it) is too concerned with weak trends and not concerned enough about encouraging independent and intelligent thought among their employees."

"Change is obviously inevitable, but this book completely ignores your ability to affect change yourself. It is always the 'other' moving the cheese instead of moving the cheese yourself. Self-will and determination are completely thrown out the window. It also completely discounts the capability of thinking about the situation to effect positive results; only unthinking reaction is held up for praise."

"While I agree with the general premise that it often works better to embrace change rather than fight it, I found the book to be rather pretentious and condescending. While I agree that simply whining and complaining will do no good, it is true that unthinking acceptance is equally dangerous."

potential positives were discussed in Chapter 2 when we addressed the literature on soliciting input during change.

We can illustrate the practice of principled dissent or resistance put to use in the story of Facebook. In a 2010 article in *Fast Company* about the world's 50 most innovative companies, Facebook is listed as number

1. In the article the culture at Facebook is described as definitely innovative. Mark Zuckerberg, Founder and CEO, makes the point that fear of failure is what drives most companies but not at Facebook, "A lot of companies are set up so that people judge each other on failure. But I'm not going to get fired if I have a bad year. Or a bad five years ... I don't worry about making things look good if they're actually not." This philosophy is clearly instilled in the Facebook culture, where having a good "fight" about the pros/cons of a new idea is a prized norm. "The sparring – which takes place at meetings, in prototype demos, and in constant online conversations, and often gets mischaracterized as staff revolt – focuses routinely on the small issues ... But the big picture stuff also looms large."

Employees understand the potential value of their own front-line experience and contributions during change and recognize the problems with ignoring or downplaying the value of upward dissent. This is revealed in the comments made by some Amazon.com customer reviewers of the book *Who Moved My Cheese?* (see Highlight Box 6.4).

Conclusion

In summary, this chapter has provided an overview of perspectives on power and resistance in organizations broadly and as they apply in the context of organizational change. This chapter has mostly dealt with the resistance of stakeholders (mostly employees in workplaces) towards manager/implementer ideas or change programs. Chapter 8 will further discuss alternative targets of resistance and the emergence of resistance as an outgrowth of social sensemaking and social influence processes among stakeholders.

My perspective on resistance presented in this chapter argues that actions stakeholders take to push back on change efforts are likely born of multiple sources: distaste for change; value of stability and staying the course of what has worked; objections or concerns about a particular change initiative; self-interested objections to change; ambivalence towards a change based on unfinished or conflicting analysis of its implications among others.

In this perspective it is unproductive and misleading to label as "resistance" any reaction of a stakeholder other than quick and complete acceptance and enthusiasm. Further, thinking of resistance as energy in change initiatives is more than putting a happy face on a problematic set of responses. Such a perspective allows us to see potential benefit in the time, focus, and attention put towards a change. At least for those who are ambivalent, practicing principled dissent, and even some who represent powerful (or latently powerful) stakeholder groups, this energy might result in improvements to the change effort if marshaled effectively. Further, it is likely from the evidence on dissent that the absence of upward channels for participating, providing input, and empowerment to engage with decision-makers is as much a cause of change resistance as anything. If input solicitations are sincere, open, and embraced by decision-makers as a resource, much of what is usually called "resistance" might be reframed and repurposed as input for improvement.

Note

1. *Who Moved My Cheese?* is praised as effective by Peter Drucker Management Center and by executives at Whirlpool Corporation, Aeronautical Science Center at Patterson AFB, Rochester Institute of Technology, Merrill Lynch International, Eastman Kodak, and Xerox Corporation. Based on the Amazon. com customer reviews, customers either loved it or hated it (791 reviews showing 4 or 5 stars, 576 showing 1 or 2 stars, with only 150 showing 3 stars).

References

Argyris, C. (2000) *Flawed Advice and the Management Trap: How Managers Can Know When They're Getting Good Advice and When They're Not.* New York: Oxford University Press.

Boonstra, J. J. and Gravenhorst, K. M. B. (1998) Power dynamics and organizational change: A comparison of perspectives. *European Journal of Work and Organizational Psychology*, 7 (2), 97–120.

Castles, J. (unpublished) Reframing resistance to change.

Contu, A. (2008) Decaf resistance: On misbehavior, cynicism, and desire in liberal workplaces. *Management Communication Quarterly*, 21 (3), 364–379.

Cooney, R. and Sewell, G. (2008) Shaping the other: Maintaining expert managerial status in a complex change management program. *Group* and *Organization Management*, 33 (6), 685–711.

Deetz, S. (2005) Critical theory. In S. May and D. K. Mumby (eds.), *Engaging Organizational Communication Theory and Research: Multiple Perspectives*. Thousand Oaks, CA: Sage.

Deetz, S. (2008) Resistance: Would struggle by any other name be as sweet? *Management Communication Quarterly*, 21 (3), 387–392.

Dent, E. B. and Goldberg, S. G. (1989) Challenging "resistance to change." *Journal of Applied Behavioral Sciences*, 35 (1), 25–41.

Emerson, R. M. (1962) Power-dependence relations. *American Sociological Review*, 27 (Feb), 31–40.

Fairhurst, G. (2011) *The Power of Framing: Creating the Language of Leadership*. San Francisco, CA: Jossey-Bass.

Fast Company (March 2010) The world's 50 most innovative companies.

Fleming, P. (2005) Metaphors of resistance. *Management Communication Quarterly*, 19 (1), 45–66.

Fleming, P. and Spicer, A. (2008) Beyond power and resistance: New approaches to organizational politics. *Management Communication Quarterly*, 21 (3), 301–309.

Ford, J. D., Ford L. W., and D'Amelio, A. (2008) Resistance to change: The rest of the story. *Academy of Management Review*, 33 (2), 362–377.

Foucault, M. (1984) *The Foucault Reader* (P. R. Rabinow, ed.). New York: Pantheon.

Foucault, M. (1995) *Discipline and Punish*. New York: Vintage/Random House.

French, J. R. P. and Raven, B. H. (1959) The bases of social power. In D. Courtwright (ed.), *Studies of Social Power*. Ann Arbor, MI: Institute for Social Research.

Garner, J. T. (2009a) When things go wrong at work: An exploration of organizational dissent messages. *Communication Studies*, 60 (2), 197–218.

Garner, J. T. (2009b) Strategic dissent: Expressions of organizational dissent motivated by influence goals. *International Journal of Strategic Communication*, 3, 34–51.

Garner, J. T. and Wargo, M. R. (2009) Feedback from the pew: A dual-perspective exploration of organizational dissent in churches. *Journal of Communication and Religion*, 32 (2), 375–400.

Gephart, R. P. (1984) Making sense of organizationally based environmental disasters. *Journal of Management*, 10 (2), 205–225.

Gephart, R. P. (1988) Managing the meaning of a sour gas well blowout: The public culture of organizational disasters. *Industrial Crisis Quarterly*, 2 (1), 17–32.

Gephart, R. P. (1992) Sensemaking, communicative distortion and the logic of public inquiry. *Industrial Crisis Quarterly*, 6 (2), 115–135.

Gephart, R. P., Steier, L., and Lawrence, T. (1990) Cultural rationalities in crisis sense-making: A study of public inquiry into a major industrial accident. *Industrial Crisis Quarterly*, 4 (1), 27–48.

Gossett, L. and Kilker, J. (2006) My job sucks: Examining counterinstitutional web sites as locations for organizational member voice, dissent, and resistance. *Management Communication Quarterly*, 20 (1), 63–90.

Graham, J. W. (1986) Principled organizational dissent: A theoretical essay. In B. M. Staw and L. L. Cummings (eds.), *Research in Organizational Behavior* (Vol. 8, pp. 1–52). Greenwich, CT: JAI.

Harris, L. C. and Ogbonna, E. (2006) Service sabotage: A study of antecedents and consequences. *Journal of the Academy of Marketing Science*, 34 (4), 543–558.

Johnson, S. (1998) *Who Moved My Cheese?* New York: Penguin Putnam Inc.

Kassing, J. W. (2002) Speaking up: Identifying employees' upward dissent strategies. *Management Communication Quarterly*, 16, 187–209.

Kassing J. W. (2005) Speaking up competently: A comparison of perceived competence in upward dissent strategies. *Communication Research Reports*, 22, 227–234.

Kassing, J. W. (2006) Employees' expressions of upward dissent as a function of current and past work experiences. *Communication Reports*, 19, 79–88.

Kassing, J. W. (2009) "In case you didn't hear me the first time": An examination of repetitious upward dissent. *Management Communication Quarterly*, 22 (3), 416–436.

Kunda, G. (1992) *Engineering Culture: Control and Commitment in a High-tech Corporation*. Philadelphia: Temple University Press.

Larson, G. S. and Tompkins, P. K. (2005) Ambivalence and resistance: A study of management in a concertive control system. *Communication Monographs*, 72 (1), 1–21.

Lines, R. (2007) Using power to install strategy: The relationships between expert power, position power, influence tactics and implementation success. *Journal of Change Management*, 7 (2), 143–170.

Lukes, S. (1974) *Power: A Radical View*. London: Macmillan.

Maurer, R. (1996) *Beyond the Wall of Resistance*. Austin, TX: Bard Books.

Mintzberg, H. (1983) *Power in and Around Organizations*. Englewood Cliffs, NJ: Prentice-Hall.

Mumby, D. K. (2001) Power and politics. In F. M. Jablin and L. L. Putnam (eds.), *The New Handbook of Organizational Communication: Advances in Theory, Research, and Methods* (pp. 585–623). Thousand Oaks, CA: Sage.

Mumby, D. K. (2005) Theorizing resistance in organizations studies: A dialectical approach. *Management Communication Quarterly*, 19 (1), 19–44.

Oreg, S. (2003) Resistance to change: Developing an individual differences measure. *Journal of Applied Psychology*, 88 (4), 680–693.

Oreg, S. (2006) Personality, context, and resistance to organizational change. *European Journal of Work and Organizational Psychology*, 15 (1), 73–101.

Pfeffer, J. (1981) *Power in Organizations*. Marshfield, MA: Pitman.

Pfeffer, J. and Salancik, G. (1978) *The External Control of Organizations: A Resource Dependence Perspective*. New York: Harper and Row.

Piderit, S. K. (2000) Rethinking resistance and recognizing ambivalence: A multidimensional view of attitudes toward an organizational change. *Academy of Management Review*, 24 (4), 783–794.

Putnam, L. L., Grant, D., Michelson, G., and Cutcher, L. (2005) Discourse and resistance: Targets, practices, and consequences. *Management Communication Quarterly*, 19 (1), 5–18.

Real, K. and Putnam, L. (2005) Ironies in the discursive struggle of pilots defending the profession. *Management Communication Quarterly*, 19 (1), 91–119.

Ruben, B. D., Lewis, L., and Sandmeyer, L. (2008) *Assessing the Impact of the Spellings Commission: The Message, the Messenger, and the Dynamics of Change in Higher Education*. Washington, DC: National Association of College and University Business Officers.

Scott, W. R. (1987) *Organizations: Rational, Natural and Open Systems* (2nd edn.). Englewood Cliffs, NJ: Prentice-Hall, Inc.

Scott, C. R., Lewis, L. K., Davis, J. D., and D'Urso, S. C. (2009) Finding a home for communication technologies. In J. Keyton and P. Shockley-Zalabak (eds.), *Case Studies for Organizational Communication: Understanding Communication Processes* (2nd edn.). Los Angeles, CA: Roxbury.

Watson, T. J. (1982) Group ideologies and organizational change. *Journal of Management Studies*, 19, 259–275.

Yukl, G. (1994) *Leadership in Organizations* (3rd edn.). Englewood Cliffs, NJ: Prentice-Hall.

Zorn, T. E., Page, D. J., and Cheney, G. (2000) NUTS about change: Multiple perspectives on change-oriented communication in a public sector organization. *Management Communication Quarterly*, 13 (4), 515–566.

Further Reading

Ainsworth, S., Hardy, C., and Harley, B. (2005) Online consultation: E-democracy and e-resistance in the case of the development gateway. *Management Communication Quarterly*, 19 (1), 120–145.

Zoller, H. M. and Fairhurst, G. (2007) Resistance leadership: The overlooked potential in critical organization and leadership studies. *Human Relations*, 60 (9), 1331–1360.

7

Antecedents to Strategies, Assessments, and Interactions

Every action must be due to one or the other of seven causes: chance, nature, compulsion, habit, reasoning, anger, or appetite

Aristotle

Habits are at first cobwebs; at last, chains

Unknown

We are half ruined by conformity, but we should be wholly ruined without it

Charles Dudley Warner

Pressures, constraints, habits, mimicry, norms, goals, values, and situational analyses all play important roles in triggering initial and ongoing communication choices, interactions, and assessments of various communicators during change. This chapter explores antecedents to strategies, assessments, and interactions during change. Communication

Organizational Change: Creating Change Through Strategic Communication,
First Edition. Laurie K. Lewis.
© 2011 Laurie K. Lewis. Published 2011 by Blackwell Publishing Ltd.

scholars have conducted a good deal of research into factors that predict individuals' choices of communication approaches (David and Baker, 1994; Hellweg, Geist, Jorgensen, and White-Mills, 1990; Morrison, 2002), messages (Greene, 1997; O'Keefe, 1988), and media (Daft and Lengel, 1986; Timmerman, 2003; Timmerman and Madhavapeddi, 2008). Explanations for choices include individual difference characteristics, e.g., gender, cultural background, communication apprehension (cf. Cai, Wilson, and Drake, 2000; Drake, 2001; Oetzel and Ting-Toomey, 2003), communication styles (cf. Ting-Toomey, Oetzel, and Yee-Jung, 2001; Weider-Hatfield and Hatfield, 1995; Wheeless and Reichel, 1990), emphasis on various communication goals (cf. Brown and Levinson, 1978; Kellerman 2004; Lakey and Canary, 2002), and the impact of social influence on communication choices (cf. Fulk, Schmitz, and Steinfeld, 1990) among other explanations. Additionally, some research (Kellerman, 1992; Timmerman, 2002) has focused on **mindlessness** – where instead of processing new information, people behave without thinking about their actions – and communication that is conditioned by scripts that permit us to repeat patterns of interaction without much cognitive processing. For example, a person familiar with dining out in restaurants can "mindlessly" go through all the motions of standing in line to be acknowledged by the host/hostess; providing necessary information about size of party and seating preferences (smoking/non-smoking); examine a menu of choices; give a drink order at a short time interval; provide a food selection at a later time, etc. without having to devote much cognitive energy to the pattern of interaction. It is a common "script" most of us know and follow repeatedly. Only in some circumstances of urgency (needing to get through a meal very quickly) or unfamiliar setting (eating at an exotic restaurant with unusual practices) would we have to become "mindful" and depart from the script.

We know less about how implementers select strategies for introducing change. However, organizational scholars (Damanpour, 1991) have found evidence that structural characteristics such as high specialization, functional differentiation, administrative intensity (high proportion of managers), internal and external communication channels, and low centralization are significantly related to both initiation and implementation of change. Further, in my original model of implementation processes (Lewis and Seibold, 1993), my co-author and I argued that the scope, novelty, and complexity of the innovation (change) will influence how implementation activities are carried out. Further, processes that implementers follow are also based on the form of the organization (e.g., its size, complexity, number of layers, degree of connectedness among its parts). These are fairly rational explanations for strategy selection – that is, that I'd pick one method over another because it is necessitated by a logistical concern such as size. However, suggesting that selections of strategy are solely made on a logical analysis of the situation is a limited perspective.

Clearly many factors go into individuals' analysis, selection, and enactment of communication strategies, approaches, tactics, and styles. From broad orientations of a communication strategy (e.g., I'm going to disseminate as much information to as many stakeholders as possible) to specific message designs (e.g., I'll avoid the use of the word "layoffs") communicators make many choices. The point of this chapter is to begin to explore some factors that might have special significance in predicting communicators' strategies, interactions, and assessments in the context of organizational change.

In the Model presented in Chapter 3, three sets of antecedents are depicted: institutional factors; implementers' perceptions of the change context; and stakeholders' perceptions of the change context. We will take each set in turn and discuss how they are especially predictive of communicators' strategy choices as well as influential in how stakeholders' assess each other, develop concerns about change, and initiate interactions with other stakeholders.

Institutional Factors

Communication strategy choices do not come out of thin air. Communicators make choices of strategies to employ towards communicative goals for a variety of reasons. As we just noted, some of these choices are doubtlessly based on individual differences (e.g., gender, personality, cultural background, age). Some choices are constrained by the individual's personal history of success with some strategies (e.g., if threats worked in the past, we may be more likely to use them in the current situation). Some strategies are not feasible for some individuals to pull off in certain situations (e.g., you can't threaten to quit a job you don't have). Further, our communication strategy choices are somewhat constrained by what we deem as appropriate given the audience, the topic, the situation, the history and nature of the relationship, and other organizational and professional norms by which we may abide.

Because organizational communication occurs in complex systems, not merely in the context of dyadic and personal interactions, we must consider how organizational environments might encourage or restrict use of some strategies. **Institutional theory** (Meyer and Rowan, 1977) argues that when components of an organization's formal structure (the ways that organizations do things and arrange leadership, decision-making, and the like) and institutionalized contexts (e.g., industries; professions) become widely accepted, deemed to be necessary or appropriate, then their presence is used as a signal of organizational legitimacy. In short, there are some things one cannot legitimately do in some contexts and there are other things that are expected. Institutional pressures act on organizations to constrain decision-makers' choices of organizational and communication structures and practices. Specifically, institutional theory posits that the three forces of **isomorphism** (a constraining process that gives rise to similarity in organizational form and practice) – mimetic, coercive, and normative – act on organizational agents to compel compliance with similar practices found in the institutionalized field in which they exist. To ignore such forces is to risk delegitimizing (making less acceptable in the eyes of stakeholders in that setting) oneself or one's organization.

Mimetic forces direct implementers to conform to established and well-known routines for implementing change and compel other stakeholders to mimic what they see as successful and common examples used by stakeholders of other change initiatives. Implementers might seek this information from popular press books, consultants, and trade publications. Scholarship is increasingly identifying the isomorphic pressure of popular guru writings and presentations in managerial practice (Clark and Greatbatch, 2004; Furusten, 1999). For example, in a review and content analysis of the popular press literature on communicating organizational change, I found with my colleagues (Lewis, Schmisseur, Stephens, and Weir, 2006) that such literature has "the potential to inspire feelings of confidence and competence in individual managers" (p. 114) when they follow the advice provided. One reason *Who Moved My Cheese?* discussed in Chapter 6, is so popular is that it provides a framework of messages and strategy to introduce change that has been adopted quite widely in corporations. Other stakeholders in change might turn to friends in the profession or family members who have faced change in their own organizations for ideas of how to approach communication strategies. They might emulate strategies that worked in other settings. The popularity of "griping" online on "Sucks. com" sites is an example of mimicry of a forum for protest of unwanted change.

Coercive forces of isomorphism direct communicators away from certain practices (e.g., public humiliation of noncompliant employees, sabotaging a change through acts of theft or damaging equipment) that would be frowned upon by authorities such as unions, legal systems, government oversight agencies, or watchdog groups. Some practices (e.g., formal notification of a change in employment policy or safety regulations) may be mandated by authorities. Coercive pressures typically come with punishment or threat of punishment for violations. For example, introducing some new policies regarding safety procedures in a manufacturing plant requires posting of detailed information in employee workspaces. Similar specifications are made for the alteration of policies concerning hiring, promotion, discrimination, harassment, and the like. Legally such policies need to be communicated in specific ways. Punishment for failure to meet such coercive expectations can range from censure by a high-profile oversight organization, to legal proceedings, to grounds for strike by a union. For individual stakeholders, certain communicative practices (e.g., screaming at your boss, discussing internal proprietary information with external stakeholders) might result in being dismissed or being sanctioned in some other way.

Finally, expectations for appropriate and standard operating procedures are established through professional socialization, training, and industry standards. These are **normative pressures**. The norms for how we introduce change might speak to the language used to discuss change; the level of openness and secrecy; the timing of change announcements; and/or the range of stakeholders informed about a change. Normative pressure often stems from various professional traditions (e.g., human resource, management, government administration, social work). Communicators trained in those professions will learn messages, beliefs, and tools about ways change should be communicated and with what goals. These powerful socializing forces of training, combined with the socialization garnered upon entry into an industry or specific organizational culture, provide a normative force that encourages certain strategy choices (e.g., give everyone a chance to have their say, use polite and constructive tones, withhold negative information) and discourages others (e.g., overt threats, public arguments, permitting rumors to go unanswered). Such normative pressure can work for or against constructive change efforts since some practices that are counter-productive can be well entrenched within standard practice (e.g., giving little notice to those who will be laid off; holding company secrets within small circles; providing few channels for upward dissent).

We must also acknowledge that those stakeholder groups who have a positive value-fit with a change also need to engage with implementers. They may be eager for the change (impatient even); be looking for details of implementation; and may want to participate in making change happen. So, implementers who wish to capitalize on these initial positive reactions need to plan strategies that foster those positive perceptions and leverage them to aid the change process. Further, many stakeholders often will have an initially neutral values-fit with change as they learn more about it and seek to make sense of it with other stakeholders. Messages that target those in this situation are also important. Such stakeholders are often uncertain about the change; are likely targets of persuasion of those who are strongly opposed to the change; and can often provide useful feedback to implementers in terms of how the change is being perceived and the questions that are being raised about it.

Klein and Sorra also point out that the relative power among groups in the organization can affect the degree to which implementers' campaigns (and other actions in support of the change such as setting up rewards and removing obstacles to participation) will succeed. Those in power whose group values do not fit well with the change can make it harder for lower power groups who are supportive of the change to participate. In the converse situation, high power groups with a favorable view of the change can bribe, encourage, or coerce participation of lower power groups who oppose the change. A good example of this is found in the Spellings case (see Case Box 7.1). Boards of colleges and universities, Congress, and state governments were among powerful stakeholders in the Spellings Commission's audience. Support for the recommendations from those stakeholders has made a significant difference in how higher education responds to the Report.

The complexity of the values-fit landscape at the outset of change initiatives may prompt implementers to make strategic choices about how and to whom to present the change. They may, for example, take a more targeted message approach when the values-fit is quite different for several different sets of stakeholders. However, if the values-fit issues are similar for many different groups of stakeholders, taking a blanket message strategy may be more effective.

Further, if we recall our discussions in Chapters 3 and 5 about the interactions among stakeholders and the sharing of counter-arguments with one another, we may also conclude here that part of the assessment of values-fit among stakeholders should concern the likelihood of the

---

Case Box 7.1: Reactions of Powerful Stakeholders

The Spellings Commission Report prompted a variety of reactions from different stakeholders. Boards of colleges and universities throughout the United States had mixed reactions to the Report. Some were generally positive and some disinterested. One interviewee noted, "I think board members who were interested in participating at a national level ... were familiar with it. I'd say they started being very negative, progressed to having a more neutral view, and ultimately have ended up with a favorable perception."

Stakeholders interviewed for this study reported mixed reactions of Congress as well: "I think Congress has been really positive to the Report. They haven't adopted all of its recommendations, but the folks that we work with think they're seeing the right direction ... however others saw a more qualified response from Congress, "You know it's ... interesting. ... you would think from the behaviors that they are actually ... [annoyed], questioning whether the Secretary has the right to push the agenda."

The study also found that state governments tended to view the Report favorably: "several association leaders noted that state governments are very interested in the themes and directions of the Commission's work because they provide a much greater portion of the support for higher education than does the federal government."

Source: Adapted from Ruben, Lewis, and Sandmeyer (2008) (quotes from pp. 53–55).

---

different groups interacting and sharing their own evaluations of the change. Where initially negative stakeholder groups are likely to influence the opinions of other key stakeholder groups, implementers may wish to inoculate those key stakeholders during initial communication campaign messages. Where such contact and lobbying from one sub-group of stakeholders to another is less likely, it may unwise to raise potential objections of other stakeholder groups. However, as discussed in Chapter 5, two-sided messages tend to be viewed as more credible.

Assessing Needs for Consensus Building

Implementers sometimes will assess the degree to which it is important to achieve consensus among stakeholders for change to be a success. In a research study I completed with colleagues Stephanie Hamel and Brian Richardson (Lewis, Hamel, and Richardson, 2001), we found that implementers frequently reported "need for consensus building" as a rationale for use of some communication strategies over others. In that article we define *consensus building* as the "effort put forth to achieve commitment to a course of action implied by a joint decision" (p. 29). Implementers interviewed for our study reported that they were more likely to perceive a need for consensus building when (a) changes were perceived to be controversial and or highly novel, (b) a history of resistance to similar change was present, (c) critical resources (e.g., expertise, money, approval) were controlled by stakeholders other than the implementers, and/or (d) ongoing support and cooperation would be needed to maintain the change. Where one or more of these conditions exist, implementers may take a closer look at the values-fit of key stakeholder groups to ensure that adequate attention is paid to stakeholders whose values may not imply support for the change initiative.

An example of a focused consensus-building strategy is provided in Lewis *et al.*'s (2001) report of one large nonprofit implementer who employed both internal and external communication tools such as sending representatives out to talk to stakeholders, using press releases and the like. Also they tried to give "mom-and-pop" shops a voice by bringing them to Austin to discuss things. The implementer commented:

> There's a lot more consensus building required within the nonprofit sector which can be a detriment to how fast change occurs. It helps to retain trust. ... That's one of my biggest challenges as a manager ... trying to move a process when we need to make change occur quickly in an environment where people want their say and want their stakes [recognized]. (pp. 19–20)

Assessing Needs for Efficiency

In the same study, my colleagues and I found that implementers sometimes felt the need for communication strategies to be efficient.

We defined communication *efficiency* as "the accomplishment of a communicative task with a minimum expenditure of time, effort, and resources" (p. 28). Implementers we interviewed reported they were more likely to perceive a need for efficiency when (a) the organization's available channels for communication were very limited in number and/or in information-carrying capacity, (b) there was an urgent need to progress through the change process and little time for interaction, and (c) resources devoted to the change were scarce and few could be devoted to the communication tasks involved with implementation. One example is provided in our research from a large national nonprofit, "During a change, I communicate with the minimum number of people, key people, and give them enough information to meet their needs" (p. 23). In fact in one study (Lewis, Richardson, and Hamel, 2003) my colleagues and I found that the vast majority of implementers followed a rule of "quid pro quo" in which high resource-holding stakeholders were given the "lion's share" of the communicative attention during change. That is, high resource-holders were given higher frequency of contact and earlier contact by implementers. However, evidence suggested that these implementers were no more successful in change efforts than those who were did not observe this pattern. This suggests that perhaps singling out some stakeholders merely for efficiency reasons may not advantage the change effort.

Although these data were collected in small to mid-sized nonprofits, we might expect strikingly similar concerns even in larger or more complex organizations. Although larger organizations typically have more resources for communicating (e.g., multiple channels) they also are more likely to have multiple change (and other) initiatives occurring simultaneously. It is likely to be more challenging to garner stakeholders' attention around any given topic for long. Also, in for-profit settings, we are likely to see a competition-driven urgency in getting changes up and running more quickly.

As discussed in Chapter 5, efficiency may be one reason that an implementer may adopt a communication strategy. Implementers may find it easier and more straightforward, for example, to design only a single mass message, delivered in a single setting (e.g., organization-wide meeting; newsletter; memo to all staff) or to isolate only a handful of truly key stakeholders for purposes of discussing the change. Further, they may see advantages to interacting with all stakeholders simultaneously and with the same message to avoid complaints that some stakeholders were favored with inside information.

Assessing Individual and Organizational Change History and Readiness

People and organizations have histories related to change. Histories may have been rife with a series of changes or absent change; scattered with both positive and negative experiences with change; or dominated by many painful or many exciting changes. Our own history is a good predictor of what we will anticipate in the future. As I argued in a study (Lewis, 2000) I once did concerning "hindsight," it is critical to understand the hindsight perspective of what one has done; done well; and done wrong. "At the conclusion of a change effort, and indeed throughout the ongoing process, the implementer glances back at what he/she has experienced, pieces together what happened by 'enacting' a reality for operative purposes. The implementer then adapts future behavior accordingly" (p. 47). The same can be said for all stakeholders in organizations.

As discussed in Chapter 1, Weick's (1979) idea of enactment suggests that stakeholders in organizations "construct, rearrange, single out, and demolish many objective features of their surroundings" (p. 164). In other words, it isn't so much what "really happened" as much as our own version of what occurred, that guides our future behavior. So, implementers will consider what they think has worked well and not so well in past experiences with change (especially in the current organization) as they construct plans for the current change. Further, they understand that stakeholders in their organization will not come to the change without biases about change. Thus, knowing key stakeholders' constructions of past change efforts is useful in anticipating how they'll approach any new initiative. An interesting example of this is illustrated in the Spellings case (see Case Box 7.2) where many higher education stakeholders expressed fear that the recommendations for change in higher education would repeat the same pattern as those employed in the No Child Left Behind Program developed and implemented in primary and secondary education.

Making sense of an organization's change history, especially as it is seen from the various perspectives of different stakeholder groups, is part of assessing the organization's readiness for change. Terms such as "openness" (Miller, Johnson, and Grau, 1994) and "readiness" (Armenakis, Bernerth, Pitts, and Walker, 2007) capture the idea that stakeholders are willing to give any specific change a chance to succeed. **Openness** is conceptualized as support for the change, positive affect about the change. Similarly, **readiness** is understood as a compilation

---

Case Box 7.2: History as Prologue? Spellings Report Triggers Comparisons to NCLB

There was a strong, shared view that perceptions about NCLB were quite significant. In some quarters, for example, there were anxieties growing out of a fear that the Report suggested a higher education version of the controversial program. While this linkage may not have been intended by the Department of Education, the high level of visibility of both initiatives, and the common themes of accountability, assessment, and transparency made this conceptual linkage quite predictable. One person interviewed noted, "particularly, with the call for some kind of standardized measure of student outcomes, the sense that this was NCLB for higher education created a fairly negative impact." Several pointed to the common core values in both places. Another described the issue by saying, "I'm not sure that people believe that NCLB has really had a significant impact ... whether or not that program is working as well ... is this going to be just another initiative like that?" ... The inclusion of the NCLB logo along with the Department of Education seal on the header of the official announcement of the Spellings Commission may also have contributed to a perceived linkage within the higher education community.

Source: Ruben *et al.* (2008).

---

of stakeholders' beliefs about the necessity and appropriateness of change combined with beliefs that the change can be accomplished and will be beneficial. At the point before change is introduced stakeholders often have a sense of the need for any change to be introduced. For some stakeholders, solutions to known problems or positive action related to a perceived opportunity may be long anticipated. For other stakeholders, organizations may be perceived as humming along in need of no remedy or aggressive ambition to alter the path.

A part of the assessment of pre-change perceptions of stakeholders may involve gauging the degree to which the historical pattern of change and change success in an organization has been tolerable or intolerable; correctly paced, too fast, or too slow; targeted correctly or incorrectly; managed well or mismanaged; anticipated or sprung unexpectedly. The Ingredients Inc. merger case in this book provides an example of a

Case Box 7.3: Flip-flopping on Anticipation of Change

Rumors that the merger was in the works persisted for months, even years, prior to the event. However, these rumors were never officially confirmed and in several cases, were actually dismissed by decision-makers. One interview informant recalled:

> ... about a year ago it [the rumor] got real strong. So much so that at the National Sales meeting, which in 06 was in January ... We wanted to hear it from the big guy. And, so I remembered asking [my co-worker] "well, ask the guy." He goes, "no, why don't you ask him?" So finally, I said "ok," so I asked him. He stood up in a room full of people and said there would be no merger. So I thought that was quite stupid for [this important organizational leader] to say this because he didn't destroy anybody else's own personal credibility except his own when he did that because then about 5 months later, the merger was announced. And I think, he probably at the time said that because he wanted to suppress anything. But what he probably should have said is, "look, right now, as far as everyone in this room is concerned, that's just not open for discussion or debate, what we do we'll do, and blah blah blah, and we'll make a decision ... I think the answer would have been the same because nobody believed me when he said it, and boy, 6 months later they announced the merger. And everybody thinks, "oh, now [this leader] of [our organization] is a liar ..." (Rick, MC).

Source: Laster (2008), p. 43.

change that was not only unanticipated for many employees but was denied only months earlier (see Case Box 7.3).

Assessing Goals for Change

Finally, implementers' perceptions of the change context include their goals of the change effort. In Chapter 4, we raised the issue of implementers' desires for uniformity and/or fidelity. To a large extent this assessment of the change context by implementers involves thinking about the degree to which stakeholders are interdependent in the ways they engage the change. Different communication messages are needed if interdependence is high. Consider the task of planning a meal with a group of friends for a holiday (say, Thanksgiving). If there is no coordination, you could end up with three turkeys, no pie, and two sets of mashed potatoes! At a minimum, you may want to share what each person plans to bring so you can eliminate duplication. If you are planning a "pot luck" meal it may not matter whether there are some duplications. You may decide that to simply assign people to a category – main course, salad, dessert – is sufficient to hit all the important goals for the meal. Each of these solutions deals with levels of interdependence differently. In organizational contexts, interdependence during change is often high. As implementers consider the goals they have and the importance that a high-fidelity use be adopted, they may design message strategies to encourage those outcomes.

Also, as discussed in Chapter 4, we need to be conscious of the fact that the degree to which goals are fixed, known, and agreed in organizations is highly suspect. Goals tend to shift as events unfold in organizations and the history of what their goals are can be reconstructed. After the party gets started and there are two turkeys and four apple pies, if everyone is having a good time, we may reconstruct the goal of the whole event to be centered on people and having fun rather than on food! Similarly, even if an organization's leaders have stressed uniformity from the outset of a change initiative, if they see widespread creative innovation with a change, they may reconstruct what they were after "all along" was ingenuity from the employees who were using a new tool. They may declare a success of initial goals.

Stakeholders' Perceptions of Change Context

Stakeholders' perceptions of the change context will drive their behavior as well as the behavior of implementers during change. We have already discussed earlier in this chapter stakeholders' change values-fit and their perceptions of change history. Here we will discuss stakeholders' beliefs about change in more detail. Achilles Armenakis and colleagues' research program over 30 years has explored "what change recipients consider when making their decision to embrace and support a change effort or reject and resist it" (Armenakis and Harris, 2009, p. 128). Their research identified five specific beliefs that are key in the change assessment made by stakeholders (especially the assessments made by employees): discrepancy, appropriateness, efficacy, principal support, and valence. Armenakis and colleagues conclude from an extensive body of research into these beliefs and the processes by which readiness is created in change contexts, that focus on "creating readiness for change rather than waiting to reduce resistance" (Armenakis and Harris, 2009, p. 129) is the most beneficial practice for implementers. Further, they support the emphasis on change recipients' active participation in change as a means to creating readiness. Early communication with stakeholders is highlighted in this approach. Here we will define each of these five beliefs and discuss how understanding them from the outset of change has potential importance for the strategic communication during change processes for both implementers and stakeholders.

Discrepancy (the belief that the change is necessary) and **efficacy** (the belief that the change is something we can successfully accomplish) were both discussed in Chapter 5. We discussed how discrepancy and efficacy beliefs work in balance. The challenge in front of the organization needs to be significant enough to warrant doing something but not so large that stakeholders think it cannot turn out well. Armenakis and Harris (2009) note that they discovered how crucial discrepancy beliefs are in the formative phase of change initiatives. In research conducted in the 1970s they found that early involvement of organizational members regarding the major issues they perceived as needing attention (gap analysis) resulted in enhancing their sense of discrepancy and making it more likely that appropriate changes were selected to address them. Thus, the discrepancy and efficacy beliefs were achieved through stakeholders' involvement and process of analysis – and sensemaking with implementers and other stakeholders – not merely through a communication campaign once a change had been adopted by the organization. Armenakis and Harris conclude about these early participatory efforts that "involving change recipients in the diagnostic process actually begins to sensitize them to the possibility of impending organizational change, and can serve to encourage change readiness" (p. 130).

To some degree the Spellings case illustrates how this early involvement can be somewhat unpredictable (see Case Box 7.4). The higher education community had long participated in conversations identifying many of the "problems" that the Spellings Report covered. Indeed, they had already identified and were working on many of these problems. They did not perceive the need for change as a "crisis" nor as a brand new problem. This cut two ways. On the one hand it made stakeholders more receptive to the messages of discrepancy, but also resulted in annoying those in higher education because the communication tended to portend ignorance of ongoing efforts.

Case Box 7.4: Discrepancy Messages Overplayed

Many of the individuals interviewed believed that the Commission saw itself as chronicling a crisis, when in fact, from the perspective of those within the higher education community, the concerns voiced were not particularly new, nor was there any particular reason for alarm or panic. This point of view was articulated quite clearly in statements from the Washington presidential associations, as for example from the American Council on Education, which noted:

> The assumption underlying the recommendations ... is the need for change. ... We agree that there is a need for change. That is not new. It is important to note that reassessment and change is a continuing process in American higher education. Many of our [leaders/institutions] are already working on the challenges facing higher education in a careful and systematic way.

Source: Ruben *et al.* (2008), p. 64.

Appropriateness reflects the belief that the specific change under consideration or implementation is the correct one to address the discrepancy. Although stakeholders may see discrepancy as large and efficacy as sufficient, they need also to believe that any particular change effort proposed to close the discrepancy gap is appropriate. In many cases, stakeholders may agree on the problem or opportunity but not on the remedy or assertive action that should be taken. Armenakis and Harris (2009) discuss the research conclusions of their work highlighting the need for correct and rigorous diagnosis. Changes that address existing discrepancies (in what needs to be or what could be) may be ideal solutions/ideas or may be "satisficing" (good enough but not perfect) solutions/ideas.

Stakeholders' values will often be invoked in the discussion and analyses of appropriateness of any given change. For example, the struggle of an organization during tough financial times might be addressed any number of ways and different values will be raised with different consideration of various solutions. In the university setting, tough financial times are being addressed through raising tuition (increasing burden on students and their families); furloughs and salary freezes for staff and faculty (increasing burdens on those individuals and their families); layoffs and decreasing services such as limiting programs, outsourcing some activity (e.g., printing), and stopping or delaying projects (increasing burdens on those who lose service, service quality, or jobs). The values that are invoked in these circumstances help guide these decisions. At some universities loss of jobs was an intolerable sacrifice, and so employees agreed to higher workloads and pay cuts (i.e., furloughs and delayed or denied merit increases) to avoid those losses. At other institutions the burden of increasing tuition on students and their families was considered a fair distribution of shared pain. Much of the ongoing discussion of any change may have less to do with discrepancy or efficacy than with the appropriateness of any given change as solution to a perceived problem. "Resistance" to change may be read in some cases as resistance to the change that was chosen over known alternatives that some stakeholders prefer. They may not "fear change" or disparage the need for change, but merely prefer an alternative change.

Principal support is the belief that high-level decision-makers share a commitment to the change initiative such that it will not become a mere passing fad or discarded change after an initial flurry of activity. Klein and Sorra's work (1996) discusses the implementation climate as perceptions of what is rewarded, supported, and expected in an organization. "Employees perceptions of their organization's climate for the implementation of a given innovation are the result of employees' shared experiences and observations of, and their information and discussions about their organization's implementation policies and practices" (p. 1060). Further, Klein and Sorra describe a strong implementation climate as one that (a) ensures skills in innovation use, (b) provides incentives for use and disincentives for avoidance of use of innovations, and (c) removes obstacles to innovation use. Essentially, principal support involves that leaders in the organization demonstrate support for the change in words and in deeds. It is one thing for a manager to claim to support a change, it is another that she provides her staff time to learn it; the resources to resolve difficulty with it; and praise and material rewards when they master it.

A supportive change climate will lead to the belief that principal support is present in the organization and serves as a motivator for stakeholders to embrace the change. Such support can be provided to non-employee stakeholders as well as employees. For example, companies will often provide discounts or free trials for customers to try new innovations in product or service provision. My own grocery store has installed a new system for shopping in which the customer is provided with a mobile scanner that they can use to scan the prices of their groceries as they go, bagging the groceries as they take them off the shelves. All they need to do at checkout is to pay the total that is recorded on the device. To assist customers in learning this new technology and process, they provide helpful tip guides and post a person at the front of the store to answer questions. The presence of this support makes it more likely that customers will try it. In our case study of Homeless Net (see Case Box 7.5) we attempted to increase the belief in principal support through providing substantive material support and tech support function of our project. We hired a graduate student to be available to people who were trying to learn the new collaborative tools and provided powerful computers and software to participating agencies. Resources talk, especially in a cash-strapped environment like homeless service provision.

Case Box 7.5: Supporting Stakeholders Through Change

Initially, it was difficult to get the provider agencies to take us seriously. They seemed to believe that we'd merely "swoop in" to get our data and then be overwhelmed with the challenges faced by the providers and quietly leave. They'd been researched before and were skeptical of what benefit they'd get out of the project or the new tools we were offering.

However, our team persisted and were able to locate funding to support high-speed Internet for some of the smaller agencies; new sophisticated desk-top computers for all participating agencies; and a technology consultant who would do training and tech support. When many of the agencies learned they would be eligible to receive equipment they could keep, and free training and technical support, their interest perked.

Attending the orientation and training was a condition for getting the equipment and it also provided a chance to learn how to use some of the software and hardware provided. Approximately 25 agencies initially signed on to be sites for Homeless Net Project.

Source: Adapted from Scott, Lewis, D'Urso, and Davis (2009).

Social support might be a part of the support that managers provide to stakeholders during change. Given what we know about the likelihood of high uncertainty during change and emotional reactions that some stakeholders can have during demanding or stressful change, providing a mechanism to promote support is also likely beneficial. Stakeholders want to know that managers support the change not only intellectually and in terms of resources, but also in terms of empathizing with those who must make it operational. However, such support can sometimes turn into emotional labor and the management of emotions. As Zorn (2002) found in his study of implementation of ICTs, implementers and managers both attempted to drive the implementation effort forward through projecting uniformly positive emotion about the technology. Further, they attempted to control and manipulate the emotional displays of others to achieve their goals. By following sanctioned display rules in the organization for what constituted "professional" behavior, the change agents were able to discourage strong expression of negative emotion.

Robinson and Griffiths (2005) studied the role of various stressors and social support-based coping mechanisms during change including instrumental social support, information seeking, and emotional social support. They assessed the effect of instrumental social support (seeking advice or assistance from others), wherein an individual might ask for concrete assistance such as more workers assigned to an area adjusting to change; more financial resources to aid in carrying out a new initiative; loosening of expectations or lightening of some work tasks while a change is being introduced. Informational support concerned stakeholders' active attempts to seek information. The ready availability of useful, clear, and accurate information was a form of social support. Third, they assessed emotional social support which involved getting "moral support," sympathy, and opportunities for employees to vent to one another. The study found that social support coping was used most frequently to address stress related to high uncertainty and ambiguity, interpersonal conflict surrounding the change, as well as feelings of loss.

The final belief in Armenakis's set of five is valence. **Valence** concerns the belief that change is beneficial to the individual stakeholder. This is the belief that speaks to "what's in it for me." Many practitioner books on implementing change argue that the key concern for most stakeholders of change is self-interest. I think it is true that stakeholders will normally concern themselves with questions about potential harm and/or benefits they would accrue from the success or even mere presence of a change effort. Some changes represent high risk (e.g., mergers, layoffs, reorganization, reskilling) for some stakeholders. Some represent high stakes changes in the benefit/cost ratio (e.g., changes to compensation or performance assessment system; changes in allocation of resources). Some changes imply winners and losers in political battles for resources, attention, opportunities, innovation, etc. It would be naïve to assume that assessments of change initiatives are cool-headed purely rational assessments of the pros and cons of the merits of the change without regard to personal benefit or costs. However, Armenakis and colleagues point out that the balance of these five beliefs drives reactions and readiness to change – not merely assessments of self-interest. In fact, there may be situations where individual stakeholders see wisdom in a change that is not personally rewarding.

In research on the Belief Scale, Armenakis and colleagues have established both reliability and validity. In a test (Holt, Armenakis, Field, and Harris, 2007) of predictive validity (whether the scale could predict logical outcomes) of the Belief Scale, results suggest that those who scored high on this scale were significantly more satisfied in their jobs and affective commitment, and had lower turnover intentions. Further, in the same study tests of convergent validity (whether the scale was related to other theoretical constructs in ways that make sense) for these readiness factors found that these beliefs were positively related to general attitudes towards change. Rebelliousness was negatively related to the readiness factors. Further, perceptions of the communication climate and management's ability were both positively related to the readiness-for-change factors.

In general, these change beliefs ought not be thought of merely as a set of topics for communication messages for change, although they certainly can be used productively in the design of methods to introduce change. They ought to be thought of as a necessary set of precursors to change readiness that can be brought about through any number of means. As noted earlier in this chapter, stakeholders can come to hold these beliefs through their own participation in analysis and diagnosis before any specific change is even selected or announced. In fact, according the research evidence of Armenakis and colleagues, such first-hand early involvement is an ideal way to build these beliefs in stakeholders. Other ways in which stakeholders may come to hold these beliefs is through sharing with other stakeholders who already hold them; exposure to the evidence that led decision-makers to these beliefs; and independent assessment of evidence gathered outside of the organization.

Conclusion

In sum, this chapter has helped us explore the antecedents to communicators' strategies, interactions and assessments in the context of organizational change. Specifically, we have discussed how mimetic, coercive, and normative forces of isomorphism can create burdens on communicators to constrain their choices in communicative strategies, and how implementers' and other stakeholders' perceptions of the change context will drive their choices of communication strategies and approaches. The presence or lack of certain key perceptions or beliefs may motivate stakeholders, including implementers, to focus on specific communication messages, channels, and/or audiences. Chapter 8 discusses how stakeholders interact with one another throughout change efforts.

References

Armenakis, A. A. and Harris, S. G. (2009) Reflections: Our journey in organizational change research and practice. *Journal of Change Management,* 9 (2), 127–142.

Armenakis, A. A., Bernerth, J. B., Pitts, J. P., and Walker, H. J. (2007) Organizational change recipients' beliefs scale. *The Journal of Behavioral Science,* 43 (4), 481–505.

Brown, P. and Levinson, S. (1978) Universals in language usage: Politeness phenomena. In E. N. Goody (ed.), *Questions and Politeness* (pp. 56–289). Cambridge: Cambridge University Press.

Cai, D. A., Wilson, S. R., and Drake, L. E. (2000) Culture in the context of intercultural negotiation: Individualism-collectivism and paths to integrative agreements. *Human Communication Research,* 26, 591–617.

Clark, T. and Greatbatch, D. (2004) Management fashion as image-spectacle. *Management Communication Quarterly,*17, 397–424.

Daft, R. L. and Lengel, R. H. (1986) Organizational information requirements: Media richness and structural design. *Management Science,* 32, 554–571.

Damanpour, F. (1991) Organizational innovation: A meta-analysis of effects of determinants and moderators. *Academy of Management Journal,* 35, 555–590.

David, C. and Baker, M. A. (1994) Rereading bad news: Compliance-gaining features in management memos. *Journal of Business Communication,* 31 (4), 268–290.

Drake, L. E. (2001) The culture-negotiation link: Integrative and distributive bargaining through an intercultural communication lens. *Human Communication Research,* 27, 317–349.

Fulk, J., Schmitz, J., and Steinfield, C. W. (1990) A social influence model of technology use. In J. Fulk and C. W. Steinfield (eds.), *Organizations and Communication Technology* (pp. 117–140). Newbury Park, CA: Sage.

Furusten, S. (1999) *Popular Management Books*. London: Routledge.

Greene, J. O. (1997) A second generation action assembly theory. In J. O. Greene (ed.), *Message Production: Advances in Communication Theory* (pp. 151–170). Mahwah, NJ: Lawrence Erlbaum.

Hellweg, S. A., Geist, P., Jorgensen, P. F., and White-Mills, K. (1990) An analysis of compliance-gaining instrumentation in the organizational communication literature. *Management Communication Quarterly*, 4 (2), 244–271.

Holt, D. T., Armenakis, A. A., Field, H. S., and Harris, S. G. (2007) Readiness for organizational change: The systematic development of a scale. *The Journal of Applied Behavioral Science*, 43 (2), 232–255.

Kellermann, K. (1992) Communication: Inherently strategic and primarily automatic. *Communication Monographs*, 59, 288–300.

Kellermann, K. (2004) A goal-directed approach to gaining compliance. *Communication Research*, 31 (4), 397–445.

Klein, J. and Sorra, J. S. (1996) The challenge of innovation implementation. *Academy of Management Review*, 21 (4), 1055–1080.

Lakey, S. G. and Canary, D. J. (2002) Actor goal achievement and sensitivity to partner as critical factors in understanding interpersonal communication competence and conflict strategies. *Communication Monographs*, 69, 217–235.

Laster, N. M. (2008) Communicating multiple change: Understanding the impact of change messages on stakeholder perceptions. Dissertation Abstracts International (UMI No. AAT 3342339).

Lewis, L. K. (2000) "Blindsided by that one" and "I saw that one coming": The relative anticipation and occurrence of communication problems and other problems in implementers' hindsight. *Journal of Applied Communication Research*, 23 (1), 44–67.

Lewis, L. K. and Seibold, D. R. (1993) Innovation modification during intraorganizational adoption. *Academy of Management Review*, 18, 322–354.

Lewis, L. K., Hamel, S. A., and Richardson, B. K. (2001) Communicating change to nonprofit stakeholders: Models and predictors of implementers' approaches. *Management Communication Quarterly*, 15, 5–41.

Lewis, L. K., Richardson, B. K., and Hamel, S. A. (2003) When the "stakes" are communicative: The lamb's and the lion's share during nonprofit planned change. *Human Communication Research*, 29 (3), 400–430.

Lewis, L. K., Schmisseur, A., Stephens, K., and Weir, K. (2006) Advice on communicating during organizational change: The content of popular press books. *Journal of Business Communication*, 43 (2), 113–137.

Meyer, J. W. and Rowan, B. (1977) Institutional organizations: Formal structure as myth and ceremony. *American Journal of Sociology*, 83, 340–363.

Miller, V. D., Johnson, J. R., and Grau, J. (1994) Antecedents to willingness to participate in a planned organizational change. *Journal of Applied Communication Research*, 22, 59–80.

Morrison, E. W. (2002) Information seeking within organizations. *Human Communication Research*, 28, 229–242.

Oetzel, J. G. and Ting-Toomey, S. (2003) Face concerns in interpersonal conflict: A cross-cultural empirical test of the face negotiation theory. *Communication Research*, 30, 599–624.

O'Keefe, B. (1988) The logic of message design: Individual differences in reasoning about communication. *Communication Monographs*, 55, 80–103.

Robinson, O. and Griffiths, A. (2005) Coping with the stress of transformational change in a government department. *The Journal of Applied Behavioral Science*, 41 (2), 204–221.

Ruben, B. D., Lewis, L., and Sandmeyer, L. (2008) *Assessing the Impact of the Spellings Commission: The Message, the Messenger, and the Dynamics of Change in Higher Education*. Washington, DC: National Association of College and University Business Officers.

Scott, C. R., Lewis, L. K., Davis, J. D., and D'Urso, S. C. (2009) Finding a home for communication technologies. In J. Keyton and P. Shockley-Zalabak (eds.), *Case Studies for Organizational Communication: Understanding Communication Processes* (2nd edn.). Los Angeles, CA: Roxbury.

Timmerman, C. E. (2002) The moderating effect of mindlessness/mindfulness upon media richness and social influence explanations of organizational media use. *Communication Monographs*, 69, 111–131.

Timmerman, C. E. (2003) Media selection during the implementation of planned organizational change. *Management Communication Quarterly*, 16, 301–340.

Timmerman, C. E. and Madhavapeddi, S. N. (2008) Perceptions of organizational media richness: Channel expansion effects for electronic and traditional media across richness dimensions. *IEEE Transactions on Professional Communication*, 51, 18–32.

Ting-Toomey, S., Oetzel, J. G., and Yee-Jung, K. (2001) Self-construal types and conflict management styles. *Communication Reports*, 14, 87–104.

Weick, K. E. (1979) *The Social Psychology of Organizing*. Reading, MA: Addison-Wesley.

Weider-Hatfield, D. and Hatfield, J. D. (1995) Relationships among conflict management styles, levels of conflict, and reactions to work. *The Journal of Social Psychology*, 135, 687–698.

Wheeless, L. R. and Reichel, L. S. (1990) A reinforcement model of the relationships of supervisors' general communication styles and conflict management styles to task attraction. *Communication Quarterly*, 38 (4), 372–387.

Zorn, T. E. (2002) The emotionality of information and communication technology implementation. *Journal of Communication Management*, 7 (2), 160–171.

Further Reading

Armenakis, A. A., Harris, S. G., and Mossholder, K. (1993) Creating readiness for organizational change. *Human Relations*, 46 (3), 1–23.

Daft, R. L., Lengel, R. H., and Trevino, L. K. (1987) Message equivocality, media selection, and manager performance: Implications for information systems. *MIS Quarterly*, 11, 355–366.

Fulk, J. (1993) Social construction of communication technology. *Academy of Management Journal*, 36, 921–950.

Kellermann, K. and Park, H. S. (2001) Situational urgency and conversational retreat: When politeness and efficiency matter. *Communication Research*, 28, 3–47.

Lamude, K. G. and Scudder, J. (1993) Compliance-gaining techniques of type-A managers. *Journal of Business Communication*, 30 (1), 53–79.

Self, D. R., Armenakis, A. A., and Schraeder, M. (2007) Organizational change content, process, and context: A simultaneous analysis of employee reactions. *Journal of Change Management*, 7, 211–229.

Wheeless, V. E., Hudson, D. C., and Wheeless, L. R. (1987) A test of the expected use of influence strategies by male and female supervisors as related to job satisfaction and trust in supervisor. *Women's Studies in Communication*, 10, 25–36.

8

Stakeholder Interactions: Storying and Framing

All organizations depend on the existence of shared meanings and interpretations of reality, which facilitate coordinated action
Warren Bennis

We live, move and have our being, marinated in our own stories
David Sims

Man is eminently a storyteller. His search for a purpose, a cause, an ideal, a mission and the like is largely a search for a plot and a pattern in the development of his life story – a story that is basically without meaning or pattern
Eric Hoffer

It takes a thousand voices to tell a single story
Native American saying

Stories are very hard to ignore, especially good stories with vivid characters, intriguing and plausible plots, twists and turns, and unexpected

Organizational Change: Creating Change Through Strategic Communication,
First Edition. Laurie K. Lewis.
© 2011 Laurie K. Lewis. Published 2011 by Blackwell Publishing Ltd.

endings. A good deal of interaction following the announcement of an organizational change involves storytelling (Brown, Gabriel, and Gheradi, 2009; Brown and Humphreys, 2003; Whittle, Suhomlinova, and Mueller, 2010). A major point of storytelling is to make sense – **sensemaking** – of a change and to give that sense – **sensegiving** – to others. This chapter will focus on how stakeholders interact about change through stories and through framing and the consequences those interactions have for how stakeholders come to regard their own stakes and the stakes of others. As David Buchanan and Patrick Dawson (2007) argue, "narratives are both about and become the change process" (p. 669). Stories capture the experiences of change, aid in creating sense of the world, influence the reactions of stakeholders, and construct the after-the-change accounts of what happened. Brown *et al.* (2009) propose:

> In a world of change … threatening forces are at play, uncertain choices confront us, unpredictable outcomes result from our actions and disturbing emotions suffuse our being. Meanings are fragile, identities require maintenance work, sense is confronted with many diverse possibilities. Stories and other narratives then help us make sense of change, explain it, domesticate it and, at times, celebrate it. (p. 328)

In this chapter I will discuss how storymaking and storytelling provide opportunities for sensemaking and framing in organizations. Stories, and the interactions involved in making them, have consequences for how stakeholders come to view a change, their stakes in the change, and the concerns they may have regarding the change. Both the process of storymaking as well as the resultant stories that are told afford opportunities for stakeholders to come together in shared stakes and/or to disassociate from others. The narratives that are created help define boundaries around "us" and "others" that may stimulate alliances or rivalries among groups of stakeholders. Further, I will discuss how some stories and other framing attempts come to hold especially strong influence in organizations. This is a subject we know the least about in the context of organizational change.

Creating Stories and Storylines that Make Sense

Larry Browning (1992) compares stories with organizational lists. He argues that lists represent standards, accountability, and certainty. In

Highlight Box 8.1: How We Make Stories

Way back when …
Every day …
But one day …
Because of that … (repeat three times or as often as necessary)
Ever since then …
And the moral of the story is … (optional)

Source: Adapted from Anecdote.com on 1/13/10.

contrast, he defines *stories* as personal experiences shared in everyday discourse. A story is "romantic, humorous, conflicted, tragic, and most of all, dramatic. It unfolds sequentially, with overlays and pockets of mystery" (p. 282). Browning further suggests that stories change over time and involve multiple voices. Czarniawska (1998) argues that narratives (used here as synonymous with stories) involve (a) an original state of affairs, (b) an action or event, and (c) the consequent state of affairs. A plot brings these elements together in a consumable whole.

In an illustration of how stories can function in organizations, a facilitator (see Highlight Box 8.1) describes an exercise he uses in teaching about sensemaking in organizations. Participants are asked to make a story about an organizational situation using a set of prompts. You can imagine how this organizational tool could produce many different stories, with different evidence and different "morals" from a given circumstance in an organization.

Using this set of prompts might produce the following story about a planned change:

> Way back when this organization was just starting out we always treated everyone as family. Every day the manager would walk through this place and call everyone he met by name. But one day after we made this change and we started calling everyone "associate" and "team member." Because of that, we lost that sense of family and we lost the sense that we really belonged to something and that we were all individuals. Ever since then we have been made into cogs in a machine that are faceless. So, I am opposed to anything that sounds like "team."

These sorts of stories tell facts of an organization's history and then frame them in a narrative that leads from point A to point B to conclusion X. Assembling "facts" and elements of a story is more than presenting a string of pearls to be appreciated independently. Such activity is more akin to creating a dot-to-dot picture that once tied together creates a vivid picture. See Case Box 8.1 for examples of stories from our merger case. Although these are abbreviated versions of more full-blown stories, they give a sense of how a set of observations can be

---

Case Box 8.1: Threads of Merger Stories

A Story of the Acquisition "News":
For hourly or plant employees, information about the merger would be communicated by their shift lead or supervising manager. In respect to the merger, both internal and external formal announcements were prepared. Subsequent changes, however, were disseminated differently to different groups and were generally based on a need-to-know basis; that is, a determination was made by a person with authority as to if and how particular groups of people needed to know about a change. For example, information about the acquisition was only shared with employees who would be directly affected by the acquisition. However, one informant recalls how he and his department, a department directly impacted by the acquisition, discovered they would be absorbing another company and their product lines. He shares, "… I realized something must be happening because we saw new products on our production list … before it was MC 3 and now you have a product name of ACQ 4412."

A Story About the Status Change of One of the Legacy Companies:
The formal follow-up communication to this initial round of communi- cation occurred about 90 days after the first announcement. At the end of July 2006, internal and external stakeholders were informed of the official name change, which included names taken from both legacies. At this time, details were provided about the new corporate office located in MC. The respondents at EC saw this as a huge defeat. As explained by Marie, one of the specialists at EC, "only one of us could be 'top dog' and when we found out that *they* (her emphasis) were getting the corporate office, we knew it wasn't going to be us."

Source: Laster (2008).

treated as evidence and fitted into a plot to develop a conclusion. Such stories are told over time, adapted as the audience and circumstances change, involve multiple parties in their crafting, and adapt to draw lessons or morals that seem appropriate to the storytellers and co-creators of the story.

Storytelling is, of course, social. However, we do not merely swap completed stories with one another. We share the storytelling and the storymaking. It becomes a co-authoring project. Shelly Bird (2007) studied collective sensemaking through story-building. She argues that **story-building** helps participants to order disparate facts, events, and experiences; create shared understanding of the past; and predict successful coping with future events and circumstances.

The authors of a study of this process investigated the stories of technology-enabled nomadic workers at Telenor, Norway's premier telecom company, in late 2002. "Nomadic workers" were those equipped with mobile phones and laptop computers for wireless or wired communication. They used paperless processes and eschewed use of private offices in favor of common space, open landscape facilities, and hot-desking options. In the wake of this change, Telenor initiated a layoff. One story shared publicly became iconic for the dangers of project management in this new environment at Telenor (see Highlight Box 8.2). A former project manager previously celebrated as a rising star in the company was under-utilized after the downsizing effort that left her without a project to manage, but still employed. Her story was repeated and circulated around the organization by other employees who used it as a lens to interpret what was the new reality.

Highlight Box 8.2: Story of Bad Treatment

She shared her story publicly, and it became iconic for the dangers of project management. She reported being bored and insulted as a result of having been assigned to a menial task, given her education and recognized talent. ... the downsizing ... had jolted her into a tedious job, she maintained an attitude of incredulity toward the process and activities that the firm had deployed during downsizing. By publicly sharing her story, she raised doubts about the meaning of project management as central to organizing.

Source: Bean and Hamilton (2006), p. 339.

Case Box 8.2: Varying Stories About What Was Announced as Change

Brian's Story:
"We found out right before it happened. They told us that we would be merging with this other company but that it wouldn't affect us ... business as usual they said. But we did see changes to our jobs, mostly more products ... we don't have the space for it, and that has really affected my job. It would have been nice to know that the merge meant more than business as usual."

Marie's Story:
"[W]e came to work and found this email with the exclamation point saying there is a meeting this morning for the entire company ... that's when they told us ... we were merging ... and that this would also mean some minor changes related to becoming a new company ... it's funny because later that day, there was a change immediately. We no longer answer to Robert. We were no longer under his supervision. We now fell into operations, so now we answer to Ronnie, which was an immediate change ... yeah, it happened immediately ..."

Patty's Story:
"[I] believe some of the employees were called out to the parking lot for a large town hall meeting. It was pretty common to have those. I wasn't at it ... from what I had heard, the downsizing was going to be followed by a merger, and then we were going to move all of our processes to the other company and that our company was no longer going to be producing the same kinds of things we used to ... I think I even heard that we were going to get a new plant."

Lisa's Story:
"[I] think the first change was going to be a location change ... we would be moving [across town] into a new building, new technology would soon follow, and once we merged, we were going get a new lab. Funny thing is, that the change I resisted the most was the adoption of new policies and procedures. They won't let me have real plants in my office and I have to whisper in what they call a 'library voice.'"

Source: Adapted from Laster (2008).

Storymaking and storytelling are more complex when we consider the organizational contexts in which they occur. As David Boje (2008) points out, many stories are being told simultaneously in many "rooms" throughout an organization.[1] A person's sensemaking is influenced by his/her travels through those rooms, the timing of his/her appearance in any room at any given point in storymaking or storytelling, and the order or "path" of traveling through rooms. Boje refers to this as **"Tamara"** – the stitching together of a sensemaking path through an organization.[2] Boje suggests that this distributed, simultaneous "storying" and narrating process has not been the subject of much empirical research.

If we think about Tamara in the context of an organizational change we can see how versions of a change rationale; descriptions of future intentions of implementers; evaluations of the capability and operational consequences of a change, among other topics of stories, might circulate in different organizational networks ("rooms") at a given time. Although it was not her intention to study Tamara, Nicole Laster's study of the Ingredients Inc. merger case (see Case Box 8.2) is a good example of how multiple versions of the "story" of what the change entailed circulated differently in the organization. As we learned in Chapter 2, employees recalled the communication about the changes differently. Some reported more forewarning about the complexity and number of changes to come, while others reported that they were only told about one change (the merger). The result was that different sets of employees experienced the ongoing change in different degrees of expectation. As these employees made sense of the change with one another as the changes unfolded, the sense they made likely depended greatly on which other stories they were exposed to and in which order.

In sum, storytelling and storymaking result in different versions of "what is going on" in an organization. Those stories have consequences for the change initiative and for the stakeholders grappling with change. We will discuss those in the next sections.

Framing

Stories and story-building are one means to construct frames for sensemaking. Fiss and Zajac (2006) argue that actors in organizations use **frames** "to affect the interpretation of events among different audiences" (p. 1174). Discourse frames are used here metaphorically. Just as photo-frames bracket off a stream of information and visual data that is available in a photo, discourse frames bracket off experiences and events into interpretable pieces. A photo-frame positions some objects in a photograph as more central and others as more off-center and thus less important. They help focus our attention on the important images. Discursive frames "simplify and condense the 'world out there' by selectively punctuating and encoding events in order to rend them meaningful" (Fiss and Zajac, 2006, p. 1174).

You can think of a frame as something that helps you make assumptions about individual pieces of experiences or knowledge about a situation. For example, you can imagine framing the relationship you have with another person as "dating." You could also frame that relationship as a "hook-up" or as a "friendship." Each frame implies different ways of interpreting the events, actions, communication, and sequencing of events that you notice. Certain activities would be seen as appropriate and natural within one frame, but very odd or ill-fitting in another frame. For example, if you are framing your relationship as a friendship and the other person kisses you passionately at your doorstep, you might conclude that either your "friend" was operating with a different frame for the relationship, or has a very different understanding of what "friendship" entails! Further, that act, if received positively by you, might completely reframe the relationship as something else – perhaps even to the point that you both reconstruct that what you've been doing all along was "falling" for one another.

In another example, a colleague of mine was retelling the story of his car's collision with a deer. At the conclusion of the story I expressed concern for him and his car's damage and then said something like, "It's a shame that you hit that deer." He replied, in a classic example of reframing, "From my perspective, it is the deer that struck my vehicle"! So, in my colleague's version of the story, the deer was on the attack, or in a careless act slammed into his innocent and legally driven vehicle. He was victimized. While amusing, this version of the story does put a completely different spin on the events than my original frame that positions my colleague as "killing a deer with his car" – doubtlessly the version of the story that the other deer are sharing with one another!

There is debate about whether frames live in our heads (as representations of reality stored in memory) or as a dynamic process of enacting and shaping meaning in ongoing interaction (Dewulf *et al.*, 2009). The former are referred to as "**cognitive frames**" and the later as "**interactional frames**." As Dewulf and colleagues describe this important difference in perspective, "Cognitive frames capture chunks of what people believe is external reality. From an interactional perspective, frames are co-constructions created by making sense of events in the external world. Framing thus constructs the meaning of the situations it addresses" (p. 164). In this chapter I adopt an interactional perspective on framing. Although Dewulf and colleagues discuss framing in terms of conflict and negotiation research, their work is useful in explaining framing in the change context as well. For example, they discuss "issue framing" where issues are not objective, but rather are discussion topics that are "named, blamed, and claimed" in interaction.

> Different parties may engage in issue framing in different ways. While they are giving information, asking questions, or arguing about a situation, actors stress specific aspects of a situation and employ particular formulations that delimit and define how the issues should be understood or labeled. (p. 171)

The interactional component of framing is what makes it so powerful. It is not enough to know stakeholder groups and their individual stakes as groups to determine the frames they bring to any given situation. In Chapter 3 we discussed how Gallivan's study of a technology change was "read" by different groups of stakeholders in very different ways. We observed at that point that membership in professional or occupational communities, prior socialization into specific jobs, and different bases of experience might have led to these different interpretations of "what was going on." Here we need to extend that analysis to include discussion of how the interaction among stakeholders (both within stakeholder groups and between the groups) may influence the sensemaking, and thus frames, that individuals adopt. As Brummans *et al.* (2008) report through their research in framing in multiparty conflict, "disputants within the same group may or may not rely on a similar repertoire for making sense of what is going on" (p. 45). People – even within groups of stakeholders – do not necessarily highlight the same aspects of experience nor make sense in similar ways. Further, there may be various allegiances operating. As discussed in Chapter 3, individual stakeholders may have "membership" in multiple stakeholder groups simultaneously, and a change effort can trigger different kinds of sensemaking regarding each "hat" they wear. Thus, just knowing their group memberships is not enough. We need to understand how frames are built, questioned, redesigned, negotiated, and undone through interaction.

During interaction the frames may be embraced by others or resisted, shaped, or realigned through interaction. Thus, these frames are created and altered through the interaction among people (not within individuals' heads). Frames are often contested in organizations and can be the source of great conflict (Brummans *et al.*, 2008). That is, one person's read on what is "really happening" may clash with another person's read on the same set of actions and events. As Johansson and Heide (2008) argue, "whilst an ideal may be that people can make sense of strategic change through a coherent narrative that is credible for all parties, actors are making sense of situations differently, and are impacting on each others' sense-making processes" (p. 296).

Whittle *et al.* (2010) provide a good example of how framing can be done through interaction (see Highlight Box 8.3). They studied a training session regarding a new controversial change in a system. As the trainers explained the new process, employees began to express objections and skepticism as to how the system worked and what implications it would have for them. Instead of immediately accepting the framing of trainers that "this will make your job easier" they argued "this will make our jobs harder." In the following exchange, the trainers attempt to reframe the complaint in ways that steer the enacted reality toward the conclusion they want the employees to draw.

Through our interactions we are constantly negotiating frames surrounding events and relationships. We and other stakeholders may be reinforcing a given frame; contesting each other's frames; exploring new frames; and/or even retroactively reinventing the frame of past events. In reflection on our previous example of the relationship between two

Highlight Box 8.3: Attempts at Framing

Employee 1: So we're gonna have to go into every record and check whether it's OK? So that's gonna be extra work.

Employee 2: So technically this means that we're gonna be doing more work and the consultants are gonna be doing less.

Trainer: But it's all about quality isn't it, and getting things right the first time … But it's all to do with an ongoing audit isn't it. So when it comes to audit time – you guys aren't sitting here doing all the paperwork.

Source: Whittle *et al.* (2010), p. 26.

people, one person might view a relationship they are in as a romantic one that is leading to a permanent commitment and the other might frame it as a casual friendship. In organizations such frame conflicts may be a function of differing perceptions of what is "going on" or it may be indicative of active attempts to shift the ground by which those around them view the world – such as in the case of the training session highlighted above.

It isn't so much about who is "right" and who is "wrong" in interpreting reality; it might be more about who will win more support for his/her version of reality; or actually creating a new reality through framing. Your "friend" might try to shift the relationship to a romantic one by kissing you. The trainer in the Whittle *et al.* study was trying to create the reality that the change represented an improvement in the work tasks of the employees. In organizations, implementers and stakeholders may attempt to frame events and sequences of events in certain ways that will enhance the chances of bringing about results, and enacting the reality, that each desires. Framing a change situation as a response to a crisis is another example. Crises invoke certain sorts of actions and have specific implications. We tend to give up some power in a crisis and rely more on leaders to make important and quick decisions; we understand that processes may be less than ideal and that sacrifices are often demanded of everyone; we are more forgiving of being left out of things; we might be less expectant to know all the pertinent information early on; we understand that urgency is required and/or drastic actions may be necessary. So, framing a change situation as a crisis response can invoke many other assumptions, expectations, and behaviors of stakeholders. In essence the successful framing of change as "crisis" enacts that reality – the situation becomes a crisis.

Scholars have embraced framing as a means to understand important organizational dynamics (cf. Bartunek, Rousseau, Rudolph, and De Palma, 2006; Cherim, 2006; Fairhurst, 2005). Typically, the change literature has addressed framing as something that implementers do to get stakeholders to accept change. This "management of meaning" approach suggests that stakeholders can individually accept, revise, or reject those meanings that implementers try to include in a frame. If accepted, stakeholders (especially employees) are more likely to be concretively controlled (monitor themselves in alignment with the goals and frames established by management). For example, in a study of change in two Canadian banks, Samia Cherim describes how managerial frames are appropriated by employees. She defines appropriation as acceptance of the frame and the identities the frame implies, including internalization of the values, goals, and means to achieving them. She details employees' willing appropriation, reluctant appropriation, and partial appropriation as ways in which employees responded to managerial frames for change. Such approaches are useful in the sense that they provide us with language and a perspective to understand the strategic attempts of managers to engage in sensegiving in organizations as well as with a means to trace "reactions" to those attempts. Further, as Fairhurst and Sarr (1996) note, "many individuals prefer to look to others to define what is real, what is fair, and what should count now and in the future. They are reluctant to manage meaning for themselves or others because there is risk involved when the stakes are high" (p. 2). Thus, the role of leaders and managers in managing meaning – especially during what can be very turbulent times in organizations undergoing change – is important.

However, an exclusive focus on leaders' or managers' or implementers' framing attempts would underplay the important strategic communication of other stakeholders in actively shaping meaning and promoting their own sense of what is going on or in manipulating others' sensemaking – including implementers. Depicting stakeholders as mere recipients of framing attempts – that are adopted, partially adopted, or rejected – doesn't consider their important strategic communication. By highlighting the framing of many stakeholders we can pay attention to the interplay of framing and the multiple frames that may exist simultaneously in an organization during change. Some of the most consequential framing that occurs during change likely happens in interactions among stakeholders without implementers being present. Zoller and Fairhurst (2007) make a similar point in discussing resistance leadership, "resistance leadership emerges from dynamic and evolving relationships *among resisters* as well as between *resisters and their targets*" (p. 1355, italics in original).

There have been several examples of framing already presented in previous chapters of this book. For example, in Chapter 2 we discussed the language used to define the state of higher education, in the Spellings case, as a "crisis" by some and as a long-understood set of problems by others. In Chapter 5 we discussed examples from the Spellings case of use of two-sided messages to frame the key issues related to changing higher education, as well as the Merger case example of framing that change as a gain as opposed to a loss. These examples illustrate that there are many "framers" of reality and many participants in framing interactions during change.

Stories and Frames Create, Maintain, and Resolve Concerns

Stories and framing attempts do more than guide our sensemaking. Stories have consequences for the beliefs and concerns that stakeholders hold concerning change. Both hearing stories and participating in their development and elaboration can encourage feelings of anxiety, stress, calm, or excitement as well as help us to put a name to particular concerns we have about a given change initiative. Further, they can help resolve concerns or minimize them. Most importantly, they can become the means by which concerns come to exist. As Whittle *et al.* (2010) argue "[stakeholders'] interests are not a fixed, essential entity that drives social action. Rather interests are negotiated and transformed in interaction" (p. 33). They argue that we should focus on how interests are *constructed in* discourse rather simply *expressed in* discourse.

In research I did with my colleague David Seibold, we identified three sets of general concerns that stakeholders have during change: uncertainty, performance, and normative. **Uncertainty concerns** are related to the problems that occur for stakeholders when they do not know what to expect or what are likely outcomes of a change. Uncertainty is nearly always present during change. As we noted, "Users and potential users of an innovation may be faced with disruptions in procedures, unsteady resource-dependency relationships and role relationships, shifting communication networks, new standards for performance evaluation, and technical upgrading, among other changes" (Lewis and Seibold, 1993, p. 333). Further, stakeholders are confronted with uncertainty about accompanying changes that might be triggered by any given change (as the Merger case illustrates) and speculation about what the future holds for the organization, unit, practice, promotion, and job security.

Performance concerns are related to issues of assessment and judgments of competence as well as to one's own feeling of mastery over tasks. In the midst of change much of what we once could mindlessly accomplish through established routines must become mindful. Think about how you drive to work or school each day. You may not even be able to recall specifics of the route after you arrive. You are able to navigate traffic, make correct turns, and obey traffic laws (hopefully!) all without much active processing of the stimuli. You can follow the same path easily over and over. If a traffic jam or weather event makes you take a new route to the same destination, you need to be a much more active processor of information. That processing requires an additional cognitive load. You may have to turn off the radio and eliminate other distractions to navigation. You are more prone to getting lost or being unsure if the route you are taking is correct. That state of uncertainty creates stress about your ability to perform. And, until you've successfully mastered the new route, you won't feel all that competent in getting to your destination. You may have to try several alternates before you find the best one.

Similarly, when organizational change forces us to forge new "paths" in our lives it creates concerns about our ability to perform adequately as well as raising our cognitive load. These performance concerns will be exacerbated if we have rewards tied to expected performance; if we are being closely monitored for signs of mastery; or if we have much personal investment in our mastery of the involved actions or tasks. Even in cases where we are told by implementers that our performance need not meet high standards for some initial period, we may simply not like to feel incompetent at tasks that we once felt mastery over.

When my grocery store implemented a new system for collecting groceries and checking out I experienced some of these concerns. In the new system the customer scans in each item with a scanner device, bags the groceries as you go through the store, and pays at a kiosk without any help of the grocery clerks. I was reluctant to try it because I didn't want to look or feel incompetent. I took my 10-year-old with me the first time so that if we had trouble I might be seen by onlookers as "helping" my child with the technology (when, in fact, it was more the opposite!). I was concerned with impression management and with the uncomfortable feelings of being incompetent at grocery shopping – something I'd got down to a science after years of doing the task. I didn't fear being laughed at by the employees at the grocery nor being penalized in some way for failing to use the new technology correctly. My hesitation was due to internal feelings of incompetence. A feeling I found distasteful.

Seibold and I also wrote about the importance of concerns about group norms that are formed and enforced with respect to behaviors that have some significance for the group. Such norms enable individuals to express central values and clarify central tenets of group identity. "Change in the organization may present reinforcement or threat to existing group norms and values, and it may trigger concerns for the protection and survival of the group in which individuals consider themselves members" (Lewis and Seibold, 1993, p. 333). Many different **normative concerns** can become salient during change. Some concern the nature of the change itself; some concern the abandonment of old ways or values for new ones; and some concern the process of change (e.g., timing, fairness, treatment of stakeholders). Further, some normative concerns are connected to the ripple effects of change – that is, those side effects that aren't central to the change, but are nonetheless a part of what occurs in the wake of change. The move to a new office building might include a ripple effect of more noise; less easy access to windows and light; increased or decreased temperature for some; lack of privacy for some; depersonalization of workspace (as more corporately approved displays and art are favored over individuals' posters and photographs). Any of these ancillary changes that are associated with the major change of a move to a new office building could trigger a normative concern.

At times stakeholders may have concerns that are not the idea of the change, perceived need for it, or its likely benefits, but relate to the manner in which it is introduced (e.g., key stakeholders not given a chance to participate in discussion of the change prior to its introduction; overly top-down approach to forcing change; the manner in which the change was framed). Thus, the process of change and not the change itself may violate established norms. We saw an example of this with the Spellings case in this book. Many in higher education did not object to several of the conclusions of the Spellings Commission. Many of the issues identified in the Report were long acknowledged by higher education leaders. However, they objected to the presentation of these as "newly discovered" and packaged as a "crisis." As we discussed in Chapter 2, "Much of the response to the Report came in the form of 'don't tell us what we already know, like we don't know it.' One respondent put it this way, 'I don't think the federal government needs to tell us that we need to offer lifelong learning opportunities'" (Lewis, Ruben, Sandmeyer, Russ, and Smulowitz, unpublished, p. 25).

In contrast, the Homeless Net case illustrates that early involvement of key stakeholders in implementing technology changes coupled with stressing the earnest effort to address community needs probably bought some goodwill and was more in keeping with the community's normative ways of initiating change. We followed the process norms of that group by making a face-to-face appeal to a central decision-making group; we brought new material resources to the network; and we involved ourselves in learning about the needs of homeless persons (which was a central value of all the stakeholders). All of those process steps bought good will. As our research team initially worked with the Homeless Net to establish common goals – to increase the collaborative capacity of the network; to increase familiarity of the agencies and organizations with one another; and to upgrade the technical capacity of organizations that previously lacked them – initial response to the project and our process was positive. However, even though the normative concerns about our process were minimal, as we saw in our discussion in Chapter 6, normative concerns did eventually get in the way of some stakeholders adopting technologies to the degree our team had hoped.

These three sets of concerns – uncertainty, performance, and normative – exist alongside specific concerns that stakeholders may have about the appropriateness of a change to address the specific challenges and opportunities presented by implementers (in messages of discrepancy, efficacy, valence, and principled support). Even without personal concerns about a given change, a given stakeholder may doubt appropriateness. Simply put, they may think that the change is flawed, poorly timed, unlikely to fix the problem it is supposed to address, likely to bring about negative unintended consequences, etc. And, as we discussed in Chapter 6, they might be right!

During storytelling among stakeholders, these concerns may be intentionally or unintentionally raised or resolved. Stakeholders' interactions have the ability to strategically or inadvertently give rise to these concerns for themselves and for others. The joint sensemaking about "what is really going" on during change will highlight certain aspects of the change experience and predict the future in ways that make some concerns more salient and important. Further, stakeholders may strategically highlight or de-emphasize concerns for other stakeholders with regards to key stakes those stakeholders value. And as we saw in the earlier example concerning the exchange of trainers and employees, the framing of claims and counterclaims can also crystallize a concern – in that case, the degree to which the process change would create more work for some employees.

An excellent example of this can be seen in the Spellings case where stakeholders had a national conversation via published articles and commentary in online journals of higher education. One story that flourished in these online environments suggested that the Spellings Commission was proposing a "one size fits all" approach to higher education reform. This portrayal of the Commission's goals hit a nerve on several fronts, but especially invoked normative concerns among those in higher education. "The idea that measures would be standardized across institutional types and then publicized struck a fearful chord among leaders of many different institutional types. In fact, since everyone could find something to dislike about this break with normative practice, it served often as a rallying cry for those opposed to the work of the Commission. Diversity and decentralization is considered a hallmark of higher education (Ruben *et al.*, 2007) and our interviewees suggested that 'the lack of appreciation for the value of diversity' was a serious problem" (Lewis *et al.*, unpublished, p. 26). Thus, the various voices trying to make sense of the Spellings Commission formed a "nutshell" understanding of "what was going on" – that the federal government was trying to take over and create one system for all to follow. That story invoked concerns about the strong norms for embracing diversity among institutions of higher education that viewed a wide array of institutions with varying missions of equal value. If marshaling resistance to the Spellings Commission was a goal, this was a provocative story to gain negative reaction.

Creating and Resolving Alliances, Rivalries, and Schisms

Sensemaking, whether in storymaking or framing, can result in activating or disintegrating connections among stakeholders and stakes. Sensemaking can lead to creation or dissolution of alliances, rivalries, and schisms among stakeholders.

> Some stakeholders will see opportunity for alignment of mutual goals with other stakeholder groups. Some may wish to disassociate from former allies and become more independent in the network. The more significant the change episode … the more strident the ripple effects throughout the network of stakeholder relationships are likely to be. As the web of relationships change, the position that implementers find themselves in changes too. (Lewis, 2007, p. 193)

Shelly Bird's (2007) investigation of a group of women coping with organizational change illustrates how alliances can be formed during change sensemaking and storybuilding. Bird found that elaborated and joint storytelling helped the women cope with uncertainty. She also found that "**terse telling**" (Boje, 1991) – a truncated form of storytelling that involves reference to an elaborated story shared by the group – reflected bonding among the group members (see Highlight Box 8.4). Stories served many functions for the group that Bird studied including social support, advice-giving, and as a means to form and solidify

Highlight Box 8.4: Terse Telling

I often heard the phrase "make like an ostrich" quietly uttered when a member became engaged in a heated debate. ... I was told of many stories about former network members who "got their heads cut off for being troublemakers." ... "it is best to keep you head underground like an ostrich and just focus on your work. Otherwise, you may lose your job in the next round of reductions." Similarly, the word ostrich ... was used to remind network members of both the futility and the perceived consequences of getting involved in internal politics.

Source: Bird (2007), p. 321.

friendships. One way that storytelling provoked social support was through engaging in "**puzzlements**" – propositional forms of storytelling where the listeners are asked to engage in problem-solving. In these stories, details of events are shared with some interpretation of the teller's response to them and concerns about them. Then, the teller invokes an opening for others to advise, help interpret "signs," or instruct on appropriate steps that should have been taken or should be taken in the future. Bird observed, "The identities of network members are informed and, to some degree, constrained by the collective stories they tell" (p. 328). Bird found that these networks of shared storytelling helped empower the women who participated and created strong ties that increased levels of internal trust and mutual support as members expressed their stories with one another. Thus, the stories that are told serve as both a rallying call for similarly minded stakeholders and as a means to solidify behind a version of "what is going on" in the organization during change. Further, stories are shared within an alliance to reinforce or even to advance a "plot line" as change unfolds. In a case of "strange bedfellows," sensemaking about change may provide an opportunity to bring together groups of stakeholders who before the change may have had little recognition or appreciation of one another's stakes.

Sharing stories that are in alignment with powerful stakeholders' perspectives on a change can have political motivations as well. In Bryant and Cox's (2004) study of "stories of conversion" some individuals highlighted particularly positive narratives of a change while downplaying negative aspects. These practices may help mark those individuals as ready for upper management. Additionally, as Whittle *et al.*'s (2010) study illustrates, stakeholders – even those tasked with promoting a change – may decide to align with resistors as they work through sensemaking interactions (see Highlight Box 8.5).

Most examples of rivalries created through sensemaking and framing illustrate how "management" and employees frame and reframe change competitively. Such work is usually described in terms of detailing how

Highlight Box 8.5: "We Don't Want It Either"

As the start of the training session, the change agents' discourse suggested that they were passionate advocates of the change, emphasizing the many benefits the change would bring for the employees and the company. As the change agents encountered increasing levels of hostility, however, this "presentation of self" … subtly shifted. The change agents began to present themselves as kind of unwilling victims of the change process by distancing themselves from the terminology involved.

Shirley [Trainer]: [reading from screen] "Performance Manager interrogates." We have an issue with that word, Catherine and I.

Catherine [Trainer]: Yeah, we don't like interrogates. We didn't put these together.

Shirley: We're just delivering this. We don't like it.

This rhetorical tactic of distancing is particularly interesting because it seems to present the change agents as being "one of you" vis-à-vis the recipients, that is a common victim of changes imposed by management and external parties. By building a sense of "being in the same boat" as the recipients, the change agents could be seen to come across as more sympathetic to the recipients and more authentic in their request for the recipients to at least comply with the change (if commitment is out of the question). In addition the process of distancing from the change could also act to minimize personal responsibility for the resistance they were facing, as suggested by the following extract:

Shirley: We're bound to get resilience, but this isn't a Shirley and Catherine thing, we're just delivering this.

Source: Whittle *et al.* (2010), pp. 27–28.

Highlight Box 8.6: Reframing and Resistance

The managerial accounts of the change project were persuasive, but the shop stewards had developed their own strategy of resistance that was based on reframing the managerial account of change. ... the stewards focused on the poor judgment of the managers in seeking a simple system that would alienate employees and would not be sophisticated enough to achieve the goals of the change project. The employee representatives were thus able to redefine the rationale given by the management based on improved competitiveness for the firm, as something that was worthy in principle but that could not be achieved in practice ...

Source: Cooney and Sewell (2008), p. 698.

resistance is manifest in communication. Cooney and Sewell's (2008) research into technology change at an Australian subsidiary of a North American carmaker illustrates what they refer to as "resistance through reframing" (see Highlight Box 8.6). The "reframing" effort of shop stewards suggested selfish political motives of the managers who implemented the change. The researchers suggest that the current management team was trying only to do a "quick and dirty job that gave them kudos for introducing the system but that left the problems to be dealt with by their successors" (p. 698). The reframing was aimed at stopping poor decision-making. The resultant process of change was marked by "discord" and high emotion where the lead manager questioned whether the union representatives truly represented their members and later characterized the conflict-ridden meeting as too emotional and that the union representatives had "few value-adding recommendations" (p. 700).

In a third example, schisms within and between groups of stakeholders may also form, increase, or dissolve as a result of change sensemaking and storytelling. Schisms refer to division, rifts, or separation among groups that don't necessarily imply the rivalry or direct conflict of the previous category. Schisms may be repaired, created, or worsened during change. Change sometimes makes visible lines around groups of stakeholders (e.g., those who have the new technology and those who do not; those who are permitted to telecommute and those who do not;

those who were laid off and those who still have jobs). At times change may erase previously clear lines separating stakes or stakeholders (e.g., elimination of previous status differences; mergers of task groups; elimination of a resource that once differentiated some stakeholders from others). These effects on stakeholder groups can have implications for the change initiative as important distinctions are relaxed or highlighted.

In sum, as we work through stories and concerns that these stories invoke or resolve, we also may discover attractions to some and repulsions from others that ultimately shape our social network in the context of the change. In short, we come to see shared fate with some stakeholders and see distance or even antagonistic goals with others. The sensemaking influences our world views of "what is going on" and those worlds sometimes collide, sometimes merge, and sometimes run parallel.

Which Stories and Frames Matter?

So, which stories and which frames matter the most in change? Does it matter who the storymakers and framers are or when the stories and frames are made? Are there characteristics of more convincing stories or less attractive stories or of more or less plausible frames? What leads one story to be cast aside for another? These questions concern how stories and frames come to be held in esteem by various stakeholders and for what window of time they are influential.

In Chapter 3, I discussed the importance of opinion leaders, connectors, and journalists who likely play key roles in the processes of sensemaking during change. Some empirical work has investigated the relationships between organizational social structure and opinion leadership during change. For example, Albrecht and Hall (1991) found that talk about innovation tends to occur within multiplex relationships (those that share multiple content such as friendship and professional tasks). They found that individuals tended to talk to friends and those they trust about new ideas. Another study by Tenkasi and Chesmore (2003) found that strong ties between implementing units and "recipient units" facilitated results that the implementers desired. Scant research has focused on the sorts of questions that are raised at the start of this section.

We probably have more intriguing questions than answers about these issues at this point. For example, questions come to mind when we consider the complexity of sensemaking interaction in organizations. David Boje (2008) asks about Tamara, "How do people find out what stories were performed in the rooms they are not in? How are the many choices of sequence of rooms to be in during just one day, by each person, affecting the differentiated sense made to a story enacted in a current room?" (p. 16). As he observes, "the implications of Tamara are in tracing the dynamics that are simultaneously distributed over time, to get at processes of emergence, pattern formation, and the ways sensemaking pathways (of room choices, and in which order) affect sensemaking" (p. 16). We can add to Boje's list of questions by investigating who is making and telling stories or creating or resisting frames together? What are "rules" for participating in any given sensemaking process (e.g., are some excluded or invited) and how do some make themselves more influential storytellers or framers?

Much of what has been written in organizational analysis of change stories, framing, and sensemaking are reports of the "sense made" of a change or the accounts given. The empirical work relies mostly on interview or participant observer interviews with stakeholders who detail their *current* descriptions of "what is going on" or what has transpired, or what the change meant or means. The limitation of this approach is that we are capturing a snapshot of a process of sensemaking and thus have a less rich understanding of the answers to the questions we have just raised. Much like photographing a basketball player mid-flight as he jumps to make a basket, without running the "video," the meaning of the action can be lost. We don't know if the player made the shot, or if not, if he or another player rebounded and then scored. Did the other team immediately return a score or was this the beginning of a series of multiple scores for the one team? Was this a pivotal point in the game, or one that didn't matter much to the final result? All of those sorts of questions are captured through investigation of the process, not in merely capturing one moment. The same can be said for the post-game analysis. If we ask a given player to report what happened in a moment or what his/her conclusion was about the game as a whole, we miss the in-the-moment sensemaking in favor of the hindsight sense made. To capture the sensemaking we might record the player of the game moment-by-moment as well as his discussions with other players and coaches as the game unfolds.

A recent study captured just this sort of sensemaking during change. Paul Leonardi's (2009) study of the implementation of a new technology in an auto manufacturing plant (see Highlight Box 8.7) was able to capture the "game as it unfolded." Leonardi argued that stakeholders

Highlight Box 8.7: Social Sensemaking Sets Up Material Disappointment

Developers framed CrashLab in ways they felt would attract managers to it emphasizing speed and how it would help PEs do their work faster. Managers who were exposed to this framing then passed such messages on to their PEs. In weekly staff meetings, crashworthiness managers would use the same talk about "speed" to pitch CrashLab as a technology that would allow PEs to build their simulation models faster than they had before ...

PE: So will it make the setup procedure faster?

Manager: Yes. After you learn to use it you'll be able to set up models much faster than you do now and there'll be more time to work on other engineering aspects. This will make your work much faster.

However, for crashworthiness PEs, "speed" was a word associated with preprocessing and not with postprocessing. The result of this framing was that PEs began to liken the technology to preprocessing applications. As one PE commented:

> My guess is that CrashLab is going to be a new preprocessor because it's supposed to make model building faster. That is normally what preprocessors do. Like, you could do it all by hand, but the reason you use a preprocessor to speed up the work. So, yeah, I guess Crashlab is going to be a good preprocessor if it speeds things up.

As the PEs began to use CrashLab they explicitly compared CrashLab's features with the features of existing preprocessors and in doing so began to interpret CrashLab itself as a preprocessor. The overall effect was for PEs to make determinations about whether or not to use CrashLab based on what they learned it could do or not do in relation to preprocessing tools already available to them.

Source: Adapted from Leonardi (2009), pp. 407–441.

develop interpretations of what a technology can do through both material interactions (actually using a new technology) and social interactions (talking with other stakeholders about the new technology and its use). In his study the users of the new technology developed one interpretation of the change that so informed these stakeholders' expectations and interpretations of the change that it seriously shaped their material interactions with it. In this case, that "shaping" led to a negative assessment of what the technology could do. This study is an excellent example of empirical analysis of sensemaking as it unfolds over time and of the consequences of that sensemaking for the results of a change effort.

Leonardi was able to capture sensemaking as it unfolded in multiple "rooms" over the course of months of experimentation with a new technology. Leonardi studied this large automobile manufacturer over a nearly two-year period during which he spent nine months conducting observations (over 500 hours total).

> Because I conducted observations during the implementation period I was able to document how informants struggled to make sense of the technology in the real-time practice of their work rather than having to rely on retrospective accounts of their interpretation formation. (p. 414)

In other words, Leonardi was able to capture sensemaking not just the sense made (at one point in time, as a version is told to a researcher in hindsight). In addition to watching the employees work with the new technology, Leonardi was also able to capture the interactions about it. He recorded talk occurring during all observations that included interactions between employees as well as "self-talk" ("I encouraged them to speak out loud as they worked": p. 414).

The stories and frames that matter during change are going to be ones that serve a pivotal role in some sense. Ones that garner attention from key stakeholders; serve to change dynamics of the thrust of the change effort; shape or enact the reality of what the change is; and endure in the organization long enough to make a difference in outcomes or at least key processes. Exactly what pathway such storymaking and framing must travel, and with which participants, to make them "important" is something we have little understanding of thus far.

Conclusion

In summary, this chapter has introduced a discussion of how sensemaking activity, carried out in interaction through storymaking and framing, is fundamentally important to enacting what the change "is" and how it moves through networks of stakeholders. Stakeholders' sensemaking activity surrounding a change shapes both the change and their concerns about it and their stakes in it. The discovery of new stakes and the understanding of joint and opposing stakes through sensemaking interaction creates opportunities for stakeholders to form alliances as well as emphasize differences – either in rivalries or schism. Understanding these processes of interaction during change is key to unpacking the entire picture of change implementation and the means that implementers and stakeholders use to engage, enact, and create change.

The next and last chapter of this book will take a practice perspective on the model presented in the earlier chapters. We will examine how a stakeholder of an organization going through a change process might make use of this model and the insights it affords. We will also discuss ways in which implementers might apply the lessons of this model and the arguments in this book.

Notes

1. Boje also refers to this idea in Boje and Dennehy (1993) and in Boje (1995).
2. "Tamara" comes from a play by the same name by John Kriznac. Characters unfold their stories in the many rooms of a huge mansion before an audience that splinters into fragments, chasing characters from one sensemaking situation to another. Audience members can only be in one room at a time. This creates the necessity of asking others about stories performed in rooms you did not attend, and pathways influence what some people interpret from the rooms they did enter.

References

Albrecht, T. and Hall, B. (1991) Facilitating talk about new ideas: The role of personal relationships in organizational innovation. *Communication Monographs*, 58 (3), 273–289.

Bartunek, J. M., Rousseau, D. M., Rudolph, J. W., and DePalma, J. A. (2006) On the receiving end: Sensemaking, emotion, and assessments of an organizational change initiated by others. *Journal of Applied Behavioral Science*, 42 (2), 182–206.

Bean, C. J. and Hamilton, F. E. (2006) Leader framing and follower sensemaking: Response to downsizing in the brave new workplace. *Human Relations*, 59 (3), 321–349.

Bird, S. (2007) Sensemaking and identity: The interconnection of storytelling and networking in a women's group of a large corporation. *Journal of Business Communication*, 44 (4), 311–339.

Boje, D. M. (1991) The storytelling organization: A study of storytelling performance in an office supply firm. *Administrative Science Quarterly*, 36, 106–126.

Boje, D. M. (1995) Stories of the storytelling organization: A postmodern analysis of Disney as "Tamara-land." *Academy of Management Journal*, 38 (4), 997–1035.

Boje, D. M. (2008) *Storytelling Organizations*. Thousand Oaks, CA: Sage.

Boje, D. M. and Dennehy, R. (1993) *Managing in a Postmodern World: America's Revolution Against Exploitation*. Dubuque, IA: Kendall Hunt.

Brown, A. D. and Humphreys, M. (2003) Epic and tragic tales: making sense of change. *Journal of Applied Behavioral Science*, 39 (2), 121–144.

Brown, A. D., Gabriel, Y., and Gheradi, S. (2009) Storytelling and change: An unfolding story. *Organization*, 16 (3), 323–333.

Browning, L. D. (1992) Lists and stories as organizational communication. *Communication Theory*, 2 (4), 281–302.

Brummans, B. H. J. M., Putnam, L. L., Gray, B., Hanke, R., Lewicki, R. J., and Wiethoff, C. (2008) Making sense of intractable multiparty conflict: A study of framing in four environmental disputes. *Communication Monographs*, 75 (1), 25–51.

Bryant, M. and Cox, J. W. (2004) Conversion stories as shifting narratives of organizational change. *Journal of Organizational Change Management*, 17 (6), 578–592.

Buchanan, D. and Dawson, P. (2007) Discourse and audience: Organizational change as multi-story process. *Journal of Management Studies*, 44 (5), 669–686.

Cherim, S. (2006) Managerial frames and institutional discourses of change: Employee appropriation and resistance. *Organization Studies*, 27 (9), 1261–1287.

Cooney, R. and Sewell, G. (2008) Shaping the other: Maintaining expert managerial status in a complex change management program. *Group and Organization Management*, 33 (6), 685–711.

Czarniawska, B. (1998) *A Narrative Approach to Organization Studies*. Thousand Oaks, CA: Sage.

Dewulf, A., Gray, B., Putnam, L. L., Lewicki, R., Aarts, N., Bouwen, R., and van Woekum, C. (2009) Disentangling approaches to framing in conflict and negotiation research: A meta-analytic perspective. *Human Relations*, 62 (2), 155–193.

Fairhurst, G. T. (2005) Reframing the art of framing: Problems and prospects for leadership. *Leadership*, 1, 165–185.

Fairhurst, G. T. and Sarr, R. A. (1996) *The Art of Framing: Managing the Language of Leadership*. San Francisco: Jossey-Bass.

Fiss, P. C. and Zajac, E. J. (2006) The symbolic management of strategic change: Sensegiving via framing and decoupling. *Academy of Management Journal*, 49 (6), 1173–1193.

Johansson, K. and Heide, M. (2008) Speaking of change: Three communication approaches in studies of organizational change. *Corporate Communications: An International Journal*, 13 (3), 288–305.

Laster, N. M. (2008) Communicating multiple change: Understanding the impact of change messages on stakeholder perceptions. Dissertation Abstracts International (UMI No. AAT 3342339).

Leonardi, P. (2009) Why do people reject new technologies and stymie organizational changes of which they are in favor? Exploring misalignments between social interactions and materiality. *Human Communication Research*, 35, 407–441.

Lewis, L. K. (2007) An organizational stakeholder model of change implementation communication. *Communication Theory*, 17 (2), 176–204.

Lewis, L. K. and Seibold, D. R. (1993) Innovation modification during intraorganizational adoption. *Academy of Management Review*, 18 (2), 322–354.

Lewis, L. K., Ruben, B., Sandmeyer, L., Russ, T., and Smulowitz, S. (unpublished) Sensemaking interaction during change: A longitudinal analysis of stakeholders' communication about Spellings Commission's efforts to change US higher education.

Ruben, B. D., Lewis, L., and Sandmeyer, L. (2008) *Assessing the Impact of the Spellings Commission: The Message, the Messenger, and the Dynamics of Change in Higher Education*. Washington, DC: National Association of College and University Business Officers.

Tenkasi, R. V. and Chesmore, M. C. (2003) Social networks and planned organizational change: The impact of strong network ties on effective change implementation and use. *Journal of Applied Behavioral Science*, 39 (3), 281–300.

Whittle, A., Suhomlinova, O., and Mueller, F. (2010) Funnel of interests: the discursive translation of organizational change. *Journal of Applied Behavioral Science*, 46 (1), 16–37.

Zoller, H. M. and Fairhurst, G. (2007) Resistance leadership: The overlooked potential in critical organization and leadership studies. *Human Relations*, 60 (9), 1331–1360.

Further Reading

Fairhurst, G. T. and Putnam, L. (2004) Organizations as discursive constructions. *Communication Theory*, 14 (1), 5–26.

Reger, R. K., Gustafson, L. T., Demarie, S. M., and Mullane, J. V. (1994) Reframing the organization: Why implementing total quality is easier said than done. *Academy of Management Review*, 19 (3), 565–584.

Sims, D. (2003) Between the millstones: A narrative account of the vulnerability of middle managers' storying. *Human Relations*, 56 (10), 1195–1211.

Teram, E. (2010) Organizational change with morally ambiguous contexts: A case study of conflicting postmerger discourses. *Journal of Applied Behavioral Science*, 46 (1), 38–54.

9

Applying the Model in Practice

You don't learn very much when you yourself are talking
Eric Schmidt, CEO of Google

The secret to managing is to keep the guys who hate you away from the guys who are undecided
Casey Stengel, baseball player and manager

Change happens by listening and then starting a dialogue with the people who are doing something you don't believe is right
Jane Goodall

This chapter is written with the practitioner in mind. After reading the preceding chapters and learning about the research and theory that informs the general model presented throughout this book, practition-

Organizational Change: Creating Change Through Strategic Communication,
First Edition. Laurie K. Lewis.

ers may be left with the question – so how to I use this model and this background to effectively and strategically participate in a change process? This chapter directly addresses that central question. The advice and frameworks presented in this chapter are aimed equally at implementers of change; those who resist a change; and those who aim to steer a change in a new direction. Any practitioner confronted with organizational change should be able to make use of the ideas in this chapter.

In this chapter I discuss a simplified way to understand the major activities that any practitioner needs to manage in order to successfully influence change in his/her organization. I also discuss four general tools that can be useful in doing so. To illustrate these tools, I will turn to a fresh, hypothetical case, that will be used in this chapter to illustrate how a practitioner could intervene, direct, influence, guide, or impact a change process. In the summary of the chapter, I will revisit important themes of this book by discussing some common myths about planned change implementation in light of what I have presented in the preceding chapters.

When working with practitioners I frequently get asked about the appropriate steps or stages of change. I get asked what period of time should be permitted for certain activities (e.g., immediate adjustment to the idea; going through a period of questioning and venting; getting to the point of acceptance and cooperation) or how long it takes for certain "phases" of a change process to unfold. For all sorts of reasons thinking about change as a set of pre-known phases or stages is unproductive. First, life rarely presents itself as neatly as that. Second, whatever set of stages a consultant provides you, it is easy then to simply cram your actual life experience into the predefined boxes – that is, enact the phases as they were given to you! It becomes more of an exercise in seeing the world in those little boxes than really moving through some set of distinct phases.

Activity Tracks

An alternative to working through stages is to think of change proceeding along *activity tracks*. We can imagine that most of our actions and reactions during change implementation run along three "meta-tracks" that account for our attention and the attention and energy of others who are effected by change. These three tracks each compete for our analytical concentration, emotional investment and preoccupation, and behavioral focus at any given time, and are defined and discussed in this chapter as managing meaning, managing network, and managing practice.

In **managing meaning**, as we discussed in Chapter 8, both implementers and stakeholders are participating in enacting realities of "what is going on" in the change process. This includes the realities of the external environment (as discussed in Chapters 1 and 7) and the internal realities discussed throughout the book: What is this change? What are my and others' stakes and how are they implicated in this change? What is "known" and what needs to be known and communicated? How do I and others feel about the change? Who is resisting? And what does resistance mean? These questions are addressed through making sense and managing the meaning of aspects of the change, the participants' roles in the change, and the context and progression of the change.

In **managing networks**, stakeholders and implementers are both monitoring and participating in shaping relationships among those who are impacted by and/or are witness to the change. As we discussed in Chapter 8, managing meaning can have implications for how stakeholders come to see one another's stakes – in alignment, in rivalry, as different but not antagonistic. In some cases, both implementers and stakeholders may reach out to specific groups of stakeholders to win compliance, support, or resources. In some cases, stakeholders or implementers may attempt to isolate some groups of stakeholders from consideration during change – to make them less central in decision-making for example. At times, implementers or stakeholders may lobby for increased participation or representation in the change decision-making process. All of these are part of managing the network of who is "in" the change; how people are connected; and the implications of how networks are being shaped during change (e.g., as more centralized; more fragmented; with new "holes" or new bridges among groups).

In the third track, **managing practice**, I refer to the more physical and material considerations for bringing about change. Implementers can make new policy official by posting it in official places; purchase and physically install new technology; alter evaluation criteria in official documents; advertise new products or services to customers, etc. Stakeholders can participate in training; attempt to master a newly required skill; perform in ways consistent or inconsistent with new policies, etc. Of course the ways in which practice gets done may or may not reflect the desired results that implementers have in mind.

Employees may not use a technology in the ways envisioned; policy may be applied unevenly or inappropriately; customers may adapt to a new procedure in an unexpected manner. All of these actions constitute material or physical responses that embody the change in practice.

We can think of these three activity tracks as running across a whole host of dynamics, tasks, strategic intentions, and efforts that give rise to the ultimate state of the change in any given organization at any given point in time. Both implementers and stakeholders who have strategic goals during change would be well advised to monitor and manage each of these activity tracks throughout change. However, different circumstances in an organization at a given point in time may demand more attention to one track than the others. For example, in a highly politically charged moment during a change implementation, demands for attention on management of meaning and managing powerful coalitions may trump our focus on managing practice in terms of installing new software, getting training up and running, and the like. In a contrasting example, if we are at a point where most key stakeholders are on board with a change and highly engaged in making it happen, the focus for implementers and stakeholders may be on managing practice rather than managing meaning or managing networks. In such a case, getting on with the tasks associated with technical fit issues; bringing in experts to train new users; and establishing necessary guidelines for use would be paramount.

Those who fail to monitor these three tracks effectively or who misread the situation in the organization may encounter more problems. Thus, ignoring brewing coalitions (managing networks) that are forming to scuttle a change effort; refusing to counter or consider sensemaking in the organization that is negative to the change (managing meaning); and putting all of the energy for the change into progressing with physical, policy, and training tasks (managing practice) might be a recipe for failure from implementers' perspectives. Similarly, implementers who focus completely on "selling" a change (managing meaning) and do very little to attend to the management of practice (creating the possibility for engaging a change and the resource support to encourage appropriate practice) will also likely fail to reach their goals.

Likewise, for stakeholders in an organization undergoing change the best strategic analysis and actions will be born of monitoring all three of these tracks and gearing one's actions to manage each towards one's goals. Let us imagine an example where a group of union workers oppose a new policy on work procedures. Implementers announce the new policy at an all-staff meeting; post it in an appropriate official document; and instruct supervisors to follow it and monitor employees' compliance (implementers are managing practice). The opposed employees could respond to that along a single activity track – they could refuse to follow the new procedures (managing practice). This would likely lead to these individuals being dismissed or punished. Alternatively, they could respond to it by complaining against the policy and discussing how poor the policy is (managing meaning) while complying with it in terms of practice. This would also be unlikely to yield any alteration of the change given that management might very well expect some "grumbling" about an unpopular policy. The opposed employees might decide to engage other union employees about the policy and/or involve the union organization in a discussion about the policy and attempt to garner their support (both managing meaning and managing the network). In this case, if they were to form a strong alliance with other employees and the union coupled with formulating and articulating a case for why the change is unnecessary or undesirable for some set of reasons, they may have a better chance of reaching their goals. Thus, managing multiple tracks is more likely to be successful than simply managing one track.

At such a point, the implementers may need to do more than manage practice. They too may need to manage meaning by creating more of a case for the change and managing the network by responding to the building coalition who may oppose the change. To ignore those activity tracks might be perilous for implementers. In fact, during highly contested change it may be wise to slow down on managing practice until more buy-in and powerful support can be secured.

In the remainder of this chapter I will work through some important tools for the management of change, both from the perspectives of implementers and other stakeholders, that work across these activity tracks. Like tools used in any context, they may be put to many uses and serve many masters. This chapter is no more devoted to helping implementers in reaching their goals than other stakeholders realizing theirs. The point is to illustrate, hopefully in a very concrete way, how the perspective represented in the earlier chapters might be put into practice. To help to do that, I introduce a new hypothetical case (see Highlight Box 9.1). We will work through this case illustrating the various ways in which the tools may be effectively used to reach the goals of the various participants.

Highlight Box 9.1: Virtual Problems

Organization: Designcorp is an architecture and design company. The culture is very professional, in part due to the high-end clients that the company maintains. The company has had a great deal of success and prides itself on quality work and quality client relationships.

Much of the work at Designcorp is done individually. However, there is also much formal and informal collaboration in the work. People frequently call meetings at the last minute to discuss issues in serving clients. There is often a lot of pressure to complete projects quickly.

Designcorp has nearly 200 employees and does not intend to grow in terms of adding staff. Their goals for the future involve growing their market share of high-end clients and developing more of a national reputation rather than the mostly local and regional one they now have.

Evelyn is the HR Director and the Implementer: Evelyn has been asked to take leadership of a new virtual work program. The program as it is proposed will permit employees in certain work roles to telework most of the days in the month. They'll be expected to be in the building for some important meetings on an infrequent basis but otherwise they will work from home or another location of their choosing.

This is a pilot program and if it is successful other types of workers may also be allowed to do telework, but only certain work roles will be able to participate even if it is successful.

The Immediate Reactions of Stakeholders: There are mixed reviews of this idea in the organization. Some are very excited and can't wait to be in line to telework. For example Susan is planning to start a family soon and sees many advantages that telework would bring to her personal life. Others, like Nathan – who works closely with Susan, but will not be allowed to telework in his role – hate the idea and think it will create chaos in their work relationships and in getting anything done (calling meetings, getting information from the teleworkers, supervising employees who aren't in the building, etc.). Some line supervisors have strongly negative opinions. Rodney, for example, believes that teleworking is a nuisance that will result only in more work for him and make his supervisory tasks that much more challenging. A few, like Claire, are at least open to the idea, but are hesitant to praise the idea and antagonize their peers who oppose it. There are many in the organization with neither very positive nor negative reactions to this idea but who simply don't understand how it is going to work. Those in favor or against it are lobbying them for support.

Tools for Managing Activity Tracks

Monitoring and Articulating Goals

As discussed in Chapter 4, goals are important in organizations for a variety of reasons. Articulating goals serves the function of charting a course for action; guiding the path that leads in a specific direction; and evaluating the distance and direction traveled in pursuit of goals. Although goals can shift over time and be recreated through actions we take, they do serve as markers and as starting points of negotiation and making sense of other stakeholders' stakes. It is important therefore that implementers and stakeholders are able to articulate, at least for themselves, what goals they have.

In Chapter 4 I discussed how change programs may be directed towards goals of uniformity and fidelity in different degrees. That is, implementers (and to some extent stakeholders) may have initial preferences or a vision for how a change will be practiced along these dimensions. In some cases there can be great tolerance for variation in practice and use across those who participate in the change. In other cases that tolerance for variation may be quite minimal. Similarly, sometimes implementers and some stakeholders may have strong preferences for a particular version of a change practice to be embraced by all. Others may see virtue in flexible and creative adoption of new practices (e.g., a new technology being used in ways not imagined by its creators). Additionally, goals will involve specific results that implementers and stakeholders wish to achieve through a change. That might include things like increases in profit margin; higher quality service for clients/ customers; increased efficiency in processes and procedures. For other stakeholders it might include improved speed of service; increased opportunities for employee development, learning, training, pay or benefit increases; decreasing supervision and monitoring to enable more job autonomy.

An important practice tool for all strategic participants in change implementation involves assessing goals for the change early, and periodically. This includes assessment of one's own goals as well as those embraced by other stakeholders and the organization's official goals. For implementers this will likely involve a formal process of writing down goals and the metrics that will be used to assess progress achieved in each area. For stakeholders with no official power to determine or measure goals, other more informal discussions and understandings of what goals might be may be developed.

Working across the three activity tracks we can think of goal setting and monitoring as involving at least two if not all three tracks. Sensemaking and sensegiving about goals is a key tool for managing meaning. To win support for a goal or set of goals, it is important for audiences to understand what those goals are and what rationale is offered to support them. Managing meaning about competing goals – either ones already embraced by the organization or ones offered as alternatives to the change goals proposed – is also necessary in order to be able to create a sense of shared and collective goals or to effectively deprioritize competing goals. Additionally, strategic participants in a change will need to manage the network in terms of understanding how different groups of stakeholders view the goals of the change; their own goals; and the competing and complementary stakes and goals of other groups of stakeholders. It is also possible that part of the management of practice will involve setting up or adjusting existing mechanisms for monitoring goal accomplishment. We can turn to the Virtual Problems case to illustrate practice tools related to goals.

As the HR Director charged with implementing this change, Evelyn should first examine the organization's core goals for implementing the change. She needs to garner the support of senior leaders for specific, measurable goals that can be shared among important stakeholders of the change. These leaders need to take part in building the belief in stakeholders that there is principal support (Chapter 7) for the change. Building a case for the change also will involve demonstrating that the change represents a necessary and appropriate change for the organization that can be successfully accomplished. These beliefs relate to discrepancy, efficacy, and appropriateness that we discussed in Chapters 5 and 7. In order to make that case effectively, it is important that senior management know what they hope to accomplish. From the case description it is not apparent how instituting telework would serve any of Designcorp's fundamental organizational goals. In fact, on first blush, it seems that teleworking might run counter to the work norms of "last minute meetings," time pressures, and team work. Not that these things couldn't be managed virtually, but that it may not be immediately obvious to stakeholders in the organization why telework is important, necessary, and potentially positive to accomplish the organization's goals. However, it is likely that stakeholders are immediately able to identify individuals' goals that would be served by the change (e.g., teleworkers gain more autonomy and flexibility). It is also likely that stakeholders would easily be able to imagine some downsides of the change for those who are not able to telework (e.g., limited access to teleworking employees, difficulty in calling meetings).

For Evelyn, it is important to think through the goals of the change initiative and the ways in which the change might line up with the current values and stakes of key stakeholders. This stakeholder analysis is an important tool in getting clarity on the goals and stakes others have in the change and determining how values fit (Chapter 7) with those goals/stakes. Table 9.1 shows how Evelyn might start such an analysis by identifying important groups of stakeholders who have a stake in this change; then identifying the most relevant values that are held by those stakeholders that seem to be impacted by the change; and finally

Table 9.1   Stakeholder analysis

Key Stakeholder	Key Values Relevant to Change	Initial Values Fit with Change from Their Perspective
Employees who may be allowed to Telework (e.g., Susan)	Job flexibility, job autonomy, high client commitment	Good
Employees who will never be allowed to Telework (e.g., Nathan)	Fairness, smooth work process, high client commitment	Poor
Supervisors of the teleworkers (Rodney and Claire)	Competency in supervisory duties, high commitment to clients, high commitment to employees	Poor to Neutral
Clients of teleworkers	Quality and timely service	Unknown
Senior Managers	Organization survival, cost savings on overhead, high employee morale, retention of talent, growth of organization's client base, high quality client relationships, development of national reputation	Mixed

estimating the degree to which the value-fit is initially poor, neutral, or good from the perspective of those stakeholders. This analysis gives Evelyn her first read on how stakeholders might react to the idea of the change and what goals might be represented in their reactions.

As Evelyn moves through her stakeholder analysis and encourages a conversation among senior leaders about the organization's goals, she is managing both meaning and the network in this change effort. She is attending to the meaning of what "we are doing" and developing an understanding of how it might be interpreted by others in the organization. She is also contributing to mapping out where potential allies and rivals might lie in the organization both for and against the change effort. Some of the stakeholder clashes and potential complementary stakes she identifies among stakeholder groups may be unknown to those groups at this early point. Further, by encouraging senior managers to thoroughly examine their core values and the ways that this change initiative is supportive or counter to those goals, she may provoke an opportunity for them to "gut check" whether this change is a good idea or not. They may end up asking themselves why they are implementing the change. Perhaps they are following a trend in the industry but without good reason. Perhaps they are responding to a single employee's request, without further analysis of the implications of the program for other employees. Perhaps there is little in the way they've envisioned the implementation of the program that is tied to any major core value or focus for the company. This is an excellent exercise for senior management to undergo before further pursuing implementing the change.

Other stakeholders need to monitor and articulate goals as well. Goals for non-implementers are more likely to be informal. For example, supervisors of the new teleworkers might discuss among themselves what goals they have for this new pilot program. In the process, they will likely discover the depth of their differences on the idea of trying telework. It might be most strategic for those opposed to the telework to gain agreement from the other supervisors on the criteria by which the pilot program will be evaluated. That is, what would it have to accomplish in order to be deemed successful and what would indicate a failure that should suggest discontinuation? Examples of success indicators might include maintaining current levels of productivity, timely processing of client accounts, number of client complaints. Examples of indicators of failure might be noticeable increase in animosity among employees, delays in resolving client issues, communication breakdowns between teleworkers and office staff. Nailing down these indicators for what success looks like would be a strategic way to force senior managers to articulate the goals for the program and to provide measurable benchmarks that the change must meet.

It might also be strategic to include individual goals that the supervisors have wanted in the past. For example, Rodney might use this opportunity to ask for other benchmarks to be met or other complaints to be addressed as the pilot goes forward. Rodney could ask that he be alleviated from some supervisory tasks or have some tasks restructured to make the transition to telework supervision smoother. In this sort of negotiation, the supervisors would be working across activity tracks of managing the network (e.g., potentially forming a coalition with some agreements about the evaluation of the change and the direct benefits all supervisors would win from the pilot should it prove "successful") as well as managing meaning of the change in forcing more commitment to terms of engagement – what is this change exactly? What is it meant to accomplish? How or when will that be assessed? – and gaining clarity on how the program adds value to those who bear the burden of the transition.

Developing Strategic Messages and Strategic Communication Plan

Another set of tools in managing across the activity tracks concern the strategic messages that implementers and stakeholders create and the general strategy framework within which those messages are created. As we discussed in Chapter 2, there are several dimensions along which message and communication plans may be based including dissemination/ soliciting input; sidedness; gain vs. loss framing; blanket vs. targeting; and discrepancy vs. efficacy.

One of Evelyn's challenges in creating messages about the change – even if she can get senior leaders to gain clarity about the goals of the initiative – is to overcome the disparities that this sort of change creates between the "haves" and the "have nots." For example, if she adopts a "gain" frame (Chapter 5) for this change, it is easy for some in the organization to question what is gained for them personally. Some of the stakeholders who are not going to be allowed to telework may see the gains as extra perks for some individual workers. If Evelyn is going to use a gain frame, she must emphasize gains for the entire organization's wellbeing or find a way to creatively identify gains even for those who are seemingly disadvantaged by this change (i.e., those who will never be able to telework themselves). Discrepancy messages will also need to be crisp and clear to the most negative of the stakeholders. If there is no message explaining the need for the change or the opportunity that the change represents (e.g., to motivate talented people who are threatening to leave to stay with the organization), it is easy for the naysayers to point out that the pain of adjustment to the new work style isn't worth the minimal organizational gains earned.

Further, a major role for Evelyn, as the implementer, is to disseminate information (Chapters 2 and 5) about what the change entails, how it will work, what processes are in place, and other core official information. She should monitor the stakeholders' understandings of the change and the questions they raise so she can both identify weaknesses in the implementation plans and correct any misunderstanding about how the change is envisioned to unfold in the organization.

Stakeholders most opposed to the change should consider strategic messages to both implementers and to powerful and well-positioned opinion leaders (Chapter 3). Targeted messages (Chapter 5) should be designed to appeal to influential decision-makers who have the power to stop the change but who may not have yet considered all the downsides to the change. So Rodney and Nathan would be wise to target undecided supervisors. These supervisors may not immediately see any problem with the change initiative and so are not opposing it initially. These participants and others like them might supply evidence (e.g., disseminate information from other organizations who have had difficulty with telecommuting) and raise issues that call attention to potential problems. Raising insurmountable problems or ones that would require a good deal of analysis and problem-solving on the part of supervisors may make the change seem less desirable. In essence Rodney and Nathan would be raising counters to "efficacy" messages – saying, "we *can't* do this."

For Susan, who is in favor of the change, strategic messages might take the form of a gain frame – what the organization stands to gain by investing in this change. She could make the case that by increasing the flexibility of work arrangements for even some staff, the commitment of those employees to the organization might be increased. She could highlight savings in physical space and other resources, as well as reduction in noise and parking lot overcrowding, as gains for the entire organization should the change succeed.

Susan and Evelyn might also apply two-sided messages (Chapter 5) that acknowledge the downsides to the change by countering with ideas for repairs for overcoming them (e.g., an inoculation message). If Susan and other supportive stakeholders worked together to target the more neutral supervisors and lobby them for support of the change they could win support from a powerful coalition. However, it might also be strategic to use the same approach with the less enthusiastic peers. Nathan might be swayed to a more supportive position if some of his concerns about the change could be alleviated. In this instance it would be useful for both Susan and Evelyn to practice soliciting feedback from stakeholders like Nathan to hear concerns, problem-solve together, and determine if problems that are being raised are insurmountable or not.

In each of these examples – Evelyn, Rodney, Nathan, and Susan – the strategic messages are geared for different audiences that these stakeholders believe will have important influence on decision-making or decision-makers. No supervisor wants to deal with a "revolt" by his/her subordinates, so even for those low-level subordinates with little power in this decision context, their support of the change might be an important contribution to the overall organization's conversation about telework. Understanding that and working to manage their sensemaking about the change involves managing meaning and managing the network.

Also, as the pilot program for the teleworking begins, those who are either opposed to or in support of the change will want to continue to manage the meanings that are constructed about how well the change initiative is working out. They will want to influence how important and influential stakeholders are constructing the reality of the change as it is practiced. For example, checking in with clients of the teleworkers to monitor for praise or complaints will be important. Further, they will want to manage the practice of the telework in terms of messages that are publicly posted and recorded about the change. Another way to manage practice is to influence who become spokespersons for the change for external or important internal audiences and how the change is represented. For example, Rodney will probably want to underscore at every opportunity that telework is a pilot program and not a finalized change. He should keep alive the discourse of tentativeness and adaptation of the program as it goes through this testing phase. He would want to correct any document or presentation that implied that the change was permanent. Symbolic markers of permanence would also need to be cautioned against – such as revising formal documents with "teleworkers" as a category of staff. For those very supportive of the change, such as Susan, moving towards encouraging normalizing practice of the telework model would be to her advantage. That might involve strategic messages that use a "future" tense. For example, she might invoke teleworkers in long-term planning documents; encourage "telework" to be advertised to new hires as a possible incentive; and encourage other non-teleworkers to make requests to be considered for a future telework slot when the pilot period concludes.

Analysis of Input

A key strategic tool in participating in a change initiative – whether the goal is to forestall the change; alter it; or support it – is to solicit and use input (Chapter 2). The implementers of a change will often consciously or unconsciously select a style of participation (see Table 2.1 in Chapter 2). Those styles will emphasize either more symbolic or sincere (resource-based) gathering of input during change. They will target very select stakeholders or wide representation of diverse stakeholders. In order to maximize the use of input as a resource, I recommend that participants adopt **USER**:

> **U**se input as a resource in the decision-making and adjustments
> **S**ystematically collect input
> **E**valuate the process by which input is collected to ensure it is working
> **R**igorously drill down and examine the input that is collected

This acronym reminds the participant to use the *input as a resource* not merely as a symbol (Chapters 2 and 6). To know if you are using the input as a resource, Evelyn could ask herself if anything she might hear in collecting input could actually alter a decision that has already been made? Could input influence important decisions going forward? Could the input influence the ways resources or responsibilities are allocated? If the answers to these and other similar questions are "no" it may be that input is merely being used to "look like" the organization is listening. Or, it might be that input is only being solicited to gauge the correctness of understanding about the change – and although that is important to do, it is very limited.

Similarly, stakeholders who hold other opinions about the change or who are not sure about their opinions during the change process should collect and use input as a resource that informs their opinions and their actions. For example, Claire should actively engage stakeholders she knows are opposed to and in favor of the change – as well as others who are uncertain – to discover what information they hold in common; what they do not share; and what concerns each has about the possible outcomes of the change initiative. Neutral participants like Claire can sometimes best manage the network by serving as important "connectors" (Chapter 3) who might broker creative solutions to identified problems or concerns.

The second piece of USER reminds us to be *systematic* in soliciting input. It is easy for us to go to those who we know will agree with us; those whose information and ideas we use repeatedly; and those who have common experiences. However, we are less likely to find new information from such people. All strategic participants in change should be wide-reaching and systematic in a search for a variety of information sources, types of knowing, and bases of experience. Part of being systematic is being active in the pursuit of input rather than passively waiting for "the usual" sources to offer up input. The noisiest, most combative or assertive stakeholders are more likely to initiate providing input. Others who are quieter, more reserved, more concerned about their self-presentation may not be eager to share perspectives, concerns, and information – especially during controversy. A systematic approach to soliciting input will attempt to overcome reluctance on the part of such stakeholders and make it easier and more comfortable for them to offer what they know and what they think. An especially strong system of soliciting input will pursue the perspectives of the skeptics and those with strong concerns (Chapter 6). Such voices are more likely to surface potential problems that might blindside the company later if not considered early in the pilot phase.

Evelyn could create input soliciting channels that would encourage widespread participation in evaluating and monitoring the pilot program. That might include time set aside during team meetings to share concerns and perspectives on how the telework is going; creating a confidential channel especially set up to discuss concerns about the teleworker relationships with peers and/or clients; a survey that asks clients to report their level of satisfaction with client services during the pilot program.

New teleworkers might create channels to monitor reactions and concerns about their new telework style. Susan could actively seek the honest feedback of her peers, routinely checking in with them over coffee or stopping by the office to ask how things are going or if adjustments need to be made in new communication procedures. Susan and other teleworkers could also encourage openness with clients about the telework program, asking for any suggestions or concerns to be surfaced so they can be addressed. Actively creating channels and opportunities for peers and clients to voice their input not only surfaces concerns, it adds perspective and information to the process of testing the new program. It also builds trust among stakeholders who may perceive their stakes to be at odds.

USER also reminds us to *evaluate the system* we are using for soliciting input to ensure that it is working to obtain the widest sample of useful input possible. We need to think through how to evaluate the system. One indicator of a poor system for soliciting input is that we are only hearing what we want to hear. If all we get is confirming input, we probably aren't doing a very good job being systematic. There should be a variety of types of input representing as many points of view as are present among our stakeholders. Also, use of input systems should encourage people to provide input repeatedly (that is, they are not soured in their early experiences of doing so). They should build a sense of trust and openness.

Finally, USER calls us to be rigorous in analysis of the input we receive. It is not enough to simply categorize or tally up those "for" and "against." It is important to ask many questions of those with various perspectives; to learn where their point of view and concerns come from; to interrogate the information (not the people) for its weaknesses and strengths before relying on it in decision-making. Rigorous analysis of any sort of data in organizations (financial, marketing, production) necessitates spending some time and using unbiased procedures. It is not that hard to "see" what one wishes to see in data. One can read the data in support of many different stories (Chapter 8). Comparing different reads on the same data and sorting through the interpretations in an honest search for a collective sense of things is challenging. Participants who invest in this level of rigor will be better able to leverage an argument though. They will be better prepared to formulate or reformulate their own position on the change. They will be better equipped to confront the change (even an undesirable one) if they have that level of data analysis behind them.

Part of being rigorous involves understanding that stories and realities are enacted not "found" (Chapter 8). As discussed in earlier chapters, the frames that are put around data can dramatically alter what they "say" to us and to others. Different stakeholders will attempt to frame data and input in ways favorable to their own interpretations of or enactment of reality. A strategic participant in change will monitor the ways in which input is being framed. For example, Evelyn could frame all the complaints of employees like Nathan as "jealousy" and dismiss it. Rodney could frame the positive or neutral responses of the non-teleworker employees as "uniformed" responses or as from people who were just reluctant to complain since this decision to do the pilot has already been made. It is important to be aware of the ways in which others are framing experiences and events so that effective counter-framing can be made if necessary.

We should also be aware that as input is solicited and interpretations form about what the data/input means, networks often are reshaped (Chapter 8). Understanding how networks can be reshaped, relationships made stronger or weaker as sensemaking activity unfolds during change, is part of managing networks. Those who come to share perspectives and stories may bond around those enacted realities. They may further search together for more stories that prove their case. Thus, as the pilot project progresses, those opposed to it may search for stories that illustrate its challenges and failures. Those in favor are likely to circulate stories about its successes. The sharing of these self-reinforcing stories may help bond the groups of stakeholders who share them. This involves managing networks as well as managing meaning.

Influencing Implementation Climate

As discussed in Chapter 2, communication is not everything in change. An important part of a change process concerns the ways in which physical, material, financial, and other resources are allocated and managed. Some authors have argued that in order to provide for a strong implementation "climate" (Klein and Sorra, 1996) participants need to know that desired behaviors are rewarded, supported, and expected. That is, infrastructure needs to be in place to create appropriate incentives (for compliance) and disincentives (for noncompliance); material and physical resources such as training, staffing, equipment, and the like needs to be in place to overcome hindrances to a smooth change process; and leaders need to demonstrate that they have expectations that stakeholders – especially employees/staff – will be supportive of the change. They need to show that they expect that the change will endure and not die out from neglect or their own lack of enthusiasm.

Many stakeholders can enhance the implementation climate through active participation, follow-through, sharing necessary resources, and the like. However, implementers are chiefly responsible for allocating necessary resources and making rewards and expectations clear to participants. Evelyn needs to think about more than "selling" the idea of teleworking to her employees and to clients. She needs to provide for infrastructure that plays a role in ensuring that telework *can* be successful at Designcorp. That could include purchasing and installing technologies that assist in smooth communication and resource-sharing between teleworkers and non-teleworkers as well as between teleworkers and clients; investing in training for all employees so they have a firm understanding of how virtual team work can be accomplished and have a chance to learn new skills; and building evaluation criteria and incentives into employees appraisal process that relate to successful management of telework relationships.

Senior leaders play a critical role in making it clear to employees that promotion of the success of the telework pilot is expected. As this is a pilot program, part of that expectation will be to report any problems so that they can be addressed. If employees feel compelled by senior managers to work with the change effort to rigorously develop the idea and "debug" processes involved with it, they are more likely to engage the change in productive ways rather than merely grumble about it. Building a strong implementation climate has to do with managing practice more than anything, but it also has elements of managing meaning since these actions bring with them a message that the organization is serious about trying out this idea.

For other stakeholders, especially those who are not in support of the change, it is wise to make clear to targeted audiences that support of their advocated position will in some ways be rewarded, supported, and at times (if negotiated agreements have been reached) expected. So, if Claire cuts a deal with Rodney that she will support him in opposing the change if certain benchmarks are not met during the pilot, Rodney would want to communicate that follow-through on that commitment is expected. Similarly, if Nathan promises to swap shifts with Susan if she drops her support for telework, Nathan would need to reward her for compliance with that request. In terms of managing practice, Rodney could create a disincentive for the telework pilot to succeed if he threatens to quit. If he could gain the cooperation of other supervisors in taking a similar stance (i.e., managing networks and managing practice) he might have a powerful tool to get his interests met.

In sum, Designcorp's implementer and stakeholders should manage the change process across the three activity tracks – managing meaning, managing network, and managing practice – by employing four general tools: monitoring and articulating goals; developing strategic messages; analyzing input; and influencing implementation climate (see Figure 9.1). As strategic and invested stakeholders (including implementers) focus on the use of these tools to manage these activity tracks they will inevitably be interacting to make sense of what is going on; be reaching for a clear understanding of multiple perspectives on the change; be working to frame the change in ways consistent with their own and

Tools of Practice

Activity Tracks	Monitor and Articulate Goals	Develop Strategic Communication Plan and Messages	Analyze Input: USER	Influence Implementation Climate
Managing Meaning	• Determine goals • Gain leader commitment to goals • Share goals with others • Manage conflicts with others' goals • Stakeholders discuss goals • Frame results from monitoring goals	• Create messages that build necessary beliefs about change / counter-argue against them • Create messages that frame the change; cope with downsides; inoculate audiences • Design information and participation strategy • Monitor reactions to messages of self/others	• Encourage the widespread understanding that sharing perspectives/concerns/ideas is useful for all concerned • Build perceptions of trust through open channels of communication • Actively frame and monitor the frames others put on input and data	• Influence stakeholders' understandings that participation in change is rewarded, supported, and expected
Managing Network	• Map stakeholders' value fit with change • Highlight shared goals with other groups of stakeholders • Map out how different stakeholders goals conflict/overlap	• Target audiences (blanket or specific) to influence process and decision-making • Raise strengths and weaknesses that speak the stakes of important stakeholders • Look to frame common stakes among allies	• Actively engage a variety of stakeholders with varied perspectives • Broker relationships among stakeholders to aid in developing overlapping stakes • Facilitate sharing of knowledge/data • Monitor the way the network is reshaped around interpretations	• Broker deals and partnerships with other stakeholders who have unique rewards or support to offer or withhold from the change effort • Monitor the key resources that various stakeholders are able/willing to bring to the change effort
Managing Practice	• Make goals official • Determine metrics to assess goals • Set up means to monitor goals • Participate in monitoring goals	• Shape official or unofficial documents about the change • Attend to the symbols, language, and spokespersons used to stand for the change	• Actively create and use channels for soliciting input • Evaluate use and opinions about system for input • Rigorously analyze input and enlist help to create shared sense of data	• Create supportive infrastructure to ensure that your goals can be met • Put in place incentives and disincentives for cooperation

Figure 9.1 Managing activity tracks with tools of practice

shared stakes; connect with and make bridges between groups of stakeholders in coalitions; and manage the physical and material resources
of the change climate in ways that support their goals in the change
effort.

These recommendations, if followed, do not guarantee that Designcorp
will have success with teleworking or that the implementers will have
an easy pathway to convincing the more reluctant stakeholders to
embrace the change. However, this prescription does encourage energy
being directed at the change initiative. Managing these activity tracks
with these tools, stakeholders will be able to thoroughly vet this change
initiative. By the end of the pilot period all the various stakeholders will
have had voice; had opportunities to help make sense of the change;
and listened thoroughly to other stakeholders. The likelihood is that all
cards are on the table through this process. Those empowered to make
final decisions about moving forward with telework should have a clear
picture of the viability and potential challenges of the change. Those
who have little or no power in the decision-making will have had opportunities to be heard and potentially have influenced outcomes.

Myths About Implementing Planned Change

In the process of writing this book, it has occurred to me that several
myths about the change process exist in our popular understanding and
to some extent surface in our research and theoretical traditions regarding change implementation. This tour of the research and theory about
implementation of change has, hopefully, debunked these myths or at
least called into question whether they are always the case.

First, the myth that planned change is inevitable. Too often popular
press books and even academic articles and books start out assuming
that the stewards of organizations must change them. They assume,
perhaps even to the point of not being aware of it, that lengthy periods
of stable practice with little variation of processes, product, policy,
style, and so on is really fantasy. Although I started this book by arguing
that there are multiple triggers for change in organizations and that
forces of regulation, marketplace, internal innovation, and environmental turbulence frequently lead to planned change as a response, that is
different from an argument of inevitability of planned change. This is a
dangerous assumption since accepting that change is inevitable sets up
the practitioner to be less vigilant in considering the soundness of arguments and pressure to bring about any specific change. If we believe

that we just *have* to change, then we resign ourselves to each new trend, fashion, and innovation as one more change we need to implement. If we take the concept of healthy stability off the table, and give into the cultural dogma that the only good organization is one that is constantly reinventing itself, we can become much less discerning about judging when change might be beneficial and when it is problematic or not worth the effort.

Further, changing organizations is an affirmative act (or more accurately a set of actions) not something that simply happens. So, in fact, change is only inevitable if we choose to change. And constant change is only inevitable if we constantly choose to change. Although certainly we don't choose the change that occurs in our organizations' environments or choose the life-cycle changes that come with the age and history of an organization, we do choose to implement planned change in response to those circumstances. Our choices to change should be vigilantly considered not merely assumed to be inevitable.

A second myth that crops up a lot in popular press discourses about change implementation asserts that it is human nature or the nature of certain personalities to fear change. This myth also suggests that such personality tendencies are at the root of resistance, and resistance is bad. As we discussed thoroughly in Chapter 6, "resistance" is probably a term that has outlived its usefulness. It is a term that groups together a varied range of behavior, attitudes, and cognition under one pejorative term. Being less than completely satisfied with, enthusiastic about, and cooperative in a change effort cannot be assumed to be a bad outcome for all cases, for all stakeholders, no matter what.

It is incumbent on the implementer to sort through hesitation, concern, push-back, negativity, refusal among other "resistant" responses to change and determine root causes and appropriate ways to manage each. For some it will be appropriate to educate and correct misinterpretations of information or intent. For others, it is more appropriate to alter the change effort to address problems and concerns that are raised. In some cases negotiation among stakeholders with competing stakes will be necessary. In others, the complete withdrawal of the change may be the wisest choice. What has been called "resistance" should be reframed in our literature and our practice as "energy" that needs to be effectively channeled in order to improve the change process and the change itself.

A third myth focuses our attention on the informational and persuasive campaigns of implementers. This myth suggests that if we offer up change in an appealing manner, we will ultimately convince most stakeholders to accept and like it. Much of this myth stems from the issue I raised in the Introduction that too many consultants and researchers assume that the change – any change – is a good idea. If that is true, then it easily follows that negative reactions must be due to misunderstanding the change. If only everyone understood the change, of course they'd be on board. So, that casts the implementer in the role of informational campaign manager. However, we know from our discussion in Chapter 2 that more information does not always resolve uncertainty nor lead to shared "knowledge" or shared meaning. We also know that there are many competing sources of knowing and information within organizations and implementers cannot just speak one-to-one to stakeholders without the influence of those competing sources. Thus, managing communication during change involves soliciting of input; managing across all three of the activity tracks discussed in this chapter; and especially understanding that meaning is managed throughout an organization and beyond – not merely by the formal messages an implementer puts in her campaign to sell the change.

Conclusion

Through this book the reader has taken a journey that has illuminated the complex social dynamics that occur when organizations attempt to implement change. While the book is somewhat ambitious in its attempt to integrate research and theory across disciplines and sub-disciplines, I hope that I have managed to intrigue the researcher and scholar of organizational change in ways that might impact the direction of future research. I also hope that this book has been able to make useful observations and provide advice for practitioners who will encounter change in their work and lives. The central argument of this book and the main take-away I hope any reader will get from it is that change implementation is essentially a social and communicative process. Further, that the negotiation of stakes, and sensemaking through interaction that occurs among stakeholders, accounts for the largest share of explanation in outcomes of change.

Reference

Klein, K. J. and Sorra, J. S. (1996) The challenge of innovation implementation. *Academy of Management Review*, 21 (4), 1055–1080.

Glossary

absorption   person adjusts self to fit role demands.

activity tracks   areas that account for our attention and energy during change.

adaptive approaches   approach to change implementation wherein the change/innovation is fit to the organization.

adoption   the term we use to describe the formal selection of the idea for incorporation into an organization.

appropriateness   reflects the belief that the specific change under consideration/implementation is the correct one to address the need expressed in discrepancy.

attribution error   occurs when an observer attributes the cause of an observation incorrectly.

authenticity   concerns the sincerity of stakeholders' compliance with implementers' expectations for their behavior.

autonomous approaches   implementation strategies that are flexible and open to redefinition/reinvention even at the lowest levels of the organization.

avoidance-avoidance goal conflicts   "arise when the message options available to respond to a question have multiple negative

Organizational Change: Creating Change Through Strategic Communication,
First Edition. Laurie K. Lewis.
© 2011 Laurie K. Lewis. Published 2011 by Blackwell Publishing Ltd.

outcomes in relation to one's aims, yet a reply must be made" (Kline, Simunich, and Weber, 2009, p. 44).

bankrupt participation describes the case where even symbolic involvement is available for only a few representative stakeholders.

boundary-spanners individuals who connect an organization with external environments.

change acceptance zone that space wherein the motivation to change is high enough to create some stress, but the perception of potential success is also high enough to provide impetus to try.

change burnout the exhaustion of an individual's capacity or willingness to continue to participate in change programs.

channel "the means by which messages get from one individual to another" (Rogers, 1995, p. 18).

coercive forces direct communicators away from certain practices that that would be frowned upon by authorities.

cognitive frames representations of reality that are stored in an individual's memory.

communication processes involve interaction, discourse, and interpretation. Processes are sometimes created through formal planned processes determined by decision makers in organizations. At other times processes are created in emergent interaction that may become normative (usual) practice over time.

concertive control concertively controlled organizations rely on the strong loyalty and identification of stakeholders (usually employees) to foster a frame of decision-making that puts the organization's interests first, above any individual interests.

connectors are those who help bridge gaps between different types of stakeholders.

corporate social responsibility scholars are concerned with describing how organizations attend to stakes of stakeholders who have claims on the organization that are not related to the bottom line.

counselors those in the organization who provide social support to other stakeholders during change.

decaf resistance looking like we are resisting while still accepting the power structure.

definitive stakeholder in Mitchell, Agle, and Wood's (1997) scheme, those stakeholders perceived to hold all three of the attributes of power, urgency, and legitimacy.

descriptive stakeholder theory   branch of Stakeholder Theory that depicts existing relationships with stakeholders.

determination   person adjusts the role to suit self.

diffusion   the process involved in sharing new ideas with others to the point that they "catch on".

discontinuance   the gradual ending of a practice.

discourse   "a system of thought with its own linguistic tool bag, or collection of terms and metaphors for key concepts and ideas; categories for understanding; themes for stories; and familiar arguments for us to draw upon to describe, explain or justify" (Fairhurst, 2011, p. 32).

discrepancy   the belief that the change is necessary.

discrepancy messages   messages focused on suggesting the urgency to initiate change.

discursive change   often involves re-labeling of practices as something new in order to give the appearance of changed practice without really doing things differently.

dispositional resistance   "an individual's tendency to resist or avoid making changes, to devalue change generally, and to find change aversive across diverse contexts and types of change" (Oreg, 2003, p. 680).

effectiveness   the accomplishment of desired results.

efficacy   the belief that the change is something we can successfully accomplish.

efficacy messages   messages promoting the sense that the change goals can and will be accomplished.

efficiency   accomplishment of effectiveness with the fewest possible expended resources.

emotional support   providing a channel for venting emotions.

enactment   in this process stakeholders "enact" or "construct" their environment through a process of social interaction and sensemaking.

equal dissemination   blanket style of communication where all stakeholders are given information with same message and style.

equal participation   blanket style of communication where all stakeholders are given equal opportunities to provide input.

equifinality   the principle that there are multiple paths to the same end.

equivocal communication   strategic use of language to give an appearance of responsiveness that if truly delivered in a clear, direct manner would create negative repercussions.

equivocality   ambiguous meanings and too many available interpretations of events/objects.

espoused theories   those we claim as the premises of our choices of action.

expertise power   relying on perceptions of one's competence, capability, and effectiveness to influence organizational or individual behavior.

exploration   there is simultaneous adjustment of role and person.

fidelity   the degree of departure from the intended design of the change.

first-order change   small, incremental predictable interruptions in normal practice.

formal communication   involves use of official channels; declarations and policy set down by organizational leaders.

frames   a means to bracket experience and elements of a story in order to impact interpretation of details.

gain frame   emphasizes the advantages of compliance with the persuader's message.

group values   vary among the groups in an organization and reflect the shared experiences, roles, interactions, and perspectives of those in the groups.

high intensity organizational values   "encapsulate strong, fervent views and sharp strictures regarding desirable and undesirable actions on the part of the organization and its members" (Klein and Sorra, 1996, p. 1063).

identity gap   the difference between the actual organizational schema and the ideal organizational schema.

implementation   "the translation of any tool or technique, process, or method of doing, from knowledge to practice" (Tornatzky and Johnson, 1982, p. 193).

implementers   are those people in organizations who take on a formal role in bringing about the change effort and translating the idea of change into practice.

informal communication   includes the spontaneous interactions of stakeholders with each other, with implementers, and with non-stakeholders.

information dissemination   involves the spreading of facts, clarifications, notices, details, rationale and the like for the purpose of increasing the knowledge about a change initiative.

informational support   providing answers to questions that are source of stress.

innovation   a creative process of generating ideas for practice.

input solicitation as resource   empowering stakeholders to have impact on the manner, rate, timing and possibly even the wisdom of implementing a change at all.

input solicitation as symbol   merely creating an appearance of participation.

institutional theory   argues that components of an organization's formal structure and institutionalized contexts (e.g., industries, professions) become widely accepted, deemed to be necessary or appropriate, and then their presence or absence is used as a signal of legitimacy.

instrumental stakeholder theory   branch of Stakeholder Theory wherein scholars test claims about how organizational actions shape stakeholder relationships (e.g., certain strategies with stakeholders are associated with certain outcomes).

instrumental support   taking on some task for another person.

interactional frames   dynamic process of enacting and shaping meaning in ongoing interaction.

interpersonal channel   channels that primarily involve face-to-face communication.

isomorphism   a constraining process that gives rise to similarity in organizational form and practice.

journalists   serve the function of investigators and reporters during change by gathering and sharing information from inside and outside the organization.

knowing   a verb: an active and ongoing accomplishment of problem-solving.

knowledge   a noun: stable facts, objects and dispositions.

latent power   available power that can be used as a threat of the exercise of power.

lateral dissent   an individual would express dissent to someone other than the leader in hopes it would get relayed to the leader.

loss frame   emphasizes the disadvantages of noncompliance.

low intensity organizational values   *organizational values* are of lesser importance to its members.

management of meaning   symbols are constructed to define reality for others. That new reality then implies certain actions and understanding over others.

managing meaning   participating in enacting realities of "what is going on" in the change process.

managing networks   both monitoring and participating in shaping relationships among those who are impacted by and/or witness to the change.

managing practice   monitoring, planning and acting on the physical and material considerations for bringing about change.

marketing   communication model where stakeholders are approached in an explicitly tailored way.

material change   alters operations, practices, relationships, decision-making and the like.

material conditions   sorts of results that change the day-to-day reality for stakeholders (e.g., pay , levels of noise, efficiency of service).

mediated channel   channels that make use of some form of mass media or technology.

mimetic forces   direct implementers to conform to established and well-known routines for implementing change and compel other stakeholders to mimic what they see as successful and common examples.

mindlessness   instead of processing new information, people behave without thinking about their actions.

multi-dimensional change   one or more changes have subsequent parts.

multifaceted change   occurs when more than one change occurs within the same temporal time frame.

multiple change   two or more independent changes occurring at the same time.

mum effect   when individuals have a distaste for delivering bad news or even previewing a message that contains bad news.

need for consensus building   the degree to which it is important to achieve consensus among stakeholders for change to be a success.

need to know   communication model where stakeholders who request information about a change are provided it.

non-refutational message   merely stating the opposing arguments without making a case against them.

normative concerns   relate to challenges to existing group norms and values that may trigger concerns for protection and survival of a group.

normative forces   expectations for appropriate and standard operating procedures are established through professional socialization, training, and industry standards.

normative stakeholder theory branch of Stakeholder Theory wherein scholars focus on moral and ethical obligations of managers to various stakeholders.

observable system concerns what is possible to notice through participation and observation.

one-sided message presenting arguments only in favor of the advocated position.

openness support for the change, positive affect about the change.

opinion leaders individuals or groups of stakeholders whose opinions tend to lead rather than follow other stakeholders.

organizational values "Implicit or explicit views, shared to a considerable extent by organizational members, about both the external adaptation of the organization and the internal integration of the organization" (Klein and Sorra, 1996, p. 1063).

peer-focused resistanced resistance efforts directed at co-workers, family, and other stakeholders in informal and sometimes anonymous settings such as underground publications including websites, cartoons, newsletters, and zines.

performance concerns relate to both issues of assessment and judgments of competence as well as personal feelings of task mastery.

personal development in which the person alters his or her frame of reference, values, or other attributes.

planned change those brought about through the purposeful efforts of organizational stakeholders who are accountable for the organization's operation.

position power relying on formal power invested in one's organizational role to influence organizational or individual behavior.

power one's ability to influence a target or capacity to effect organizational outcomes.

principal support belief that high-level decision-makers share a commitment to the change initiative such that it will not become a mere passing fad or discarded change after an initial flurry of activity.

principled dissent expression of dissatisfaction for reasons of justice, honesty, or organizational benefit.

privileged empowerment implementer style wherein select stakeholders are approached for input in a resource-based way.

programmatic approaches approach to change implementation wherein the organization and the organization are altered to accommodate the change.

psychological contracts   the "good-faith" relationships between stakeholders and organizations that stipulate an understanding of what is expected of each party.

puzzlements   propositional forms of storytelling where the listeners are asked to engage in problem-solving.

quid pro quo   communication model where stakeholders who provide the most resources get the most communication about the change.

readiness   a compilation of stakeholders' beliefs about the necessity and appropriateness of change combined with beliefs that the change can be accomplished and will be beneficial.

reciprocal interdependence   concerns the situation where one stakeholder's inputs are another stakeholder's outputs and vice versa.

refutational message   not simply referring to opposing arguments, but making the case against them.

replication   minimal adjustment to personal or role systems – repeat what you did before.

resources   ways of doing, organizational beliefs, and important possessions in an organization that can be invoked in order to move along a new idea or to make a case for staying the course on an action.

results   concern whether the implementation effort achieves intended/ unintended or desired/undesired consequences.

ripple effects   the impacts that organizational actions and presence bring to stakeholders within and surrounding the organization.

ritualistic participation   describes the case of diverse stakeholder symbolic involvement where many different types of stakeholders may be asked to provide input, but it is routinely ignored in most or all cases.

role development   in which the person tries to change the role requirements so that they better match his or her needs, abilities, and identity.

role schema   individuals beliefs about what such a role typically requires.

routinization   when the innovation/change has become incorporated into the regular activities of an organization and is no longer considered a separate new idea.

rule-bound approaches   implementation strategies that are centrally controlled and designed.

rules   simple, but powerful ideas that guide process and action.

schema   a cognitive structure that represents what is known about some object including its attributes.

second-order change   large transformational or radical changes that depart significantly from previous practice in ways that are somewhat frame-breaking.

self-concept   how the individual views him/herself.

sensegiving   giving the sense made to others.

sensemaking   assorting observations and stories into a coherent understanding of what is going on.

sequential interdependence   a special type of interdependence wherein stakeholders affect each other in sequence.

socialization   concerns how organizations shape the understandings its members have to the values, priorities, procedures, job tasks, culture, and formal and informal expectations.

solicitation of input   asking for opinions, feedback, reactions about change and change process.

stakeholders   those who have a stake in an organization's process and or outputs.

story   a means to capture and share experience, to create sense out of the world, to influence others' sensemaking.

story-building   collective activity of sensemaking wherein two or more individuals work together to order disparate facts, events, and experiences and create shared understanding of what is going on.

structured implementation activities   a set of actions purposefully designed and carried out to introduce users to the innovation and to encourage intended usage.

structures   rules and resources that create organizational practices.

system requirements   organizational expectations.

tamara   the stitching together of a sensemaking path through an organization.

targets of identification   groups and subgroups with which individuals may identify with within or relative to an organization.

terse-telling   a truncated form of storytelling that involves reference to an elaborated story shared by the group.

theories-in-use   those theories we actually act out in real life.

third-order change   involve the preparation for continuous change.

two-sided message   presenting arguments supporting arguments as well as discussing opposing arguments.

uncertainty   a lack of information or as confusion related to many available possible interpretations of events /objects.

uncertainty concerns   relate to problems occurring when stakeholders do not know what to expect or what likely outcomes will be.

uncertainty reduction   lessening of the sense that information is lacking.

uniformity   the range of use of the change across adopting unit(s) or stakeholder groups.

unintended consequences   unforeseen and /or unpredicted results of change.

unplanned change   those brought into the organization due to environmental or uncontrollable forces.

valence   belief that change is beneficial to the individual stakeholder.

values fit   key stakeholder groups will initially consider the change a good fit with their high intensity values and other key stakeholder groups will consider it a poor fit.

widespread empowerment   exists where solicitation of input is done in a manner consistent with a resource approach and is widespread.

Index

Organizational Change: Creating Change Through Strategic Communication,
First Edition. Laurie K. Lewis.
© 2011 Laurie K. Lewis. Published 2011 by Blackwell Publishing Ltd.

Printed in the USA/Agawam, MA
August 9, 2012

568350.011